New Francophone
African and Caribbean Theatres

AFRICAN EXPRESSIVE CULTURES
Patrick McNaughton, *editor*

New Francophone African and Caribbean Theatres

JOHN CONTEH-MORGAN
WITH DOMINIC THOMAS

Indiana University Press
Bloomington and Indianapolis

This book is a publication of

Indiana University Press
601 North Morton Street
Bloomington, Indiana 47404-3797 USA

www.iupress.indiana.edu

Telephone orders   800-842-6796
Fax orders   812-855-7931
Orders by e-mail   iuporder@indiana.edu

♾ The paper used in this publication meets the minimum requirements
of the American National Standard for Information Sciences—
Permanence of Paper for Printed Library Materials, ANSI Z39.48-1992.

Manufactured in the United States of America

Library of Congress Cataloging-in-Publication Data
Conteh-Morgan, John.
New Francophone African and Caribbean theatres /
John Conteh-Morgan with Dominic Thomas.
    p.   cm.   — (African expressive cultures)
Includes bibliographical references and index.
ISBN 978-0-253-35513-3 (cloth : alk. paper) —
ISBN 978-0-253-22226-8 (pbk. : alk. paper)
1. African drama (French)—History and criticism. 2. Theater—Africa,
French-speaking Equatorial. 3. Theater—Africa, French-speaking West.
4. Caribbean drama (French)—History and criticism. 5. Theater—
Caribbean, French-speaking. I. Thomas, Dominic. II. Title.
PQ3983.C63   2010
842'.914099—dc22
2010000638

1 2 3 4 5 15 14 13 12 11 10

To Nyo, Dé, and Mei

Contents

ACKNOWLEDGMENTS

John Conteh-Morgan was unable to complete the manuscript and asked Dominic Thomas to do so. The following acknowledgments are Conteh-Morgan's.

Without Nyo's prodding, this book would have taken even longer to write. With tact, patience, and sometimes barely concealed despair when it looked as though I would not heed her advice to stop taking on new projects, she kept up a gentle but persistent pressure, encouraging me to focus on the completion of this book. I also wish to thank her for being such an attentive listener and stimulating intellectual sparring partner.

Let me also register my appreciation to the students in my graduate seminars on francophone and postcolonial literatures at Ohio State University with whom I rehearsed many of the ideas contained in this work. Their often well-argued and persuasive thoughts, not only on the theatre, but on issues of postcolonial criticism in general, forced me to reconsider and refine mine.

This book is the product, in part, of research I conducted in 2002 as a W. E. B. DuBois Fellow at Harvard University. A version of the public lecture I delivered in the institute's lecture and seminar series (which has since been published under the title "The Other Avant-Garde: The Theatre of Radical Aesthetics and the Poetics and Politics of Performance," in a collection of essays edited by James Harding and John Rouse, *Not the Other Avant-Garde: The Transnational Foundations of Avant-Garde Performance* [University of Michigan Press, 2006]) included several key arguments developed in the introduction to *New Francophone African and Caribbean Theatres.* I thank the institute's director, Professor Henry Louis Gates, Jr., for providing such a stimulating work environment. Not only did I benefit from discussions with other fellows during that year, but I was able to take maximum advantage of the splendid resources at the Widener Library, including little-distributed journals and primary materials published in various countries in Africa.

My thanks also go to both my department and the College of Humanities at Ohio State University for the congenial working conditions and for the travel grants which enabled me to participate in national and international conferences where portions of this work were presented. The manuscript benefited enormously from the suggestions of Carrol F. Coates and Judith G. Miller, who evaluated the manuscript for Indiana University Press. Thanks also to Professor Pius Ngandu N'Kashama (Louisiana State University) for providing the translation of the lines included in Kikongo in Tchicaya U Tam'si's play *Le bal de Ndinga*.

I am greatly indebted to the work of my colleagues in the field of francophone and postcolonial theatre criticism; there are too many to mention here, but their names and works are listed in the references.

NB: All translations are John Conteh-Morgan's
unless otherwise indicated.

PREFACE

John Conteh-Morgan and Dominic Thomas

In his influential essay "Is the Post- in Postmodernism the Post- in Postcolonialism?" (1992), K. Anthony Appiah explored both the anti-colonial and early postcolonial nationalist tradition associated with African novels of the 1950s and 1960s (in which one finds a unitary conception of identity and a celebration of the nation with the aim of forging national culture and a common cultural past) and the process of "delegitimation," which characterized a second stage in the development of postcolonial literature and in which growing anxieties relating to the shortcomings, indeed failures, of nationalism were already becoming apparent. The literature of this stage shed the celebratory optimism of the earlier period and in its place appeared a spirit of critique or even cynicism (at the very least, skepticism) with regard to the nationalist project whose legitimating myths or master narratives —"development," "nation building," "modernization"—now came in for parody and transgressive subversion and both challenged and delegitimized its precursors. Indeed, while *Theatre and Drama in Francophone Africa: A Critical Introduction* (Conteh-Morgan 1994) essentially focused on the nationalist phase, *New Francophone African and Caribbean Theatres* updates the framework by incorporating the second stage of postcolonial literary production.

Various trends in francophone post-1970s theatre will be approached as movements whose coherence can be determined from their genealogical history and features, but the objective is also to improve our understanding of various cultural meanings by considering the contexts in which these plays emerged. Plays will therefore be examined in terms of their development, genealogy, and features; individual readings will offer concrete expression to these movements; and, finally, an elucidation of the meanings of the movements and plays and how these are mediated and filtered will be provided through analyses of dramatic practices in both Africa and the Caribbean that will shed light on their wider meaning, alongside critical insights provided by such fields as cultural, postcolonial, and performance/theatre studies.

Although *New Francophone African and Caribbean Theatres* explores sub-Saharan African writing and the works of playwrights from the French Antilles (more specifically from the three *départements d'outre-mer* known as the DOM, namely, Guadeloupe, Guyana, and Martinique, which hold national administrative status and offer their own citizenship for residents), the primary objective is not geographical coverage but rather the examination of a specific and widespread type of postcolonial and post-*departmentalization* theatre. This 1970s and 1980s theatre has been described as a "culturalist" theatre and characterized by the instrumentalization and retrieval of indigenous/folk performance idioms in a process of reculturalization. Thus, the chapters are not structured according to geography or the nationality of individual authors, but rather according to theatrical categories.

Pressed into the service of a reconfigured national identity rooted in the performance cultures of postcolonial francophone countries, this theatre is directed at the nationalist generation of playwrights who, though practicing an oppositional politics to empire, remained nevertheless wedded to the language and dramatic procedures of its theatre. Just as one must, in the twenty-first century, invoke the plurality of theatres from Africa, the same applies to the Caribbean context, where no monolithic francophone theatre exists. Haiti can boast similar developments, although they occurred much earlier— beginning in the 1920s in ethnography and fiction, and in the 1950s in the theatre, specifically in Félix Morisseau-Leroy's translations into Haitian Creole of such Greek plays as Sophocles' *Antigone.* In other words, Haiti, whose culturalist trends in fiction (Fouchard 1988) and the theatre emerged over a century and a half after its independence and long before Africa and the Antilles ceased to be colonies, is outside the temporal frame of interest in *New Francophone African and Caribbean Theatres.*

Also, the conditions for the culturalist revival in Haiti were not as directly related to France and its immediate successor local elites as they were in Africa and the Antilles. The U.S. military occupation of Haiti (1915–1934) coupled with that country's complex, long-standing, and ongoing internal cultural/racial politics—embodied in the Christophe-Pétion rivalry of the early nineteenth century—are perhaps more germane explanations for this development. Of course, the use of Creole in both Haitian and Antillean theatres might be grounds for an inclusion of Haiti in a discussion of the culturalist dimension in francophone Caribbean theatre (as we shall see, the geo-political dimension of relations between the French Antilles and Haiti is central to Simone Schwarz-Bart's play *Ton beau capitaine*). While this idea is attractive, unlike those in Haiti, few Antillean playwrights (excluding in this context the popular repertoire of unpublished plays) actually write, produce, and direct plays in Antillean Creoles in the way that Morisseau-Leroy or, more recently, Frankétienne or Syto Cavé have done. Antillean dramatists insist (in French) on the need to write in Creole, but they rarely do. Instead, in spite of all the declarations and manifestos, plays are at best a mixture of French, creolized French, and French-based Creole, interspersed occasionally with Creole words and expressions. As we shall see, the Guyanese Elie Stephenson's play *O Mayouri* is something of an exception; our focus on the translated French version of the play, which includes Creole text, as indeed does Patrick Chamoiseau's *Manman Dlo contre la fée Carabosse*, will help to elucidate these complex questions.

Furthermore, while Creole may serve as a marker of identity both in the Antilles (only very recently) and Haiti (much earlier), it is, as Martinican novelist and theorist Edouard Glissant has argued in *Caribbean Discourse*, a far more embattled language in the Antilles, where it is completely dominated and being replaced by French:

> There are, as we have seen, no languages or language spoken in Martinique, neither Creole nor French, that have been "naturally" developed by and for us Martinicans because of our experience of collective, proclaimed, denied, or seized responsibility at all levels. The official language, French, is not the people's language. This is why we, the elite, speak it so correctly. The language of the people, Creole, is not the language of the nation. . . . Our problem is therefore not to create an awareness of an obvious linguistic phenomenon—Creole—that could have preceded the

disfiguring influence of French and would await the moment of its rebirth. Creole was not, in some idyllic past, and is not yet our national language. (1992, 166–67)

Evidence of this is available in the education system and in the media, where battles continue to rage with an intensity and political relevance that they no longer have in Haiti (although Spanish and other European languages do inflect these debates, particularly in the border territory between Haiti and the Dominican Republic). In Haitian literature, the use of Creole constitutes less an act of anti-colonial resistance and identity formation than an act of realism—that is, acknowledgment of its status as a fully-fledged language and a practical medium of communication with a mass audience. In short, Haitian dramatists are succeeding in establishing Creole as a legitimate language of literature and the theatre in a way that Antillean dramatists have not been able to.

Similarly, if we had extended the analysis in this volume to the Haitian diaspora in mainland North America, the result would have been an unwieldy and incoherent book without any regulating idea except for coverage, much as exploring other diasporic frameworks, such as the Haitian diaspora in France (where dramatists such as Jean Métellus would have received critical attention), would have undermined the focus on post-nationalist francophone African and Caribbean theatres. Naturally, compelling points of commonality exist among these multiple theatrical practices and some are discussed in this book, but ultimately they remain for other scholars to explore.

The nationalist theatre's mainstream French stage conventions and use of the French language exhibited authoritarian, messianic, statist tendencies and a paternalistic view of the emergent nation that were embedded in dynastic, regal, epic, and heroic conceptions of the African and Caribbean past. Of course, the theatre of nationalism, with its procession of seers, divination and coronation scenes, folk dances, and plumed figures could also be said to evoke and embrace oral idioms. However, there is a difference between the nationalist use of indigenous cultural performances and those that would come later. Consistent with the colonial era tradition from which nationalist theatre proceeded, these indigenous performances were exotic and decorative elements rather than meaningful or substantive components. These idioms would later be redeemed from their status as folklore or "proto-theatrical" forms waiting to be developed into "real" (that is, French-based) theatre and to be consumed by westernized francophone elite or foreign audiences. They would ultimately be perceived instead as the site of new and "authentic" theatrical cultures whose structure, function, and theatricality constituted the foundations of an alternative French-language tradition of playwriting.

The formal features of the leading practitioners of the second generation and the specific ways in which their avant-gardist plays broke from the hegemonic theatre of nationalism will be analyzed in this volume. While united in opposition and repudiation of the earlier nationalist theatre and sharing overarching goals, the significant writings and practices of this period were expressed in different ways: on the one hand, aesthetic and cultural critiques were foregrounded, while on the other, political critiques were privileged. Playwrights and theatre practitioners became notable for their conscious struggles to break free from the French-based theatrical conventions of the dominant theatre of nationalism, conventions first introduced into francophone Africa in the early 1930s at the École William Ponty, and for the ways in which they inaugurated a new and "authentic" idiom of theatrical expression. A key aspect of this alternative, culturalist theatre (including a genuine return to cultural roots) was the inscription of the excluded "native" or nonliterate Other into the symbolic order through the incorporation of marginalized cultural performance forms: sacred rituals, dramatized epic and folktale narratives, and concert party spectacles. The recovery of practices such as audience participation, the decentralization of text, and authorial authority effectively reduced the centrality of European influences—a paradox, as we shall see, given that European theatrical innovation has been inspired by such practices.

Similar developments were witnessed in the francophone Caribbean within the context of independentist agitation and post-departmentalization politics where a "new," post-Césaire, performance-based theatre emerged. This will provide a comparative framework that will enable us to explore various conceptions of what could be termed the "postcolonial performative," notably cultural and economic globalization and its concurrent discourses of indigene-ity and differential performance modes. Various models of distinct indigenous cultural events will be examined in chapters focusing on the ritual/ceremonial in Werewere Liking's *Les mains veulent dire*, the epic narrative in Eugène Dervain's *Saran, ou La reine scélérate*, and folktale performance in Bernard Zadi Zaourou's *La guerre des femmes*, Patrick Chamoiseau's *Manman Dlo contre la fée Carabosse*, and Elie Stephenson's festival-inspired *O Mayouri*. Among the questions addressed in the reading of both African and Caribbean texts will be the selection processes at work in the appropriation of specific per-formative events and the areas of continuity and divergence between these performance resources and the plays derived from them.

If the theatre of cultural critique focused on issues of theatrical form and cultural agency, the theatre of political critique turned its attention to issues of governance and attacked the political vision of the theatre of the nationalist state and its goals of sociopolitical trans-formation or the heightening of political consciousness. Thus, the struggle for the social, as opposed to the national, liberation of civil society became the primary concern, and strategies were implemented through which the authority, leadership, and vision of the nationalist state might be subverted. The charismatic leader and father-of-the-nation figure, so popular in the earlier theatre, was now featured as a dictator and buffoon whose pompous solemnity and epic grandeur had yielded to the boundless irreverence, ribald excess, and grotes-queries of carnival. With the drama of political critique, the theatre moved from the exalted, "high" politics of the state to the "low" poli-tics of derision of the streets, which became a privileged modality for the apprehension of the ambiguities of contemporary national discontent. The earlier cast of princes, courtiers, and generals was now replaced by suffering and tyrannized citizens, and playwrights such as Tchicaya U Tam'si, Sony Labou Tansi, and Simone Schwarz-Bart explored these new sociopolitical circumstances and their impact on society. Perhaps not surprisingly, the once avant-garde playwrights of the 1970s and 1980s were also the object of theatrical repudiation by their successors in the 1990s.

A third and chronologically distinct generation emerged in the twenty-first century and has variously been described as the theatre of "cultural hybridity" (Chalaye 2004), "of crossings" (Chalaye 2004, 22), and "of the in-between" (Makhélé in Chalaye 2001, 10). Unlike the culturalist theatre of roots of the 1970s and 1980s, the transgressive theatre of the 1990s rejected all discourses of authenticity. Koffi Kwahulé, one of its most prolific exponents, characterized all such discourses, with their advocacy of a return to, and appropriation of, an originary source of pure "African" theatre, as a mark of "cultural fundamentalism" (1995, 30–31). In his work, and that of such dramatists as Kossi Efoui (Togo), Koulsy Lamko (Burkina Faso), Caya Makhélé (Congo), José Pliya (Benin), and Michèle Rakotoson (Madagascar), binaries such as performance/text, the French Other/the African self, and orality/literacy are put into question, and processes of mutuality and intermeshing are instead emphasized. As one of its practitioners observes, "these new dramatists have built pathways towards the Other, in his or her alterity" (Makhélé 2001, 11).

The new theatre of transgression does not celebrate a preexistent and prescribed Africanness, but rather "a nomadic Africanness" (Makhélé 2001, 11). Some of its other features include a concentration on the individual rather than the collectivity, an expansive thematic range deployed in urban and cosmopolitan cityscapes (New York and Paris) rather than in rural imaginaries, and an unabashed mixing of cultural forms. The latter's development can be traced to a number of factors, including the processes of accelerated globalization, reflected in the flow of people, images, and cultures across national frontiers. Playwrights often reside in diasporic or translocal spaces, shuttling between capitals and moving across cultures. Far from being burdened by the anxiety of foreign influence, or preoccupied with purging or nativizing theatre in the name of cultural authenticity like their predecessors had, the 1990s and twenty-first-century dramatists joyously embrace and appropriate that influence, while borrowing liberally from the world's various theatrical traditions. Of course, as the Beninese philosopher Paulin Hountondji has shown in *The Struggle for Meaning: Reflections on Philosophy, Culture, and Democracy in Africa* (2002), anti-ethnographic philosophy has also served to underscore the ways in which deracialized characters and aesthetically hybrid styles necessarily share points of commonality with African intellectual traditions in the same way that mechanisms of reculturalization have been infused with elements of modernist drama that challenge paradigms or claims to absolute originality.

As Michel Le Bris stated in "Toward a 'World-Literature' in French":

> With the center placed on an equal plane with other centers, we're witnessing the birth of a new constellation, in which language freed from its exclusive pact with the nation, free from every other power hereafter but the powers of poetry and the imaginary, will have no other frontiers but those of the spirit. (2009, 56)

Likewise, as Franco-Djiboutian novelist Abdourahman Waberi has argued, the aim is to "undo the suffocating knot" that supposedly binds together "French" as a language, a "race," and a nation, that is (citing Achille Mbembe), to "denationalize the French language" (2007, 72).

Francophone African and Caribbean theatres in the age of globalization are characterized by this mobility, celebrating the hybrid and the interstitial, global connectivities (Amselle 2001) rather than the authenticity associated with the earlier modalities of experimental theatre. One is left wondering how conceptualizations of national or regional consciousness or distinctiveness are likely to operate or predominate over *or* be replaced by global diasporic networks and creolized spaces, how these will be manifested by authors from distinct national backgrounds, and in turn what kinds of points of commonality may emerge in terms of performance discourse. These economic, political, and social developments therefore closely parallel the evolution of theatres from Africa and the Caribbean from the territorial to the extraterritorial, from embedded to unbounded identities, and from the local to the global.

New Francophone
African and Caribbean Theatres

Instrumentalizing Performance and the Francophone Postcolonial Performative

The 1970s and 1980s saw the emergence in francophone Africa of a post-nationalist radical theatre which, in a strictly chronological sense, denoted an act of "coming after" the "first"-generation theatre of nationalism of the late colonial period and early 1960s. That earlier corpus was embodied in dramatic works such as Léopold Sédar Senghor's *Chaka* (1956), Seydou Badian's *La mort de Chaka* (1962), and Jean Pliya's *Kondo le requin* (1966), and the generation that followed made a conscious effort to achieve a radically different kind of theatre. Its "post-nationalist" quality confirmed its indebtedness to its predecessor; rather than denying the centrality of the nation, it criticized a certain bourgeois nationalist conception of it. Thus, this post-bourgeois nationalist movement, associated with playwrights such as Werewere Liking, Bernard Zadi Zaourou, and Souleymane Koly of Ivory Coast; and Sony Labou Tansi and Tchicaya U Tam'si of the Republic of Congo, is marked by a desire to forge a new idiom of theatrical expression, independent of those French-based traditions of playwriting that were introduced to francophone sub-Saharan Africa during the 1930s at the École William Ponty and that would eventually come to define the dominant, nationalist practice of francophone theatre up to the early 1970s.

New Francophone African and Caribbean Theatres builds on the arguments and observations formulated in my previous book *Theatre and Drama in Francophone Africa: A Critical Introduction* (1994). Whereas in the latter the focus was essentially on plays performed and published during the 1960s and 1970s, the contextual framework under investigation in this volume has been updated and broadened to include works produced in the late 1970s and 1980s by both African *and* Caribbean playwrights. This introduction therefore provides an in-depth engagement with the theoretical significance of these newer directions, and subsequent chapters will explore their practical implications in the works of individual playwrights. The conclusion extends this analysis even further by providing an overview of francophone theatre in the age of globalization, and it will suggest several new and exciting challenges that contemporary works provide to audiences, critics, and readers. Naturally, as will become evident, the work of the dramatists on whom we will focus inscribes itself in a long historical process of mutual influence, and readers should not be surprised that certain playwrights explored in my earlier book (such as Liking, U Tam'si, and Zaourou) also receive critical attention in this context. This does not imply interchangeability since the works studied belong to completely different phases in the authors' development; they have remained active over several decades and accordingly illustrate new aesthetic and political trends in francophone theatre in response to the transformations provided by the sociocultural modes in which they operated. For example, both U Tam'si and Zaourou were notable exponents of 1960s and 1970s historical and political drama, but both playwrights had resolutely turned their backs on this genre by the 1980s, and their later works took a decidedly culturalist turn, moving to folk narratives and ritual drama, popular urban music and funerary laments.

Post-Nationalist African Performances: History, Poetics, Politics

The members of this movement were united in their desire to create what they understood to be a new and "authentic" theatre, although of course they did not all adhere to the same guidelines in the pursuit of these objectives. Two interrelated, but distinct, cultural, aesthetic, and political directions can be identified. Certainly in works such as Sony Labou Tansi's *Qui a mangé Madame d'Avoine Bergotha?* (1989), Tchicaya U Tam'si's *Le destin glorieux du Maréchal Nnikon Nniku, prince qu'on sort* (1979), and Michèle Rakotoson's *La maison morte* (1991), the political strand of the new, post-nationalist theatre is notable for its critique of the 1950s and 1960s theatre of nationalism which, because of its exalted political vision of an all-powerful state to which individual rights must be sacrificed, it holds responsible for some of the illiberal excesses of the post-independence era. Using the techniques of satire, the grotesque, and fantasy, this subversive vision was deployed in the name of democratic rights and social liberation.

This political dimension was accompanied by a more artistically oriented theatre of cultural and aesthetic critique. Rather than attacking the post-independence political dispensation, these plays were experimental and formally self-conscious in a way that their earlier counterparts had not been, and were directed instead at the dominant theatrical aesthetic and, by extension, at the cultural order that constituted one of that dispensation's legitimating tools. The revolt against this order and the passionate advocacy for its overthrow were explored in fictional works such as *Elle sera de jaspe et de corail* (1983) by Liking. In this work, one of the characters, Grozi, poetically lashes out at the prevailing theatre conventions in his artistically barren and alienated fictional African society, called Lunaï:

> In the theater they should stop tempering words by adding purely illustrative gestures. . . . Other vibrations should come into play and move us to the core. The sound of vowels should strike our pituitary gland and put us back in touch with other worlds. . . . Smells should make our mouths water. . . . And silences should allow us to meditate and to widen our horizons. May we receive the ecstasy of the original explosion that created worlds. (*It Shall Be of Jasper and Coral*, 2000, 73)

Grozi's call for new theatrical practices is one in which the imagination is teased into contact with "other worlds" through the interplay of "smells," "[vowel] sounds," and "vibrations." His impatience with the prevailing instrumentalist theatre found in his society, in which art has become a mere handmaiden to politics, echoes the real-life sentiments of Liking, Zaourou, Senouvo Agbota Zinsou, and Souleymane Koly on the nationalist practice of playwriting. As one of Grozi's friends (Babou) observes, "And above all, they must stop clamoring electoral speeches on stage. There at least may we have the pleasure of seeing beauty and ugliness as they are in themselves and in us" (*It Shall Be of Jasper and Coral*, 2000, 73).

The culturalist dimension and genealogy of post-nationalist theatre have not been the object of sustained scrutiny. In order to redress this critical imbalance, my analysis will focus on dramatists from across Africa and the Caribbean, and central to the discussion will be a consideration of the most important historical moments in the development of this theatre, the formal specificities of the practices it attempted to delegitimize and replace, its multiple forms of expression, and finally, both the intersections with and divergences from analogous theatrical movements in other regions of the global francophone world.

Ivory Coast hosted or produced many of the most representative and gifted practitioners of the 1970s and 1980s and provides an interesting micro example of the developments that occurred. The many transitions that took place in that context also serve to highlight analogous phenomena in other francophone regions of the world. Although no decisive date or event can serve to mark the origins of the conscious attempt by dramatists to distance plays from nationalistic concerns, 1969–1970 is generally considered important to its emergence. This is when a new performance and acting style known as the "griotique" was created in Ivory Coast, a style rooted, as its etymology suggests, in the techniques of the West African griot (oral narrative performer; Kotchy 1984; Hourantier 1984). The creators of this style, Dieudonné Niangoran Porquet and Aboubacar Touré, proceeded to marry the spoken poem with gesture, movement, and facial expression during French poetry recitation sessions at their school's poetry club. This practice seemed perfectly natural to them and valid in the context of their cultures of orality, but much to their surprise, the French teachers sternly rejected it and criticized them for "moving about too much" during rehearsals (Kotchy 1984, 241). This early discovery on the part of Porquet and Touré of a conflict of assumptions with regard to performance inspired their desire to find in the indigenous traditions of their country a style which would not involve their having "to do violence to their bodies to respect the wishes of their French teachers" (Kotchy 1984, 241).

This period also saw the organization at the University of Abidjan in 1970 of an important colloquium which allowed for productive discussions on the nature of francophone theatre. Prominent African theatre critics at the conference, such as Thomas Melone, Christophe Dailly, and Barthélémy Kotchy, urged francophone dramatists to put an end to their "ignorance of their [indigenous theatrical] traditions"

(Melone 1970, 152), and to recreate in their plays "the connivance between actors and spectators" characteristic of those traditions (Kotchy 1970, 175). As Kotchy argued, dramatists faced two problems: French as a "foreign language . . . eliminates 80% of the population," and theatrical spaces inhibited the traditional interactive flow between audience and spectators (Kotchy 1970, 177).

Nevertheless, it was most likely the production on Radio France Internationale (RFI) in 1972 of the prize-winning play by the Togolese playwright Senouvo Agbota Zinsou, *On joue la comédie* (1975), that crystallized the latent dissatisfaction with local theatre as it was then practiced and inaugurated the emergence of an "avant-garde" francophone theatre. Intensely self-reflexive, and in that respect alone a radical departure from the referentialism of 1960s theatre, this play features performers engaged in intense exchanges about the problematic nature of the French-inspired bourgeois nationalist tradition of playwriting. Central to the play is the proclamation of a form of participative expression that corresponds to the needs of a wider and not just French-literate African audience. Zinsou's character Petit Monsieur embraces "readerly" plays in the tradition of nationalist theatre, complete with its illusion-of-reality techniques and determinate meanings. Instead, he is presented with a "writerly" text that invites him—and metonymically the public itself—to be part of the very process of play making. Incensed by endless arguments concerning performance methodologies, he chastises his fellow performers: "I have the impression, I must say, that you are taking us for fools. I paid two hundred francs to watch a play and not such childish goings-on" (Zinsou 1975, 19). Furthermore, his expectations have not been met: "This to me isn't theatre. . . . The theatre has to instruct, and educate" (16). Indeed, striking parallels can be made between Petit Monsieur's reaction and those of Parisian audiences to Roger Blin's controversial production of Beckett's *Waiting for Godot* (1952) or of the Older Gentleman in the Box in Pirandello's *Tonight We Improvise* (1932). In all three cases, a disgruntled spectator, whether fictional or real, faced with a work that is not consistent with his expectations, either reacts angrily or quite simply leaves the theatre.

The meta-theatrical playfulness amounted at the time to a determined assault on the dominant idiom, one whose didactic and realist character were nostalgically evoked by Petit Monsieur. As such, this play can be seen as paradigmatic of the culturalist strand of post-nationalist francophone theatre. What started as a lone experiment quickly developed into a theatrical movement; two of the most innovative practitioners included the director and actor Sidiki Bakaba of Ivory Coast (Kotchy 1984) and Jean-Pierre Guingané of Burkina Faso. Referring to this development, Liking observed, "By 1980, a number of groups led by academics had launched an entire movement that was quickly christened 'Experimental Theatre'" (in Pillot 1990, 58), and she also defined her own work in the context of these developments: "to participate in the growth of contemporary African arts ... means striving to live authentically, without copying models" (in Pillot 1990, 58). The Central African dramatist Vincent Mambachaka also displayed a sense of being part of a larger movement in the francophone African theatrical world when he remarked: "Our generation is getting into a period of real creativity; what matters to me is to develop my own style, to reinvent a language" (in Boiron 1993a, 17). To create, to reinvent, to live authentically without copying models—such then were the watchwords of the new theatre of cultural critique and aesthetic innovation.

The development of this theatre as a self-conscious movement, complete with media pronouncements, declarations of (not always fulfilled) intent, and programs of action articulated by some of its practitioners from what could be considered the center of gravity in Ivory Coast, was perhaps not unexpected (Hourantier 1984) as a response to the efforts being made by France to establish a modern "high" culture in its overseas territories. France not only insisted that its colonial subjects speak what a poet from French Guyana, Léon-Gontran Damas, called the "French of France/the Frenchman's French/French French" (1939), but also that the budding dramatists among them write plays according to (some dehistoricized) "European" dramatic conventions, "closest to European tastes" (Traoré 1958, 49). But which "European [theatrical] tastes" exactly, one might wonder, did France transmit to and encourage in the dramatists in its colonies? It was certainly not the modernist avant-garde practice of influential figures such as Antonin Artaud who, at about the same time as the French were introducing literary drama in Africa through the school system (in the 1930s), was advocating the re-theatricalization or re-oralization of French literary drama, whose textual "tyranny" he was busy denouncing. While he was calling for the birth of a new theatre infused with the energies of (Balinese-type) performance traditions from the "primitive" societies of the non-industrialized world (which also happened to be colonized societies, a reality that often remains invisible; Jameson 1990), official and imperial France pursued the ideological *and* physical repression of those very traditions and, not uncommonly, the looting of the "art" objects connected with them (Barkan and Bush 1995). Justification was provided by the belief that these traditions were not "theatre," but at best pre- or proto-theatre that needed to be stripped of its magico-religious dimension (never mind that some of them were secular and had nothing religious about them) and developed into proper "the-atre" (Béart 1960; Conteh-Morgan 2001).

French colonial educators were certainly not recommending the fairground, music hall, or vaudeville traditions in French theatre either. With their *commedia dell'arte* roots, these genres (which in many ways share points of commonality with African oral perfor-mances) were considered "popular" or "low" cultural categories by the French authorities who, through church and state institutions, had visited similar treatment on their own popular performance traditions as far back as the seventeenth century (Scott 1990; Elias 2000). These were thus not deemed a worthy cultural export to the colonies, any more than Artaud's musings on the theatre of the absurd, which were officially characterized as symptomatic of the "negrophilia" (Laude 1968) afflicting French modernist culture (Clifford 1988; Shelton 1995; Taoua 2002), a culture which in the name of reason, progress, and the "civilizing" mission, France was endeavoring to eradicate. Thus, the European theatrical taste that French educators sought to transmit to their African colonies was quite simply the one associated with the literary theatre of French "high" culture from the French classical age. Pointing to the influence of this taste on his early plays— *Les Sofas* (1974) and the unpublished *Sory Lambré* (1968)—Zaourou wrote: "They resemble French Classical plays, with grand tirades in the manner of Corneille" (in Kotchy 1984, 239). In his book of theatre criticism and personal recollections, *Le théâtre négro-africain et ses fonctions sociales,* Bakary Traoré also wrote about his efforts as a college student in colonial Senegal to produce plays in French, which continued to be demanded of students of the generation of the founders of the griotique movement in the sixties: "Drawing our inspiration from the masters of the seventeenth century, we sought to link events in a relationship of cause and effect that would give the plot a beginning, a development, and an ending" (Traoré 1958, 81).

Given the deliberateness and doctrinaire nature of the French approach, it is not surprising that the revolt against it and the literary theatrical tradition it sought to teach, which began in the 1970s, adopted the self-conscious form of a theatrical movement or school, complete with manifestos, public declarations, and even doctrinal splits among some of its members (Touré 1987, 46–54).

A movement, however, does not necessarily have to point to a coordinated effort to impose a unified practice. The post-nationalist theatre movement of aesthetic critique and renewal was never a unitary project. Its practitioners may well have had the same aim—to reenergize African theatre through the stage adaptation of African cultural performances—but they resorted to a diverse range of performances and conventions shaped by national traditions and personal choices to promote this aim. That said, it remains equally true that the overwhelming majority of plays within this movement exhibited combinations of certain features that make it possible to distinguish a corpus of works. Arguably, the single most important feature was the new theatre's rejection of the textualist and literary bias of the dominant theatre tradition in favor of a performance orientation. Souleymane Koly, a popular practitioner, described the change in the following terms: "the shows that are best received are those that *contain the least text*" (in Boiron 1993a, 17; emphasis added). Sony Labou Tansi was even more explicit, declaring:

> The intention, really, is to *break up the "classical" text,* if I may put it that way. A wonderful text is not necessarily a good pretext for a show. . . . During rehearsals, the work with the actors can lead to changes in the text, which is then little more than a "scenario." It is a question of mixing *mise en scène* with text. *Theatre is not about writing texts.* (in Boiron 1993a, 19; emphasis added)

So, unlike the French-inspired practice, which emphasized the textual (with its focus on plot construction, character depiction, elevated language), the new theatre of aesthetic and cultural critique privileged the performative: spectacle, *mise-en-scène*, music—those elements that Aristotle and many after him have pejoratively characterized as "the least artistic" and the most dependent on "the art of the stage machinist [rather] than on that of the poet" (Aristotle 1997, 13–14). The shift from text to performance in the new theatre took the form of a systematic return, in what might be considered an interesting example of theatrical intraculturalism, to indigenous African oral performances.

Examples of the many plays in the mold of this performance-based avant-garde theatre modeled on ritual ceremonies include Liking's *Les mains veulent dire* (1981), Zaourou's *Le secret des dieux* (1984), and Sony Labou Tansi's *La rue des mouches* (1985); based on the Togolese concert-party spectacle, Zinsou's *On joue la comédie* (1975); inspired by epic or folktale narratives, Liking's *Un touareg s'est marié à une pygmée* (1992b), Zinsou's *La tortue qui chante* (1987), and Birago Diop's *L'Os de Mor Lam* (1966); and built on puppet theatre and the Malian *kotéba* folk theatre idioms, Liking's *Dieu Chose* (1985) and Souleymane Koly's *Adama Champion* (1979). These non-elite/non-westernized idioms, which emerged from colonial oppression and its reformulation in the hands of nationalist counterparts, appealed to subaltern populations in the postcolony and have been celebrated and textualized by francophone dramatists since the 1970s as the site of "authentic" African theatrical cultures because of their spirit of creative independence. One could argue that the textual character of the French-derived theatre has been exaggerated, and that even as it aspired to produce dramatic literature, it never completely turned its back on oral performative resources as is evident in the many music and dance scenes and in the procession of griots, diviners, shamans, and their performing arts and crafts in 1960s and 1970s francophone plays, including Guillaume Oyono-Mbia's *Trois prétendants, un mari* (1964), Jean Pliya's *Kondo le requin* (1966), Cheikh Ndao's *L'exil d'Albouri* (1973), Guy Menga's *La marmite de Koka Mbala* (1969), and Amadou Cissé Dia's *Les derniers jours de Lat Dior* (1947). However, such objections are based on a widespread misconception concerning the place and function of indigenous theatrical resources in francophone theatre. The issue is not so much whether such resources have been present in the drama, since of course they have been, but rather the manner of that presence. In the examples above, the elements are designed to create atmosphere or to accord a touch of local color to the proceedings. On some occasions, such as during the "whodunit" divination scene in Oyono-Mbia's *Trois prétendants, un mari,* they even become the butt of satire. In the William Ponty student productions, they were employed to illustrate and exhibit in nearly ethnological terms (for the theatre's foreign audience of French teachers and colonial administrators) aspects of African culture. In most cases, though, they rarely complement the dramatic action, from which they remain disconnected. Jacques Schérer's observation is relevant in this regard:

> Speech, which for better or for worse was the motor of European theatre, has been a handicap for African theatre. On the other hand because music and dance scenes are so lively, a gap emerges between the text on the one hand and the staging on the other with the two never meshing satisfactorily. (Schérer 1992, 47)

In other words, in the French-derived tradition, lexical items are extracted from the various indigenous performance "languages" and then mapped onto a theatrical syntax that itself remains mainstream French. These elements therefore do not affect the structural integrity of the plays. They are more decorative than meaningful, ultimately entertaining, but dispensable exotica used by elite dramatists for equally elite audiences anxious to reassure themselves of their Africanness even as they are busy turning their backs on it. Instead, dramatists "nativized" the syntax of the play in an attempt to recreate the source performance "language." In other words, a play like *Les mains veulent dire* does not only use elements of a ritual of affliction (Liking would consider this mere tokenism), but actually aspires to the condition of that ritual in its form, structure, performance style, and function. Liking's primary concern, like that of her fellow theatre practitioners, is to de-folkloricize indigenous idioms, rescue them from the margins of theatre to which they have been relegated, and reinscribe them at the heart of the new theatre.

A second important feature of these newer performances concerns the changed function they advocated for the theatre. Their goal was no longer purely sociopolitical transformation nor the heightening of political consciousness, as was the case with plays of the anticolonial nationalist tradition, but rather cultural, spiritual, and psychological conversion. Theatrical performance becomes an act of worship or devotion during which a (culturally) alienated community of celebrants is reconnected, after a rigorous process of guided self-investigation, to a primordial, but obscured or repressed, source of selfhood (cultural, psychological, and spiritual). Theatrical performance thus becomes a form of ritual initiation into self-understanding, on whose successful outcome the regeneration of both self and community depends. As Liking's one-time collaborator, Marie-José Hourantier—a well-known theatre practitioner and theorist—puts it in connection with one of the plays of the genre:

> *Les mains veulent dire* seeks to initiate all the participants by making them discover the why and how of a social ill. . . . By tracking down the malady, describing it, denouncing it . . . the Patient takes her first steps towards lucidity and, to the rhythms of soothing incantations, can dance her way to good health. (Hourantier and Liking 1987, 85)

So where the 1950s and 1960s theatre made social or political revolution a condition of collective progress—"my aim," wrote Cheikh Ndao about his play *L'exil d'Albouri*, "is to contribute to the creation of myths that galvanize the people" (1973, 8)—the newer performance-based theatre reversed the order and turned cultural and spiritual well-being into a prerequisite for social progress and self-directed development.

The focus on the spiritual and subconscious dimensions of human experience explains the preference of this specific current of performance theatre for the nonrational techniques of trance, dreams, and fantasy—techniques that speak to, or even assault, the senses. This focus also explains its mobilization of an expanded range of languages, which includes the nonverbal: masking, costuming, symbolic gestures, and objects. For Zaourou, "theatre is a total art form whose principal treasure is its plurality of languages" (in Kotchy 1984, 239), while to Liking, "[o]ur songs are also acts of speech" (in Boiron 1993a, 17). In plays such as *Les mains veulent dire*, even musical instruments take on a meaning beyond the purely utilitarian, functioning as characters endowed with the power of speech. The use of paralinguistic forms is not limited to ceremonial plays. In the secular works of practitioners such as Dieudonné Niangoran Porquet and Aboubacar Touré of the griotique movement and Souleymane Koly, speech is used sparingly (Kotchy 1984, 241–46). The action, like in a *kotéba* performance (the model for Koly's *Adama Champion* [1979] and Porquet's "griodrame" *Soba ou grande Afrique* [1978]), is narrated through dance, mime, and body movements, a technique they use not merely for reasons of cultural authenticity, but also, as Koly specifically states, for ease of communication with multiethnic audiences (in Boiron 1993a, 17).

Thus, to focus attention on the use of a plurality of languages by the practitioners of performance theatre is not to deny the use of such elements in the plays of the literary tradition. The difference lies in the use to which music, dance, and gestures are put in each practice. In the French-inspired nationalist tradition, the burden of communication is carried by speech. When music and dance are used to communicate and not just to entertain, as is usually the case, they play a subordinate role to speech as illustrators, in images and movement, of meanings that are encoded primarily in the verbal. In the newer non-logocentric performance theatre, on the other hand, words are decentered. No longer occupying place of pride in the communicative scheme as they do in the literary theatre, they are simply one mode of communication among many others and, as such, are valued more for reasons of euphony and incantation than communication. Ultimately, the total meaning of each play can only be accessed through performance. It is thus not a coincidence that many of the late 1970s and 1980s playwrights were also theatre directors. Liking directed the Ki-Yi Mbock Theatre, Koly the Kotéba Ensemble, the late Sony Labou Tansi the Rocado Zulu Theatre, Zaourou the Didiga Theatre, and Jean-Pierre Guingané the Théâtre de la Fraternité. For them, the theatre offered a crucial departure from the literary tradition in francophone drama and was not so much about re-presenting texts, but rather about the process of situating bodies in performance, a physical activity that simultaneously combines spatial, temporal, visual, and auditory components. Traditionally, the actor is not supposed to draw attention to the body lest s/he distract the audience from the message that s/he is supposed to declaim, and the challenge is to achieve transparency, playing a role with which s/he becomes one, and the meaning of the performance in this context is *illustrated* in gestures and movement. But in the newer performance theatre, the actor is not a self-effacing signifier, and s/he maintains distance vis-à-vis the role s/he is playing. In *On joue la comédie*, for example, the actor grudgingly playing Chaka often slips out of role to remind the spectators of his real name (Zinsou 1975, 22), and he draws attention to himself as mime, musician, and even boxer (38–40) and to his body in its material expressiveness (Graver 1997).

The focus on the body of the actor is particularly important in Liking's ceremonial theatre, where acting is *not* the art of impersonation nor an attempt to remain emotionally detached from the role, in the manner theorized by Denis Diderot in the eighteenth century in *Le paradoxe sur le comédien:*

> The great dramatic poets especially are assiduous spectators of what is going on around them in the physical and the moral world. . . . Great poets, great actors, and perhaps in general all the great imitators of nature, whoever they may be, endowed with a fine imagination, great judgment, tact and sensitivity, very assured taste, are the least susceptible of beings. . . . they are too busy looking, recognizing, imitating to be acutely affected within themselves. (1988, 309–10)

This paradoxical split between a self that stages troubled emotions while remaining untroubled is one that Liking's theatre rejects. For her, acting, whether as role-play or otherwise, is the art of interrogating and emotionally expressing the innermost self, and helping the spectators to do the same. In its most successful incarnation, it exceeds role-play to become "a means of self-realization" (Kotchy 1984, 239), an acting out of personal phantasms, an activity that additionally makes of the actor "an awakener of consciousness" (Hourantier 1984, 183), a sacred figure who helps the spectator to discover his or her creative potential, the divine within:

> [The actor triggers] a process of self-revelation in the audience. Just as the actor revealed himself to himself, so he will try to show how one can rid oneself of the masks of daily life and take

control of oneself. He tears off masks in order to reveal the real person. . . . He knows he can fill the void by helping the other, his brother, to realize himself by making transparent that which is murky. (Hourantier 1984, 224)

Such activity is not conducted through words but instead through mudra-like movements of fingers, hands, feet—in short, through the body, which in its slightest twitches, gestures, postures, and costumes constitutes a broad range of signifiers: "The repetition of the gesture, its constitutive moments, various segments, and rhythms are that many signs for the spectator, signs that compete with speech" (Hourantier 1984, 181). However, the body in Liking's practice of ritual theatre is more than a "textual surface" (to borrow Judith Butler's expression) on which the individual's inner being and community values are inscribed; it is also a site of knowledge and communication, a sacred organ which keeps the individual attuned, like an antenna, to the nonmaterial, spiritual plane of existence. The need for actors to be aware of the potentialities of their bodies in order to discharge their true function explains the importance Liking attaches to physical exercises (such as yoga) in their training (Hourantier 1984, 226–41).

Concomitant with the emphasis on the actor as the center of the theatrical event was the newer theatre's predilection for collective creation. Many of its plays were the product not of a solitary author whose text was handed over for execution to a director and then to a passive group of actors, but rather of the collaborative effort of actors, directors, and sometimes spectators (as in Zinsou's *On joue la comédie*). Once a scenario (a "textual site/plan") was laid out, explained Zaourou, it was up to the "actors to familiarize themselves with it and build the show from it" (in Boiron 1993a, 19). Thus, to the practitioners of the radical aesthetics of performance theatre, the actual process of play making was more important than the finished play itself. In fact, this approach not only informed their practice but was also the subject of some of their plays. For example, Liking's *Quelque Chose-Afrique* (1996b) stages a group of actors putting together a play two weeks before its scheduled/commissioned performance. Because no architect/author has supplied them with a design, the performers themselves have to come up with one. This entails not just determining the dialogue and subject, gestures, costumes, sets, and so on, but also navigating an additional layer of complication in the guise of a fictionalized sensitive censorship issue. Although the play contains an internal stage director, Sita, her role, like that of the avant-garde dramatist, is basically that of coordinator or midwife. She prods the performers to bring forth ever more daring and creative ideas and improvisations, and she weaves their suggestions into a harmonious whole: "Let us give free rein to our passion without interruption. I'll note down the best suggestions. Let us not hesitate to bring in old dances and choreography that have not yet been used in other plays" (*Quelque Chose-Afrique*, 90).

The artistic self-consciousness in this instance is non-illusionistic, having recourse to a range of de-narrativization techniques, such as fantasy and trance, the disruption of linear plot and hence the illusion of reality, a variety of acting styles and strategies that draw attention to the presence of the performer and discourage total identification between the actor and the character portrayed, and the incorporation of the actual play within the play. The aim of the newer theatre was thus not to rehearse, as in the realist manner, social and political meanings. It was rather to throw into relief the processes of signification by which those meanings are produced and naturalized, and to encourage actors and audiences to join in the construction of new ones.

A final feature of the newer theatre, connected with its predilection for collective creation, was its use of theatrical space. Unlike the "spatial contract" (Upton 1997, 240) observed by the establishment theatre, a new contract permitted fluidity between the acting space and the viewing space, allowing for the "mobile and spontaneous intervention of the spectators" (Upton 1997, 235). However, while many of the plays in this new practice called for a circular performance space, the buildings in which they were performed rigidly divided stage from audience, thereby creating a conflict of traditions and staging challenges. This is a dimension to which we shall return later when our attention shifts to individual authors and to the various ways in which they have responded to the danger of anarchy that haunts any true participatory literary theatre, even assuming that the spatial configuration of the theatre building was not an issue.

Performance Theatre in Diasporic Perspective: The Francophone Caribbean

Thus far, the focus of *New Francophone African and Caribbean Theatres* has been the ways in which dramatists from francophone sub-Saharan Africa sought during the 1970s and 1980s to reenergize their region's theatre by foregrounding performance. Such transformations were not, of course, confined to the African context; in fact, they align themselves with a multiplicity of other theatrical initiatives and practices in the societies and subcultures of the West Atlantic African diaspora (Gainor 1995; Crow and Banfield 1996; Gilbert and Tompkins 1996; Etherton 1982; Kerr 1995; Balme 1999; Harding 2002; Olaniyan 1995; Hill 1990; Boon and Plastow 1998); in postcolonial nations in Asia such as India (Bharucha 1993; Schechner 1993), Singapore, and Malaysia (Lo 2004); and even in the intercultural practices of avant-garde Euro-American theatre practitioners (Bharucha 1993; Harding 2000b; Pavis 1996; Innes 1993, 2000). Let us briefly recall the manifestations and geocultural coordinates of this phenomenon in the area of concern to us in this section, namely "black Atlantic" societies.

Theatre historians and critics trace its earliest mature manifestations in Africa to the work of Wole Soyinka and John Pepper Clark. Already in the 1960s, they were producing plays such as *A Dance of the Forests* (1963) and *Ozidi* (1966), respectively, performance-based drama about which francophone playwrights (then still writing according to European tastes, as we saw earlier) could only dream. By the time that the latter came to fulfill that dream in the 1970s, the type of playwriting initiated by Soyinka had become current practice in anglophone Africa as exemplified in the work of Efua Sutherland, Ngùgì wa Thiong'o, Mukotani Rugyendo, and Femi Osofisan (Etherton 1982; Kerr 1995), and later (in the 1980s) in the plays of the Black Consciousness movement of South Africa (Steadman 1998). In the United States, Amiri Baraka's (LeRoi Jones's) 1960s Black Arts movement is considered to be one of the most sustained attempts at a return to the "traditional" roots of black diasporic theatre. To him and his fellow Black Arts movement practitioners—Barbara Ann Teer of the National Black Theatre, Paul Carter Harrison, and Ed Bullins—these roots were directly traceable to Africa. The aim of their movement, wrote James Hatch, was "to set in motion a Black theatre revival that was to develop a strong mythic and ritual wing *based in African religious and secular life*" (Hatch 1987, 19; emphasis added).

The situation was no different in the Caribbean where, in the words of Elaine Savory writing about Earl Lovelace, Derek Walcott, and Trevor Rhone, "*African forms of expression*, love of the word and the inventive use of music, masking, dance, possession, and ritual" were to "provide important vocabularies for theatrical expression" (1995, 24; emphasis added), a statement that can be applied with equal validity to the work of such (francophone) playwrights as Ina Césaire, Michèle Montantin, and Simone Schwarz-Bart. In short, the reconnection with an "ancestral" heritage of performance—one that was supposedly "African" but in reality often refashioned or outright invented—can be said to be one of the most important features of the African and African diaspora theatrical performative.

Compelling links are found within the Caribbean framework: the African ancestry and African-descended culture of the majority population of the region; a common imperial language born of a shared experience of colonial domination by France; transnational exchanges and reciprocal influences among artists, intellectuals, and political activists (Edwards 2003); historical links characterized by the presence of Caribbean people in Africa as colonial administrators (such as the Guyanese René Maran and Felix Eboué in Central Africa and the Martinican Louis Placide Blacher in Niger), influential teacher-activists, and revolutionaries (Frantz Fanon); and of course Africans in the Caribbean (for example Béhanzin, the deposed king of Dahomey exiled in Martinique). However, establishing connections between francophone African and Caribbean theatres and in turn between these regions and the global African and African diasporic upsurge of interest in, and return to, performance of the last forty years is emphatically not to suggest, even remotely, some undifferentiated sameness among these performance theatre practices. Gilbert and Tompkins rightly caution against any such meaningless suggestion:

> Post-colonial studies are engaged in a two-part, often paradoxical project of chronicling similarities of experience while at the

same time registering the formidable differences that mark each former colony. . . . A theory of post-colonialism that fails to recognize this distinction between "differences" will recreate . . . spurious hierarchies, misreading[s], silencings, and ahistoricisms. (Gilbert and Tompkins 1996, 5)

In other words, it is *not* enough to observe, for example, that the Ivorian Bernard Zadi Zaourou's *La guerre des femmes* (1985) and the Martinican Patrick Chamoiseau's *Manman Dlo contre la fée Carabosse* (1977) are both derived from African folktale performances. Neither is it appropriate to posit that Cameroonian Werewere Liking's *Les mains veulent dire,* the black American August Wilson's *Joe Turner's Come and Gone* (1986), and the anglophone Caribbean author Derek Walcott's *Dream on Monkey Mountain* (1967) are all derived from African ritual dramas and therefore are somehow expressions of an essential Africanness of black diasporic theatre (Okagbue 1997). Several analytical and conceptual questions challenge such a metaphysics of blackness, such as which healing, inhumation, or sacrificial rituals are used, or which trickster, etiological, or satirical tales adapted. What are the differential "strategic transformations" (Quayson 1994) wrought upon these idioms? Which discursive functions within their political and cultural locations do these transformations fulfill? What are the implications of locality, of operating from a minoritarian position within the French nation or, like their African counterparts, from a majoritarian one in an independent state, however nominally so? These considerations must be addressed.

At about the time that African playwrights were reverting to indigenous traditions, a "new francophone Caribbean theatre" (Ruprecht 2003, 20) based on a similar reversion was also emerging in the islands of Martinique and Guadeloupe and in French Guyana. Like in Africa, a number of key events, dates, and practitioners mark this enterprise. French-Guyanese dramatist Elie Stephenson's play *O Mayouri* was produced in 1975 by the culturally radical troupe Le Mouvement des Jeunes de Mirza, an event which inaugurated what he called "un théâtre authentiquement guyanais" (1990, 79) [an authentically Guyanese theatre]. The staging of this play was the culmination of cultural developments that he dates back to the founding, between 1970 and 1972, of the first indigenous Guyanese theatre company by activist students. Their black cultural nationalism was evident not only in the symbolic resonance of the name they chose for their group—the Angela Davis Troupe—but also in the type of works they performed, namely, African works by the francophone African theatre practitioner Jules Nago, originally from Benin and resident at the time in French Guyana. The breakup of this group, partly because it was not thought to be "African" enough by some of its even more radical members, led to the founding of the Mouvement des Jeunes, whose objective, Stephenson explains, was the creation of "a theatre in Guyanese Creole" (1990, 78).

Like in French Guyana, Martinique witnessed in the 1970s what Chamoiseau and Confiant term "the birth of a theatre truly anchored in our reality" (1999, 184). By this, they mean a theatre that sought its inspiration from such indigenous resources as the "traditional skit," which developed from the performances of the storyteller of slave plantation society. Chamoiseau and Confiant write:

> The storyteller's folktale performance at a wake marks the origins of our theatre: his language, intonation, onomatopoeias, gestural language, silent or voiced mimicry, dance movements, chants, his symbolizations for water, wind, and rain made for a near complete theatricalization. The skit developed on the stage the theatricalizations of the living folktale. (1999, 183)

Although such "theatricalizations of the living folktale" had given rise to some written plays—a few of them in Creole—as far back as the eighteenth and nineteenth centuries (Graver 1997), a strictly speaking *literary*, folk-inspired theatre remained on the whole a marginal cultural activity in francophone Caribbean plays. It was practiced only by a few pioneers until the founding in the 1970s of troupes dedicated to its development, such as Henri Melon's Théâtre Populaire Martiniquais and Jean Lerus's Théâtre du Cyclone in Guadeloupe (Chamoiseau and Confiant 1999; Ruprecht 2000, 2003; Montantin 2003; Jones 2003). By the 1980s, this theatrical stream had grown in both volume and importance, producing notable works such as *Mémoires d'îles* (1985) and *L'Enfant des passages; ou, La Geste de Ti-Jean* (1987) by Ina Césaire; *Manman Dlo contre la fée Carabosse* (1977) by Patrick Chamoiseau and *La Nef* (1992) by Michèle Césaire in Martinique; *Vie et mort de Vaval* (1991) by Michèle Montantin and *Ton beau capitaine* (1987) by Simone Schwarz-Bart in Guadeloupe; and Elie Stephenson's *O Mayouri* (1974b), Odile Pedro Léal's *La chanson de Philibert* (1997), and Gerty Dambury's *Lettres indiennes* (1993) in French Guyana.

Two features of this new Caribbean theatre, much like its African counterpart, were its rejection of the official French theatre of texts and its recourse to oral resources in the service of various techniques of performance, including corporeal expression (miming, acrobatics, coded dance movements, and a gestural language), call and response, improvisation, and collective creation. Other resources included (in Guadeloupe) the *lewoz,* an evening of theatricalized dance and drum music; the *gwoka* ("ka," meaning drum, and "gwo," meaning "big" from the French *gros*), originally a secret association linked with slave revolts but now a public event integral to a *lewoz* evening (Pradel 2003); folktale performances; *timtims* (riddles); and (in Guyana) carnivals such as that described by Odile Pedro Léal (2000), which provided the basis for her play *La chanson de Philibert* (1997).

That all of these developments took place in the 1970s was not fortuitous. This "fiery anticolonialism and independentist nationalism" had begun in the 1960s (Chamoiseau and Confiant 1999, 179), and with the accession to formal independence for many colonized countries in Africa during this decade, the radical, anti-departmentalization sections of francophone Caribbean societies (students, intellectuals, workers) identified with the aspirations of these countries and called for similar decolonizing efforts in their region. Intellectuals and dramatists such as Frantz Fanon, Sonny Rupaire, and Daniel Boukman preferred to seek refuge and live in Algeria rather than take up French arms against a liberation movement. The idea of a Guadeloupean or Martinican independent nation, something very much taboo up to that period, only became thinkable with the founding of independentist organizations like the Organisation de la jeunesse anticolonialiste de Martinique (OJAM) in 1965, the Groupement de l'organisation nationaliste guadeloupéenne (GONG) in 1967, and a few years later, the Guyanese Movement for Decolonization (MOGUDE). With the establishment in the 1970s of the worker movement the Union for the Liberation of Guadeloupe (UPLG), which, in an assertion of cultural Otherness, insisted that its meetings and artistic creations would henceforth be conducted in Creole rather than in French, the cultural dimension of the independentist movement had moved to the fore.

It is in the context of this political agitation that the newer Caribbean theatre must be understood, more precisely as the cultural expression of the francophone Caribbean's will to independence. We shall have occasion later to examine in more detail the cultural politics of this new theatre, but what needs to be emphasized at this juncture is that, while francophone African and Caribbean movements both orchestrated a return to traditions of performance deemed indigenous—a similarity that constitutes what Stuart Hall has called the axis of "continuity" (1990, 222) between home and diaspora—not all returns are identical. In fact, major differences or discontinuities exist between the two.

The first distinction concerns the relatively limited range of performance idioms mobilized by Caribbean dramatists. It is often said that if enslaved Africans arrived in their new world empty-handed, they did not arrive empty-minded. While this observation is true, it remains equally true that with the passage of time and through the lack of reinforcement available through constant exposure to, and participation in, cultural practices, these transplants were effectively reduced in their efforts to forge a new culture to acts of re-membering fragments of their "home" culture. To say this, of course, is not to imply that the resultant hybrid, diasporic culture is any less authentic than its home African counterpart. But it does offer a possible explanation for the relatively narrow range of performances at the disposal of francophone Caribbean playwrights. Unlike their African counterparts and contemporaries, who can draw on a broad spectrum of idioms that includes, in addition to folktales, intricate religious and secular rituals, festivals, and epic and mythic narratives, francophone Caribbean playwrights were limited to relatively minor popular genres: "odd bits and pieces of raggedy oral forms" (1994, 155), as Chamoiseau has described them.

In this respect, new Caribbean theatre is more consistently grassroots in nature. It is a theatre of the ordinary individual and not of mythic, majestic, or priestly figures. It is also interesting to note its consistently secular nature. What spirit figures and gods exist in it (like in *Manman Dlo*) function more in the mode of enchantment and allegory than instrumentality, a fact explainable by the ambient scientific and secularized environment and the absence (unlike in Haiti, for example) of a supporting and coherent infrastructure of magico-religious beliefs. In a statement of particular relevance to francophone Caribbean theatre and not just to his troupe's vain attempt to enact possession in its production of Soyinka's *The Road,* Derek Walcott writes:

> We tried in the words of [Soyinka's] professor to "hold the god captive," but for us Afro-Christians, the naming of the god estranged him. *Ogun was an exotic figure for us not a force.* We could pretend to enter his power, but he could never possess us, for *our invocations were not prayer but devices.* (1998, 8; emphasis added)

A second element of discontinuity between francophone African and Caribbean theatres relates to the question of language. Caribbean dramatists returned to, or at least were strong advocates for, a return to Creole in its multiple expressive forms. Their francophone African counterparts, on the other hand, while targeting a broad popular audience, made no such move and were even reluctant to theorize its desirability because what they argued (unlike certain anglophone practitioners) was the linguistically heterogeneous nature of African audiences. African dramatists (even assuming African-languages literacy on their part) were also aware of the problems attendant on the use of any indigenous language, given the accompanying alienation and exclusion of important sections of their multilinguistic audience and the risk of the devaluation of their work into a form of ethnic theatre.

But perhaps a more significant reason for the use of an indigenous language (Creole) in one region and French in the other lies in the differential role of language in the 1970s and 1980s conceptions of national identity in both geocultural spaces. For the playwrights of the Caribbean, Creole, or at least some form of creolized French, had become the principal mode of expression of the national community and its identity, unlike in francophone Africa where identity was increasingly predicated on aspects of culture other than language. As

Richard Burton and Fred Reno succinctly put it, "to be [French] West Indian is to speak Creole and vice versa" (1995, 153). If Creole came to stand as a metaphor for Caribbean identity, it is because of its syncretistic nature born of various interactions (technical questions that continue to preoccupy linguists) between the languages of enslaved Africans and the French dialects of the earliest colonists, and between these sets of languages and remnants of Carib Indian languages, which themselves had been in relation with Spanish (Chamoiseau and Confiant 1999, 66–72; Chaudenson 2001, 145–93). Thus, it was less the source of the elements of French Creole's constitutive languages that was of interest to identity formation than the fact that Creole offered a language system that was autonomous and original in relation to the languages from which it evolved. This syncretistic conception of Creole makes it, to performance-oriented dramatists, not only the preferred medium of theatrical communication with francophone Caribbean audiences, but also the appropriate signifier of a culture that is more than the sum of its many "African," "French," and local Carib cultural parts. No more relevant example of this cultural Creoleness can be given than that of the "storyteller," a figure generally accepted as the creator of Caribbean drama.

Although a descendant of the West African griot, the Caribbean storyteller, as Ina Césaire and Joëlle Laurent have shown, quickly had to adapt to meet the challenges of the new environment: "He adapted the original African folktale to slave and colonial society" (1976, 11). The repertoire of African animal characters (elephants, hyenas, lions, and so on) grew to include rabbits and mules, which were closely associated with European lore. Also, European human and fairy figures like Ti-Jean from Brittany (who becomes a composite of Brer Rabbit and Anansi the Spider), Carabosse (the Wicked Fairy), and Cinderella found their way into these new tales. The functions of the characters also changed, reflecting the new slave and colonial realities of race hierarchy and economic exploitation. The rabbit and the mule now represented the mulatto and the slave, respectively, and the Good Lord became the slave owner (Césaire and Laurent 1976, 7–15).

But perhaps the clearest transformation of all was in the function of the storyteller. With the urgency of the new context of enslavement, that function became unmistakably political (unlike African tales, where it is social), namely, to promote a counterculture that would "spatter the system of dominant values with all the muck of immorality or indeed of amorality" (Chamoiseau and Confiant 1999, 74). But living in the disciplinary setting of the plantation where the storyteller is simultaneously a slave and, because of numerous artistic skills, a minor personality, enjoying the freedom to tell stories and yet under surveillance and scrutiny for the slightest hint of subversion, the storyteller had to practice the ambiguous art of both accommodation and revolt (Chamoiseau and Confiant 1999, 76).

In his theory of the operational logics of resistance (a subset of the practices of everyday life where the "consumer" plays the figure of the dominated), Michel de Certeau distinguishes between "tactic" and "strategy":

> I call a *strategy* the calculation (or manipulation) of power relationships that becomes possible as soon as a subject with will and power . . . can be isolated. It postulates a *place* that can be delimited as its own and serve as the base from which relations with an *exteriority* composed of targets and threats . . . can be managed. . . . By contrast a *tactic* is a calculated action determined by the absence of a proper locus. . . . The space of the tactic is the space of the other. Thus it must play on and with a terrain imposed on it and organized by the law of a foreign power. . . . it is a maneuver within the enemy's field of vision. (2002, 36–37)

It is precisely this second style of action, the tactic, which characterizes the storyteller's artistic practice, because he "must play on and with a terrain [the plantation] imposed on [him] and organized by the law of a foreign power," namely, the master or the overseer, and the spaces of his operation are provided by the interstices in that terrain which he invests to his advantage. In his struggle for dignity, which is a struggle to outwit the master, the storyteller, powerless and vulnerable, has to make do, like one of his culture's favorite trickster figures, the rabbit, with the only weapons at his disposal: wit and ruse. His rhetorical technique of choice is circumlocution, which involves using aspects of the master's language, symbols, and values even as they are cleverly diverted from their original meanings and infiltrated with subversive ones. But because the new meanings are rhetorically encoded, they remain inaudible to the master. Like the trickster figure of Afro-American folk narratives and vernacular English with whom he clearly bears comparison in certain respects (there are significant differences, of course, including the "toastful" and "boastful" qualities of the signifying monkey, who delights in his rhetorical power to triumph over such powerful enemies as the lion and the elephant by tricking them to do battle; Gates 1988, 55–64), the francophone Caribbean storyteller's performance sessions become what Henry Louis Gates calls "language games" (1988, 52). *Games* because information is conveyed to a complicit audience of fellow slaves through all manner of playful tricks like indirection, double meanings, and allusion. Chamoiseau and Confiant sum up the storyteller's strategy in these words: "Elle n'attaque pas mais elle piège. Elle ne frappe pas mais elle mine" (1999, 74) [It does not attack, it ensnares. It does not strike, it undermines]. This ancient power, "to act as the delegate of the voice of the enslaved people," to install "maroon resistance within the plantation" all the while providing "enchantment," "distraction," and "hope," is what performance-based Caribbean dramatists have sought to recapture (Chamoiseau 1994, 76, 74). As we shall see later, two significant examples of such an attempt are Chamoiseau's *Manman Dlo contre la fée Carabosse* and Elie Stephenson's *O Mayouri*.

Differential Politics and Policies

As we have seen, a multiplicity of factors contributed to changes in African and Caribbean theatre during the late 1970s. General references have been made to the material conditions of possibility, but these conditions were not specified with regard to any particular francophone territory or country. Neither was the possibility discussed of a differential cultural politics *within* francophone zones. The cultural politics of theatre in Africa and the Caribbean is particularly interesting given issues of political economy and of various discourses of indigeneity that developed in the 1970s and 1980s. Thus, beyond their commonalities, certain differences *within* and *between* francophone theatrical avant-garde practices and politics warrant further exploration.

By the late 1960s, less than a decade after independence, Ivory Coast had acquired what Patrick Manning described as "a reputation for abject neo-colonial submission to France and foreign capital" (1988, 195). Of course, this reputation was not new. Already in 1957, when neighboring Ghana was proudly proclaiming its independence from Britain, Ivory Coast had rejected any such option, choosing instead what its then leading politician, Félix Houphouët-Boigny, described as "the difficult path of creating with the [French] metropole, a community of people equal in rights and duties" (in Losch 2000, 5). Although the Franco-African Union that he dreamed of never came to fruition and Ivory Coast became independent three years later, Ivory Coast's original policy orientation did not change. This orientation comprised first of all a liberal economy open to French capital, citizens, and know-how, what Bruno Losch has characterized as "the opening of its frontiers to capital and men, and the pursuit of close links with the former metropole" (2000, 11). Second was "an alliance with companies" (9), and third "a policy of free access to the factors of production—land and labor" (10). While this policy choice yielded enviable results from the 1960s to the mid-1980s, leading to the so-called Ivorian miracle—impressive growth rates, the rise of a prosperous planter class and an articulate French-educated bourgeoisie, important urbanization and public works projects—many commentators, even the most sympathetic, were mindful of that miracle's real and potential problems. These included a loss of political sovereignty, with the state essentially "accepting to serve as a relay for foreign, in particular French, interests" (Losch 2000, 9). With respect to domestic and foreign policy, Marcel Amondji provides examples of a country in which the heads of most strategic departments and policy-making bodies were French nationals charged with executing France's policy objectives in Africa.

Other scholars, such as Samir Amin and Patrick Manning, have pointed to the fragility of a model of development which encouraged the production of commodities which the general population itself did not consume (coffee and cocoa) and the ostentatious consumption by the elites especially of products they did not produce and could ill afford. Clearly, because of its extreme dependence on volatile external factors beyond its control, such a model could not be sustainable:

Ivory Coast's evolution in the last fifteen years . . . can be characterized by an expression "growth without development"; that is, growth generated and sustained from the outside, with no prospect of the economic structures put in place automatically moving to the next stage, which is that of a self-sustaining dynamism. (Amin 1967, 31)

Amin's analyses were confirmed twenty years later when, as a result of the collapse of the world prices of its export commodities, the country's growing indebtedness, and France's radical shift of priorities from Africa to the European Common Market, the Ivorian economy went into crisis. The attempt to manage that crisis saw the entry, as major new overseers, of transnational financial institutions like the World Bank (Losch 2000). Compounding the above-mentioned problems were Ivory Coast's "reliance on as many as a million guest workers from Burkina Faso" (Manning 1988, 196). This last point is not insignificant as it later colored, as we shall see, the discourses of indigeneity of the 1980s and 1990s that culminated in the contemporary ideology of *ivoirité,* or Ivorianness.

However, the loss of national control was not just economic or political, even if that was its most visible aspect. The domination of the national culture—an area of particular relevance to the politics of avant-garde theatre—was no less crucial. In his book *La civilisation quotidienne en Côte d'Ivoire,* Abdou Touré analyzed the compulsive obsession of Ivory Coast's official culture with all things French or Western (a "Western-alienation syndrome" [1981, 107]), irrespective of their appropriateness to the local context: "the elites, experiencing a real passionate affair, an uncritical love-passion with things Western, . . . serve as the conveyor belts of imported values" (178). Direct consequences of this mindset included the neglect of Ivorian languages in favor of French (Touré 1981, 119–20), the elimination from francophone literature anthologies and syllabi of passages and texts critical of France (138–43), and the systematic presentation of local values and institutions as the irrational Other of an essential French rationality (150–55). This information is crucial to better contextualizing the argument in *New Francophone African and Caribbean Theatres* because it is in the context of—and in opposition to—such practices of "civilization-imitation" (Touré 1981, 243) that the 1970s Ivorian new theatre, and the various discourses of indigeneity of which it is an integral part, emerged.

To readers familiar with the situation in France's overseas departments in the Caribbean (collectively known as the DOM-TOM, or Départements d'outre-mer–Territoires d'outre-mer), the similarities with Ivory Coast stand out, other divergences to which we shall return notwithstanding. What differences exist in the areas under discussion is a matter of degree not of kind. Because the Caribbean territories are constitutionally part of France, their dependence on that country is direct. In Ivory Coast, on the other hand, as in many francophone sub-Saharan African countries, the French influence is mediated through the state, the local elites, and the realities of political independence, however nominal that independence. As Edouard Glissant has shown in *Le discours antillais* (*Caribbean Discourse*), the directness of Caribbean dependence grew with the region's 1946 change in constitutional status. This opened the Caribbean market to French goods and investment (and, after the Maastricht Treaty was signed in 1992, to other European ones as well), bringing the potential for material prosperity. However, as had been the case in Ivory Coast, this prosperity attracted migrant labor from poorer neighbors: from Haiti (consider Wilnor in Schwarz-Bart's *Ton beau capitaine*) and the Dominican Republic or, in the case of French Guyana, from Brazil. But again, like in Ivory Coast, the impressive performance of the DOMs came at a price.

The most immediate opportunity cost that resulted from incorporation in a larger global economy was observed in the destruction of the region's productive, even if modest, local economies whose principal agricultural products—sugar and fruits—now proved uncompetitive in the face of cheaper imports from France and elsewhere. With this destruction also came the loss of what little control the territories exercised over their local affairs (Burton and Reno 1995, 4–6). Partly to tackle the resulting high rates of joblessness, especially between 1965 and 1975 (an issue thematized in Elie Stephenson's *O Mayouri*), France encouraged Caribbean emigration to the metropole (Anselin 1995, 112–18) even as it exported thousands of metropolitan citizens to the Caribbean to take up jobs in government and the expanding service industry sector. But the second price paid was, according to

Glissant, cultural dispossession. As traditional Caribbean culture and its arts lost their supporting economic base and functionality, they became increasingly folklorized. With the decline of Caribbean productivity, the stage was set for the blind imitation and consumption of foreign products (economic and cultural), which was encouraged by various subsidies and social allocations from France. Culture, as understood in official Caribbean circles, now took the form of tours by visiting French classical orchestras, art, fashion or other exhibitions, and theatre troupes. People assumed, in other words, the higher quality of a manufactured object shipped ready-made from France for local Caribbean consumption or reproduction.

The desire to possess these objects and to assimilate into the French identity they express has not always been consumerist, Glissant admits. Prior to 1946, to want to be French corresponded to a calculated project of accession to political rights, of acquisition of a certificate of humanity, so to speak. It was an act of emancipation. But this act later lost its liberating thrust to become, like in Ivory Coast, a mere marker of social distinction and privilege, one powerfully realized in Véronique's parents in Maryse Condé's novel *Hérémakhonon* (1976). Of course, the degree of what is known as "Frenchification" (Glissant 1981, 482) experienced by elite Caribbean residents and by Ivorians in these areas is not the same. The Caribbean is much smaller and therefore a more easily controlled territory with nearly 400 years of continuous French rule (as opposed to 132 for the longest French-colonized territory in Africa, Algeria), and there is the presence of an economically and culturally influential white, originally slaveholding, settler class (the so-called *békés*), which became the local embodiment of French cultural standards. But perhaps the most important factor is the absence in the Caribbean of a countervailing and supportive infrastructure of deeply rooted, vital indigenous cultures. And this is a crucial factor in understanding the differences in avant-garde responses between the African and Caribbean contexts. In a reflection on the absence of such an infrastructure in the francophone Caribbean, Glissant writes:

> If the Martinican intuitively grasps the ambiguity of both his relationship with French and his relationship with Creole—the

imposed language and the deposed language, respectively—it is perhaps because he has the unconscious sense that a basic dimension is missing in his relation to time and space, and that is the Caribbean dimension. As opposed to the Metropolitan relationship with the Metropolis, the multidimensional nature of the diverse Caribbean. As opposed to the constraints of one language, the creation of self-expression. (1992, 165)

But whatever the differences in levels of alienation, they pale in comparison to the shared fact of neocolonial domination, experienced and measured by oppositional elites in the respective regions not in degrees of pain, but as *absolute* pain. The context of the loss of economic and cultural control gave rise in Ivory Coast as well as in the Caribbean to various dis-assimilationist discourses and movements of indigeneity, including of course the new performance theatre, but also such ideologies as *ivoirité* (Ivorianness), *antillanité* (Caribbeanness), and *créolité* (Creoleness).

Peter Geschiere and Francis Nyamnjoh have explored movements of indigeneity, or of "autochthony," in ways that are relevant to the newer theatre. For them, these constitute responses to the processes of globalization. "The flows of people, goods . . . images [and capital] on a truly global scale," they write, "not only lead to globalization, they trigger equally potent tendencies towards localization" (2000, 425). In other words, the more intense mobility becomes (of people, goods, and capital) *across* national boundaries, the greater the sense of loss of sovereignty experienced by the national authorities. Such loss in turn provokes economic, cultural, and migratory closure and protectionism. Although the phenomenon is not limited to postcolonial societies, economic asymmetry usually privileges unidirectional and unequal global flows of economic but also cultural goods from the industrial North to the developing South. As Abdou Touré has shown:

> The West haunts the world. The dominant civilization whose originality resides in the fact of having given rise to capitalism —a capitalism that spread across the borders of the West and imposed itself on others—capitalist civilization has been the center in relation to which other world civilizations have sought to define themselves. (1981, 253)

Geschiere and Nyamnjoh locate the 1980s and 1990s African discourses of autochthony as situations in which either the nation as
a whole or a group are represented as dispossessed vis-à-vis another
group or nation within this nexus of "flow and closure" generated
by capitalist globalization. But more than a crisis of national sovereignty, these discourses also express discontent with a transnational
capitalist modernity whose collateral burden of displacements, frag-
mentations, and cultural dislocations triggers a project of emancipation from domination and a quest (cultural, physical, symbolic) for
home, belonging, and groundedness.

In the specific case of Ivory Coast, Karel Arnaut distinguished
three distinct but overlapping autochthonic trends (2004, 217–19).
The first was expressed in the form of organized political action against
Ivory Coast's perceived enfeoffment by France. The second concerned
scholarly research into aspects of Ivorian indigenous cultures, as radical intellectuals called for a cultural renaissance (Arnaut 2004, 217)
and established a specialized African Studies Institute in 1967, the
Groupe de Recherche sur la Tradition Orale (GRTO), at the University
of Abidjan. Examples of the work done in, or loosely inspired by, the
institute included research and publications on "drummology" (the
study of the language of drums; Bouah 1987a) and the performance
traditions of various indigenous African peoples. Finally, the third
movement, the one most relevant to the present discussion, was
cultural and artistic. It involved the creation of new, African-rooted
forms of artistic expression. The most well-known examples are
Ahmadou Kourouma's and Jean-Marie Adiaffi's experimental novels,
Les soleils des indépendances (1968) and *La carte d'identité* (1980), and
in theatre, the productions of such companies as Werewere Liking's
Ki-Yi Mbock, Souleymane Koly's L'Ensemble Kotéba, Marie-José
Hourantier's Bin Kadi-So, Rose Marie Guireaud's Les Guérivoires, and
Bernard Zadi Zaourou's Didiga. Many of these productions drew on
research carried out by the directors of the various companies at the
African Studies Institute referred to above.

Like in Ivory Coast, a similar movement of cultural dis-
identification from France and localization also took place in the francophone Caribbean in the 1970s and 1980s, and the rise of discourses
of Caribbeanness is seen by many as one of the expressions of this

trend (Burton and Reno 1995; Glissant 1992). Other manifestations came in the form of a revival of interest in francophone Caribbean Creole culture, the founding of the Groupe d'Études et de Recherches de la Créolophonie (GEREC) at the University of the Antilles and Guyane in the mid-1970s for the study of Creole, the creation of a university diploma in Creole studies, and the use or incorporation of that language in literary and theatrical works. Whether in Africa or in the Caribbean, the proponents of movements of indigeneity shared the belief that national sovereignty could only be recovered through reculturalization and relocalization, gestures which presupposed a delinking from French and Western global cultural and economic influences. The statement by the Ivorian academic and theatre critic Barthélémy Kotchy that Africa "could be reborn and rediscover itself through its own language, modes of thinking, and art" (in Arnaut 2004, 217) must be understood within this context. This also explains the rejection by such playwrights as Chamoiseau, Liking, Stephenson, and Zaourou of the French-based theatre culture of their respective Westernized elites, on the grounds that it was foreign and therefore inauthentic, and their stance that it should be replaced by the performance idioms of the disenfranchised majority population. In the eighteenth century, the French revolutionary Abbé Sièyes, in his fiery pamphlet *What Is the Third Estate?* (2001), had argued for the exclusion of the French nobility from the nation-in-the-making on the grounds of their unjust social privilege and idleness (Hunt 1996). Performance dramatists of the 1970s and 1980s in the Caribbean and Ivory Coast adopted a similar approach to the dominant French-inspired theatre of their day because of what they saw as its incapacity to offer national cultural representativeness. The "indigeneity" or "authenticity" of theatrical form thus emerged as a criterion for national cultural belonging.

Francophone avant-garde dramatists may well have advocated a return to the local and the autochthonous, but they did not all arrive at the same cultural destination. Caribbean dramatists had a narrower range of forms to which to return (mostly folktales as opposed to the rituals, epics, and legends of their African counterparts), and their vision remained consistently naturalistic and secular as opposed to the supernaturalism of African drama. In Ivory Coast, for instance,

Liking and Zaourou showed a predilection for religious rituals, but this choice was not exclusive and they also experimented with other idioms like puppetry, legends, dance dramas, and folktales. Koly, for his part, sought inspiration essentially from Malian secular folk forms and dance dramas, and Zinsou studiously avoided religious idioms of performance (which he saw as no less elitist in their "traditional" context than French-inspired theatre) and concentrated instead on concert party and storytelling genres. Caribbean dramatists insisted on the usage of Creole as an essential index of cultural identity, a precondition for any authentically Caribbean theatre, whereas in Africa, playwrights have for the most part failed to translate this conviction into theatrical practice. Their theatre owes its Africanness more to the performance forms they have textualized than to the language in which they are expressed. But perhaps the greatest difference between African and Caribbean avant-garde theatre resides in the cultural identity expressed by the indigenous idioms. For francophone African dramatists, that identity—held to be common to *all* Africans, especially by Pan-Africanists like Liking—is variously represented as a precious object to be dug from the earth (*Elle sera de jaspe et de corail,* 1983), a state of being with which to reconnect (*Une nouvelle terre,* 1980), or a repressed memory to be brought to consciousness (*La mémoire amputée,* 2004). Unless such excavations and reconnections are made, the cultural community stands to remain entrapped in a state of anomie.

In this regard, Zaourou's conception is no different. For him, African identity is a preconstituted reality, waiting to be retrieved and salvaged from subjugated traditions. However, he refuses to be what he calls "a prisoner of the ancient ideology served by our old arts" (2001, 132) and advocates borrowing "what is best in other cultures" (2001, 132). Where differences exist between African playwrights, or even between plays by the same dramatist, they concern the degree to which a specific recovery should take the form of wholesale restoration, or adaptation, or even rejection. There is little doubt, for instance, that Liking opts in *La puissance d'Um* (1979a) for the outright rejection of the world view embodied in the funerary rituals demanded of women in Bassa society, even as she models that play on them. Yet, in *Une nouvelle terre,* she emerges as a proponent of the selective retention of ancient practices. Nevertheless, consensus is to be found among playwrights when it comes to their conviction that the "original" culture must be the regulator of all cultural borrowings, and a commitment must be made to reactivating it following centuries of dispossession. A community that proceeds differently imperils the sense of direction provided by the compass of that original culture and thus runs the risk of drifting rudderless.

African dramatists have embraced a transcendent African culture that is posited in opposition to an equally transcendent Western culture, but the diasporic Caribbean counterpart advocates no such thing. Dramatists such as Patrick Chamoiseau, Gerty Dambury, Odile Pedro Léal, and Elie Stephenson do not exhibit a consciousness of or nostalgia for a global Africanness or blackness in the same way that Aimé Césaire did in *A Tempest* (1969). In this play, the fate of the enslaved Caribbean is linked culturally and linguistically to that of colonized Africa and politically to a segregated black America. Similarly, Césaire's *La tragédie du roi Christophe* (1963) included shifts that suggested synonymity between Africa and Haiti as well as the eponymous hero's wish to be buried on Mount Ifé (the spiritual home of the Yoruba of Nigeria), references that unmistakably reveal a traditional diasporic desire to return to an originary African home, considered the source of his authentic being. But no such desire, with its hint of ethnic absolutism, is discernible in the work of post-Césaire theatre practitioners. For them, the Caribbean cultural identity they defend and embrace is not unproblematically derived from a "straight, unbroken, line, from some fixed [African] origin" (Hall 1990, 226). It is rather plural, "framed by two axes or vectors, simultaneously operative: the vector of similarity and continuity and the vector of difference and rupture," both engaged in a "dialogic relationship" (Hall 1990, 226–27). Caribbean cultural identity is thus neither identical to nor totally different from Africa's; it is creolized, a hybrid identity born of multiple transactions but reducible to none. It is the truth of this mulatto identity, hitherto "put under lock, in the depths of our being" (Bernabé, Chamoiseau, and Confiant 1989, 14), that Caribbean avant-garde theatre seeks to recover from the French universalism which first put it "under lock." This is where one finds the fundamental difference between the African and Caribbean avant-garde, namely, in the refutation by the latter of a global Africanness/blackness, which it perceives as a mere figuration in the West Atlantic.

The Postcolonial Avant-Garde: Problems and Prospects

We have by now gained some familiarity with the kind of cultural politics intrinsic to francophone avant-garde theatre. We have also seen a number of problems emerge relating to questions of accessibility and to the systematic appropriation of indigenous performance media. Such measures can be understood as worthy acts of cultural reclamation, but they do not necessarily guarantee access to the contents of avant-garde theatre. This has been especially true in the case of African theatre where some of the media are esoteric and thus only available to initiates or community elders in "traditional" contexts. Also, because of their embeddedness in specific ethnocultural communities, neither these esoteric practices nor their secular equivalents are intelligible to all members of the national—let alone continental or global—black community, a problem made more acute for the nonliterate sections of (African) audiences by the fact that what little text exists in these plays is still overwhelmingly in French. Statements made by dramatists such as Souleymane Koly, according to whom recourse to dance, body movements, and so on provides access to "every African whatever their ethnic background" (in Boiron 1993a, 17), or Liking, claiming that "we privilege gestures and sounds; these are things that can appeal to everyone and can go across frontiers, cultural barriers" (in Boiron 1993b, 52), must be judged with caution, at the very least because of their facile Pan-Africanism. This reductive and unanimist vision of African societies, one that erases history and national, ethnic, gender, and class differences and that subsumes all Africans under an undifferentiated and generalized sameness, has been incisively discussed by the Beninese philosopher Paulin Hountondji (2002, 107–8, 131–33).

This problem, though probably less acute, is also present in the francophone Caribbean. The idea of a core identity common to a monolithic Caribbean people and expressed in Creole is as much a myth as is its African counterpart. While a theatre in Creole based on the resources of that culture is accessible to audiences in Guadeloupe and Martinique irrespective of class and race, it is much less the case in Guyana where Creole and its performance traditions are limited to a particular section of the population (albeit the largest and most influential), namely, the descendants of the plantation slaves. Creole is therefore not necessarily accessible to other Guyanese ethnic groups nor expressive of the identities of the Amerindians, the so-called bush Negroes (the Saramanca and Boni Maroons), Caribbean Asians, and so on. Thus, even if communication with spectators were facilitated by the new drama's shift to performance in the respective regions, it is not clear that anything of interest will necessarily be communicated. Indeed, there is a real danger that the imperative of reaching the broadest audiences possible could result in having to empty the plays of all engaging and radical content. Such a move would effectively reinscribe at the heart of francophone theatre what Dean MacCannell has termed the "performative primitive" (1992, 17–73), a racist category produced by the commodification by Western entertainment and tourist industries of the performance traditions of non-industrial peoples. Such cultural events include "charging visitors admission to their sacred shrines, ritual performances, and displays of more or less 'ethnologized' everyday life. [This is the] commercialization of ethnological performance and display, co-developed by formerly primitive peoples and the international tourism and entertainment industry" (1992, 18).

Of course, there is no guarantee that the most politically subversive theatre will not be transformed into a commodity by Western audiences in the grip of "the postmodern fantasy of 'authentic alterity'" in an increasingly "global monoculture" (MacCannell 1992, 19). But when the francophone theatre practitioner is an accomplice to such a transformation by deliberately emptying his or her stage work of all meaning (in the name of ease of communication), then s/he unwittingly promotes the idea of francophone theatre as an exotic product and its performers as nothing but dancing bodies. This problem, as Boiron has pointed out, is intensified by the need to also satisfy the tastes and expectations of the Western audiences on the international festival circuits, where francophone theatre is in high demand: "A complicated text . . . can constitute a serious impediment to Japanese and American *buyers*. A musical or gestural show will have a better chance of responding to the needs of the 'market'" (1993a, 17; emphasis added).

The evolution of some performance-based theatre into mere signs without referents was already noticeable in some of Liking's work that seemingly abandoned intellectually challenging, oppositional, and subversive drama. Plays such as *Dieu Chose* (1985), *Les cloches* (1988b), and *Perçus Perçues* (1991a) increasingly veered toward a feast of colors, drumming, and movement. The same could be said of Koly, according to Hourantier (1984, 50), who after early and well-received efforts to create a new theatrical language based on the *kotéba* idiom then took the easy route of using song and dance purely for entertainment. These examples are perfect illustrations of the phenomenon of "the postcolonial exotic" analyzed by Graham Huggan (2001), with the result that the global market place of the international theatre festival circuit is gradually being transformed into a commodity through world tours and the entertainment industry.

The danger of exoticizing an originally subversive theatre is also acute in the francophone Caribbean, even if the reasons for this trend are not the same. Richard Price and Sally Price, following Glissant, have shown how the francophone Caribbean's rapid modernization and cultural absorption into France and Europe and the growth of tourism there has resulted in an intense need for the "representation" (1997, 15) of Creole arts and culture. This need has been met in a number of ways: through the opening of museums and the creation of mass media programs, theatre groups, and cultural associations devoted to celebrating the local cultural heritage. Instead of culminating in the revitalization of that heritage, however, the net result of these efforts, of which avant-garde performance theatre is an ironic example, has been the "museumifaction" of that heritage and its conversion into spectacle—not just for tourists, but also, more disturbingly, for the Caribbean people whose heritage it is.

The lesson that emerges from this development is that, without a corresponding renationalization of the economic and political infrastructure that sustains a cultural heritage and makes it meaningful (a near impossibility for the Caribbean which is part of France), the reculturalization solution advocated by avant-garde dramatists both in Africa and the Caribbean seems fated to fail. At best, it becomes a coping mechanism, or an exercise in "nostalgia for people who are otherwise busy adjusting to the complexities of a rapidly modernizing lifestyle" (Price and Price 1997, 15), or at worst, as we have seen, it becomes pure spectacle. The risk of commodification and of a lurch to tourist-oriented entertainment—rather like the Western "neo-avant-garde," which uses modernist avant-garde techniques but without their oppositionality—is not the francophone avant-garde's only (potential) weakness. The situation becomes even more complex when it is recalled that what passes for "authentic" and "indigenous" and therefore necessarily acceptable is, on close inspection, of foreign provenance or externally induced. Such is the case, for example, with the representation of the performing body as a locus of knowledge, a point of intersection between the physical and spiritual realms of human experience. This emphasis on, and mystical conception of, the body—especially in the African drama of religious ceremonial—ironically reproduces one of the most tenacious discourses by which the modern West both constructed and marginalized the colonized, namely, the juxtaposition of the "rational" European with the "spiritual" African, whereby the former is all mind and the latter all body. One of the weaknesses therefore of the vision of the new drama is that it does not challenge and subvert this dualism on the grounds of its ahistoricity or the limits it sets to human self-definition, among other points. Rather, it reproduces the structure of invented identities, satisfied with reversing the valences of them. The rational and the spiritual are considered human attributes and not a function of skin color. In this framework, a truly radical and progressive drama does not dance to imposed identities, but refuses to amputate itself of important dimensions of human experience.

Even if aspects of the African and Caribbean identities asserted by this drama were not of foreign origin, its vision would not be any less vulnerable to criticism. One particular area where this is the case is in the prescriptiveness of its conception of cultural identity. It is a conception in which to be African or Caribbean is to conform, under pain of exclusion, to a predefined set of values, modes of behavior, cultural practices, and so on. In the case of theatre, it is also to use specific performance idioms, language (Creole in the case of the Caribbean), performance techniques, and acting styles, all derived from the ambient cultures of orality. While such a conception is necessary in situations of domination and plays an important role in the constitution of an autonomous collective or individual self, it does contain the potential for excess. By privileging the constructed categories of the autochthonous or the indigenous, new ways of self-imagining and becoming are foreclosed, yielding the potential for exclusionary cultural politics. An instance of such exclusion is found in Chamoiseau and Confiant's view of the theatre of Césaire, Glissant, and Boukman as being insufficiently Caribbean (1999, 189–90) because of their "inability to forge a language that is not overly external (or foreign) to the average Caribbean reader/spectator" (190). However, Arnaut has persuasively shown (2004, 224–49) that Ivory Coast provides the most instructive example of the pitfalls and degeneration of the avant-garde culturalist discourse of theatrical authenticity through its co-optation into the larger political discourses and movements of indigeneity, a co-optation to which it lent itself, let it be said, through its privileging of the notion of "authenticity."

When it first emerged in the 1970s, this culturalist discourse had a clear Pan-African bent. It sought to constitute an Ivorian culture rooted in African performance as opposed to the elite culture that derived from France. Its target, therefore, was France and the "inauthentic" francocentric culture of the local elites. In the oppositional political critiques of the Houphouët-Boigny order (Amondji 1984; Gbagbo 1983; N'Zembele 1984), these elites were labeled "fake locals" (Arnaut 2004, 222) in opposition to the "real locals," whose resistance to French/global domination was allegorized in such Ivorian historical plays as Laurent Gbagbo's *Soundjata: Lion du Mandingue* (1979) and Bernard Zadi Zaourou's *Les Sofas* (1974). In these plays, the heroes that inspired theatre practitioners were all cultural figures such as the griot or the renowned hunter Djergbeugbeu. By the 1990s, however, with the increasing liberalization of the political system in Ivory Coast and competition for power, the notion of cultural authenticity took a more regional and national turn. The South, from whence came *all* the dramatists of the Ivorian avant-garde, the first post-Houphouët-Boigny president of Ivory Coast (Konan Bédié, 1993–1999), and the current occupant of that position (the playwright Laurent Gbagbo), represented itself and its performance traditions (Bouah's "drummology,"

Zaourou's "*didiga*," and Jean-Marie Adiaffi's "bossonisme" or study of traditional Akan religious practices) as *the* site of authentic Ivorian identity (Arnaut 2004, 228–29). The North, some of whose heroes and traditions had been celebrated on the Pan-Africanist Ivorian stage of the 1970s—by the same southern dramatists who now repudiated them—henceforth explicitly became the abode of "fake locals," people of questionable loyalty to a country to which, in any case, they were said *not* to be indigenous.

The trajectory of Dieudonné Niangoran Porquet's work is revealing in this context. He was credited with launching the notion of *ivoirité* in the early 1970s when he founded with Aboubacar Touré the troupe Masques et Balafons (Masks and Drums), finding inspiration for this new theatre movement (the griotique) in the techniques of the griot of the Mandé cultures of northern Ivory Coast. By uniting in his troupe's name the cultural symbols of northern and southern Ivory Coast—the drum and the mask, respectively—he demonstrated a desire to create a national culture from the country's diverse cultures. However, by 1994, he had reversed course. His long dramatic poem *Masquairides-Balanfonides* (1994), in whose title can be detected the name of his 1970s troupe, no longer staged unity but rather conflict and dissension between the dispossessed "indigènes" (represented by the southern character Seu Gueu) and usurpatory "strangers" and conquerors, that is, between an autochthonous and authentically Ivorian South and an allochthonous North. Thus, for Dieudonné Niangoran Porquet, the avant-garde, once an emancipatory and progressive anti-neocolonial Pan-African artistic movement, had taken a narrowly national and then an ethnic turn (Arnaut 2004, 234–35).

I have drawn attention to some of the weaknesses of the politics of francophone avant-garde theatre in order to show that a return to roots is not the panacea to the problems of francophone theatre and identity that it is sometimes heralded to be. A play based on French/Western models should not be automatically condemned as un-African and therefore unprogressive, any more than one inspired by indigenous African performance resources can necessarily be hailed as liberating. While a certain rootedness of form and vision in the humus of the local culture is important in establishing communication between audience and playwright, it is not a sufficient criterion for a politically progressive avant-garde theatre.

Having considered some particularities, as well as some moments, events, and practitioners that have marked the development of francophone African and Caribbean theatre, the actual cultural meanings of this theatrical phenomenon require additional attention. A number of important questions must be addressed: What is the cultural politics articulated through the indigenous performance poetics of the new theatre? Does the adoption of such a poetics necessarily make for a progressive politics? How do positionalities vary between dramatists such as Liking or Zaourou working under conditions of limited cultural and political sovereignty and those such as Chamoiseau or Stephenson who find themselves under conditions of cultural and political subordination? And finally, how can one begin to compare avant-gardist theatrical practices in a postcolonial context with those in a postmodern one?

Experimentation, Avant-Gardism, and Post-National Theatre

Western theatrical modernism offers an interesting counter-perspective, given that several decades before dramatists from Africa and the Caribbean chose to revitalize their theatre through the incorporation of indigenous performance traditions, Antonin Artaud had advocated a similar practice for European theatre in his groundbreaking collection of essays, *The Theatre and Its Double* (1938). Describing the "Western" theatre of his time as "decadent" because of its subordination of "everything . . . that is theatrical to the text" (41), he called for that theatre's renewal through a return to "a concrete physical language" (37) of "music, dance, plastic art, [and] pantomime" (39), namely, a language "addressed first of all to the senses instead of being addressed primarily to the mind as is the language of words" (38). For Artaud, this concrete physical language could be found in the "primitive" performances of the non-industrialized world, in his particular case, as we saw earlier, in Balinese theatre. Although Artaud was more of a theorist than a practitioner (and has been criticized for making hasty generalizations about "Western" and "Oriental" theatres), his celebration of performance over text found favor in the United States and France in the experimental work of such performance art troupes as Julian Beck and Judith Malina's Living Theatre, Ariane Mnouchkine's Le Théâtre du Soleil, Peter Brook's International Centre for Theatre Research, and Richard Schechner's Performance Theatre (Carroll 1986; Innes 1993, 2000).

Western theatrical modernism both in its contemporary and historical performance art phases is also of interest because several critics have argued for its influence on postcolonial theatre. This position is based on a notion of cultural exchange in which cultural influence flows unidirectionally from metropolitan center to postcolonial periphery, such that aspects of francophone performance theatre surface as the expression and extension of these practices outside Europe. Chantal Boiron, for example, reads Sony Labou Tansi's work against the backdrop of "the avant-gardist experiments of a Craig or Appia . . . and, closer to us, of the Living Theatre, the Bread and Puppet, Eugenio Barba and Foreman, and of the famous 'performances' of the 1970s" (1993a, 19). Boiron even feels compelled to caution Sony Labou Tansi against too uncritical an emulation of these avant-garde experiments, notably their anti-textualism. "Let us remind Sony Labou Tansi," she writes, "that most of these experiments turned out to be ephemeral and sterile" (Boiron 1993a, 19). Michelle Mielly puts the onus on Werewere Liking to dispel the belief "held by more than one critic" (2003, 54) that her work— Mielly specifies Liking's fiction but could just as well have evoked her theatre—derives from that of "Artaud, Mnouchkine, or Brecht" (2003, 54). "For the Western reader," Mielly tells Liking, "your novels have a postmodern feel to them, even a surrealist quality with hints of automatic writing" (2003, 54).

Clearly then, for some critics, the immediate and significant sources of postcolonial (francophone) avant-garde theatre have to be metropolitan. There are, of course, convergences, intersections, and parallels, but also significant differences between postcolonial and Western avant-garde performance theatre, patterns that delineate spheres of influence as products of cultural circulation, but such approaches and interpretations of theatrical tradition contain the hallmarks of an imperial gesture of annexation while potentially voiding the theatre's originality and even radicalness of meaning. Indeed, the chapters that follow on individual playwrights will highlight the commonality of formal features but ultimately argue that the sources of those features are different, traceable to local rather than global cultures.

A list of shared formal features can be easily drawn up. These include a nonliterary, anti-textualist orientation (Innes 2000, 62–69); a spatial conception of theatre as "a concrete physical space which asks to be filled, and to be given its own concrete language to speak" (Artaud 1958, 37); a predilection for collective creation; a valorization of the director and the actor and a corresponding de-privileging of the playwright; a flexible use of theatrical space that aims to break down the barrier between actor and audience; an emphasis on the sensory and perceptual as opposed to the disembodied and intellectual; a non-naturalistic, self-reflexive conception of the theatre; and, finally, a view of performance in certain cases as sacred, as an act of worship. These commonalities are not recalled to imply, given their historical ante-riority, an influence of Western modernist theatre; such an influence might in fact seem anachronistic given that Euro-American modernist theatre derived components of its stylistic and formal techniques from the "primitive" performance idioms of postcolonial societies (Innes 1993, 6–18; Schechner 1969, 209–28; Steins 1976; Smith 1992, 1–13). Indeed, one of the ironies of transnational cultural relations is that what has sometimes been considered modernist, postmodernist, or avant-garde is in fact quite simply traditional or premodern, as crit-ics have shown in connection with the anglophone postcolonial the-atres of India, Nigeria, and the Caribbean (Awashi 1989; Rotimi 1990; Savory 1995). Richard Schechner makes this point when he writes:

> Generally, among the world's cultures an emphasis on drama-script has occurred only occasionally: ancient Greek drama, the Sanskrit drama of India, various Chinese and Japanese tradi-tions, the modern drama of Europe and its cultural extensions from the Renaissance on. Even among these, only "modern drama" since the late nineteenth century has so privileged the written text as to almost exclude theater-performance altogether. (in Harris 2006, 118)

Perhaps a more appropriate way of discussing the influence of the modernist avant-garde on African and Caribbean playwrights would be to emphasize the manner in which archaic idioms of performance that had been devalued by colonial culture as anything but theatre were later incorporated and celebrated on the culturally influential Western stage, providing a kind of ideological authorization in the eyes of postcolonial theatre practitioners. In short, as Peter Hawkins has pointed out, the encounter with, or the detour through, the modernist avant-garde was the catalyst that strengthened postcolonial theatre practitioners in their voyage of rediscovery of their repressed and devalued heritage (1992, 233–41).

Although the embrace of the "non-Western," "primitive," "exotic," "indigenous," "traditional," or "local" by various practitioners is one of the shared and defining characteristics of both the modernist and postcolonial avant-gardes, the politics of this embrace remains significantly different between the two movements. In the strand of modernist avant-garde represented by Artaud and his performance art followers, non-Western-inspired dramatic spectacles provided the tools for a critique and radical subversion of modernity. In their masterful use of the wordless "language" of trance and hieratic gestures and of a "poetry in space" (Artaud 1958, 38), these spectacles constituted pathways to "an unknown, obscure and fabulous reality" (Artaud 1958, 61) "from which man has been tragically severed with the advent of an impoverishing 'logos,' self-consciousness and reflexivity" (Conteh-Morgan 1994, 31–32). For those countercultural sections of Western societies of the 1960s in revolt against the repression of desire by instrumental rationality, the spectacles of faraway exotic lands came to be seen as holding the key to the spiritual Eden of a world before alienation, of "[s]peech before words" (Artaud 1958, 60).

The longing for anarchistic freedom, expressed in spontaneous behavior unrestrained by social norms, was a central feature of the performance theatre art movement (Innes 1993, 167–81), and the Living Theatre's collective creations were perfect illustrations of this longing. In defiance of social taboos, actors in these plays/ceremonies went naked, imitated copulation, and encouraged the spectators to join them in doing the same. The quest for spiritual transcendence, the struggle to overthrow the "repressive machinery civilization constructs to keep itself intact" (Schechner 1969, 217) by using ceremonial theatre might very well constitute a worthy politics for Western avant-garde theatre practitioners operating in conditions of postmodernity and late consumer capitalism, which they consider dehumanizing. But these concerns are probably considered luxuries by their postcolonial francophone counterparts who operate in conditions not of postmodernity but rather of pre- or, at best, peripheral modernity. Theirs is a condition of uneven and unequal insertion in the processes and networks of global capitalism, negatively impacted by underproduction and unequal commodity exchange. The objective is therefore to press indigenous performances to quite different ends, not so much in the direction of a revolt against commodification or in search of some vague spirituality, but instead in the creation of new theatrical cultures that could enable the creation of productive, self-sustaining economies and sovereign communities. In other words, theirs is ultimately a political project concerned with imagining a new community, a community brought into being by an act of what Christophe Dailly and Zaourou have labeled "reculturalization" (1977, 478).

The reversion to indigenous forms, even when they adopt mystical or religious overtones (like in Liking's theatre), is nothing short of a political struggle for national self-retrieval and cultural re-enfranchisement, elements that are a precondition for any act of self-directed, national development, the necessary foundation for the construction of an alternative, African needs-driven modernity. It is the displacement of a political and economic drive onto the realm of culture. The postcolonial francophone avant-garde is a movement of return to the local and the indigenous (African or Caribbean Creole culture, for example) and a rejection of the foreign or allochthonous (Western/French) that is seen as inauthentic and a threat to indigenous identity. On the other hand, the modernist avant-garde represents a flight from the (Western) local that is seen as effete and alienating, whereas the non-Western (foreign/primitive) is seen as regenerating. One paradigm is narrowly nationalistic (and sometimes even ethnic) and celebrates in various degrees "roots," "territoriality," and cultural "authenticity" (consider, for example, Bernabé, Chamoiseau, and Confiant's *Éloge de la créolité* [In Praise of Creoleness]); the other is rootlessly cosmopolitan and advocates the "undo[ing] of the closure of [social] textuality" (Heuvel 1991, 83) in favor of a world of social indeterminacy and liminality. In both instances, rootlessness is central, either to be excoriated or to be defended, and both movements reflect the contrasting historical and sociological circumstances of their emergence and development: a cultural, economic, and political crisis of national sovereignty brought about by the domination of the postcolony by the forces of French and global capital and cultural homogenization (hence the rejection of the culture of the French/ West, mimicked in its original form or its variants by the nationalist elites), and by an imperial economic and cultural hegemony that informs the construction of "a new and universal [read: European] art" (Smith 1992, 9).

The fundamental differences between the two movements are in their respective uses of primitive performance idioms. For the African and Caribbean playwrights, recourse to these idioms is meant to make modern theatre more accessible to a wider audience. The dominant literary drama inherited from France has remained, even at its most politically radical, an elite preoccupation cultivated only by the tiny minority of Western-educated members of the population because it is scripted and in French but also because of its formal procedures. The character called the Spectator makes this point in the 1975 version of Senouvo Agbota Zinsou's *On joue la comédie:* "You would understand if you thought of our compatriots who in principle have the same rights as you and me, but who in reality do not enjoy the privilege of going to the theatre because they lack the material or intellectual means, or the time" (109). It is thus partly to restore to the theatre a function equivalent to that enjoyed by performances in indigenous communities—a privileged medium of communication with a popular audience—that postcolonial dramatists of the francophone avant-garde opted for the textualization in their works of ancient idioms. "I want to create a drama," Souleymane Koly explained, "in which every African can participate and which can be understood by every African whatever their . . . social level" (in Boiron 1993a, 17). This objective was diametrically opposed to that of the modernist avant-garde, which cultivated an elite, vanguard audience of devotees who stood out for their rejection of the commercialized and conventional theatre of mass consumption. As Peter Bürger argued (1984, 55–82), in the cult of the new, recourse to the exotic, the nonconventional, and the obscure became the formal expression of resistance to mass appropriation and commodification.

Pragmatic considerations relating to communication were not the only concern of the postcolonial avant-garde. Presenting *local* idioms onstage—beyond artistic inspiration and spiritual renewal—was of profound political significance since these had been previously repressed or marginalized as the native Other of the "civilized," French-inspired, literary drama. This was consequently a measure designed to rescue these idioms *and* the ordinary people whose cultural heritage they represented from the cultural and political margins of national life. Literally and metaphorically, this process would bring these matters to theatrical and political center stage. Likewise, the widespread use of the technique of group participation and collective creation functions to create a festive atmosphere, but it is also an attempt to promote a countercultural ideal of social existence based on communal structures and not on individualism. Theorizing this sentiment in the period of rising modernity, almost a century before the period we're discussing, Nietzsche had written:

> Under the charm of the Dionysian [performance drama], not only is the union between man and man reaffirmed, but nature which has been alienated . . . or subjugated, celebrates once more her reconciliation with her lost son, man. . . . Now, with the gospel of universal harmony, each one feels himself not only united, reconciled and fused with his neighbor, but as one with him. (1967, 37)

Unlike its predecessors, embodied in the visionary and charismatic leadership found in such plays as Seydou Badian's *La mort de Chaka* (1962) and Césaire's *La tragédie du roi Christophe* (1963), where the leader formulates a political program that is then imposed through a monological relationship on a passive population whose input is irrelevant (a politics that presupposes an active custodian of the truth and a passive recipient of that truth), collective creation is a more pointedly political technique that fosters a democratic, participative, and consensus-based politics. Just as actors and audiences contribute to the creation of a play, so too in the real-life theatre of politics, rights are extended to citizens, who are not just left with the burdensome duties of "subjects." As the character Third Spectator argues in *On joue la comédie:* "The theatre will remain the worst of imperialisms if only a minority of individuals has the right to work out all the details, organize everything, and definitively determine a text, gestures, and the smallest details of an illusion that is imposed on a passive audience" (1975, 109).

The sense of irony displayed by many of the works in this tradition, their meta-theatrical playfulness and non-illusionism, do not signify mere entertainment or lack of seriousness. Rather, these aesthetic features reflect an awareness of the contingent nature of the constructedness of social and political "truths." This awareness, while disconcerting for certain audience members in search of the 1960s grand narratives of national liberation, nation building, and progress, could make for a more negotiable and tolerant politics.

Finally, another aspect worth considering is the political significance of the corporealization of dramatic action, a technique taken from indigenous performances. The performer, especially in connection with the theatre of religious ceremonial, does not always illustrate a character, and is performing an act not of mimesis, but rather of catharsis, that is, a psychologically and spiritually transformative experience. What then, one may wonder, is implied in this focus on the performing body and on perceptual values, and in the corresponding de-privileging of speech or logos? What emerges is a politics of resistance to the ideology of modernity and, by extension, its progenitor, Enlightenment rationality, according to which the body, as a source of obscurity, is an impediment to true knowledge. A site of the sensual and of appetites, the body is associated in Cartesian thought with the state of childhood and in Enlightenment rationality with women (Sala-Molins 2006; Conteh-Morgan 2006), and it is the obstacle to be transcended through acts of purification if true and certain knowledge or civilization, associated with cognition, is to be reached.

The devaluation by the French of the corporeal and sensory values of the theatre they encountered in Africa, and the corresponding emphasis on the word, causality, psychological coherence, and observable reality in the theatre they introduced, is the objective correlate of this rationalist vision. By creating a modern theatre that valorizes the senses and the body as a source of true and certain knowledge, francophone avant-garde theatre was able to defiantly reassert those values of the sensorium associated with Africa by a certain nationalist identitarian discourse. However, while the theatre of the mid-1970s and early 1980s offered a critique of the then-dominant nationalist drama, this corpus of plays was by no means monolithic. The artistic/ cultural axis provided an alternative theatrical imaginary that rejected French dramatic authority as this had come to be mediated by the nationalist elites of the pre- and early post-independence periods, and advocated instead a rediscovery and (nondecorative) stage deployment of local performance idioms. These forms were accompanied by ideological and political plays in which the focus was provided by analyses of society and politics. The target of this theatre's critique was the post-independence sociopolitical order and especially the discourse of anticolonial nationalism from which that state derived part of its legitimacy.

To contrast the artistic avant-garde and the political avant-garde within the theatre of this time period is not to suggest that both trends lived in splendid isolation of each other, nor to imply that the former eschewed politics in favor of experimentation while the latter foregrounded political commitment at the expense of artistic innovation. The major difference between the two trends lies, perhaps, in their conception and use of artistic creativity. Whereas in the plays of the artistic avant-garde (Liking and Zaourou, for example), the subversion of the French formal legacy of play making is the defining preoccupation (a fact that in part explains their pronounced formal self-consciousness), formal exploration takes place alongside sociopolitical statement in the plays of the political avant-garde (notably in the plays of Tchicaya U Tam'si and Sony Labou Tansi). Theatrical creativity serves an instrumental function by rendering the critique accessible to a broad audience *and* by translating into the language of the stage the tenets of its oppositional vision. Both, however, engage in transgressive revolt against the earlier generation, underscoring the need for both reculturalization as a condition of national development (local performance forms and cultural symbols) and sociopolitical transformation as a way of encouraging cultural autonomy and agency, the latter often emphasizing democracy and pluralism

(Fischer-Lichte 2000). These particularities will become all the more evident when we turn our attention in the following chapters to the analysis of plays by Chamoiseau, Dervain, Liking, Stephenson, and Zaourou, and subsequently to those of U Tam'si, Sony Labou Tansi, and Schwarz-Bart.

We have thus far examined some artistic components of late 1970s and 1980s theatre—the theatrical practices of the "second" generation of African and Caribbean playwrights—and I now want to concentrate on the post-nationalist theatre of political critique and its specific attempts at demarcating itself from what I have called the "theatre of the nationalist state." I use this term not so much to qualify a theatre whose function it is to reflect and disseminate state policies slavishly—not therefore in the sense of the "state-sponsored theatre" characteristic of the kind of official literary production that Dominic Thomas explored in Congo-Brazzaville with reference to the Marxist-Leninist regime between 1969 and 1991 (Thomas 2002, 1–51)—but instead to characterize a theatre whose independent commitment to, and promotion of, the values of anticolonial nationalism identified it with the political formation in which those values found their most complete juridical and political expression, namely, the national-ist state. Put differently, the relationship between the francophone nationalist theatre of the 1960s and early 1970s and the state was not one of subordination of the former to the latter, but rather a con-vergence of interests between an intellectual/artistic elite, on the one hand, and a political elite, on the other, united by a common vision and a pursuit of national self-realization and political liberation.

A key component of this vision was the notion that the achieve-ment of nationalist objectives was contingent upon the rediscovery and reactualization of an ancient, precolonial order of values and political organization. This primordialist vision, which saw the nation as a preexistent unit, fully formed and only waiting to be resurrected and reinstated (after the disruptive interlude of empire), accounts for the restorative dimension attached to the discourse of francophone nationalist theatre. It also accounts for that theatre's preoccupation with the past, with history, a preoccupation confirmed, as has often been noted, by the preponderance of historical plays. This was espe-cially true of the plays from Sahelian countries such as Mali, Niger, and Senegal, but also of those from the equatorial countries, such as Benin, Congo-Brazzaville, and Ivory Coast. Examples of such plays include Seydou Badian's *La mort de Chaka* (1962), Bernard Dadié's *Béatrice du Congo* (1970), Massa Makan Diabaté's *Une si belle leçon de patience* (1973), Jean Pliya's *Kondo le requin* (1966), and André Salifou's *Tainimoune* (1973).

Contrary to its primordialist convictions, francophone nationalist theatre did not so much resurrect a preexistent nation as imagine and perform one into being, all the while promoting national self-awareness. Nationalist theatre was, in other words, a discursive practice, a political meaning-producing endeavor that was deeply embedded in a contest with empire for power. Some of the models deployed included repeated allusions to the existence in precolonial national communities of strong and charismatic figures—for the most part, aristocratic or of warrior-class lineage—who were impelled by noble ideals and a sense of self-sacrifice. Another such mythic figure was the resistance leader or fighter, who was also often associated with nation building. While the precolonial leader was linked with sacrificial action, the image of his people in nationalist drama included unquestioning obedience and adherence to the ideals of the state. "You think obedience lowers you," N'Delebe suggests to one of the conspirators in Badian's 1962 *La mort de Chaka*. "You are mistaken. Obedience lowers no one; on the contrary, it makes you great" (115). This view is ratified by the warrior-emperor himself when he admonishes his followers shortly before his murder: "Keep alive the memory of this victory and never forget how we won it. I repeat: we won it because we knew how to obey . . . because we were able to forget ourselves for the sake of the unity we believed greater than the individual" (126).

There is no room in Badian's play, nor indeed in the theatre of nationalism in general, for individual autonomy or dissent. The public realm of national "resistance" against the enemy, "duty" to the homeland, and the "glory" of the state completely encompasses the private sphere. Individuals receive harsh treatment as they are consistently caricatured as selfish pursuers of sensual pleasure and materialism, values that are presented as somehow un-African and, at the very least, as a threat to the security of the national community. The statist or Chakaesque ideal, on the other hand, is never critically explored in nationalist drama, even for the potential dangers inherent in its hegemonic impulse to "totalization" (Bayart in Chabal 1992, 91). The political imaginary of francophone nationalist theatre, then, like the postcolonial state in which this imaginary was embodied, was distinctly hierarchical. There is, on the one hand, the world of sovereign authority, *le père de la nation* or *le guide providentiel* (father of the nation or providential guide) who lays down the law, and on the other, the subjects who unquestioningly obey. Like the colonial state that it replaced, the postcolonial state has now become what Achille Mbembe (2001) has described as a "family state" based not on a contractual relationship or negotiated dialogue among a plurality of opinions, but instead on an authoritarian and paternalistic exercise of power between a paterfamilias and his family, a sovereign and his subjects. In the political world of this theatre, the individual is not a citizen but, like in the antecedent colonial era, is a "protégé caught up in the family guardianship ... [who] can only think of his/her enfranchisement at his/her own risk and peril. For a protégé cannot be a subject of law. Consigned unilaterally to a sort of minority without foreseeable end, he/she cannot be a subject of politics, a citizen" (Mbembe 2001, 35). This statist model of politics, presented as a precolonial African formation and thus as authentic, was comprehensively repudiated and burlesqued in the post-nationalist theatre of political critique of the late 1970s and 1980s.

The reconceptualization of the state emerged in the context of a broader crisis of legitimacy of the nationalist state characterized by a drift into authoritarianism—the product of neocolonial economic and cultural dependency, paternalistic politics, successive coups d'états, the geopolitics of the Cold War, elites' greed and corruption, kleptocracy, and criminality (Bayart 1989; Bayart, Ellis, and Hibou 1999)—political instability, and the ever-deepening immiseration of the population. Perhaps the most notable manifestation of the crisis was the response to it by intellectuals, artists, and citizens themselves. One example was the work of a new wave of francophone African thinkers, of which the best known, arguably, was the Beninois philosopher Paulin Hountondji. In his work, but also in that of Cameroonian philosophers Marcien Towa and Fabien Eboussi Boulaga, the cultural nationalist idea of a precolonial African heritage to which conflict and pluralism were foreign, an idea performed on the theatrical stage of the period and theorized in Senghor's negritude, was subjected to detailed critique. Hountondji qualified this idea as imaginary and dismissed it for considering African cultures solely in synchronic terms, in the process denying them the creative tensions and transformations characteristic of all human cultures. Hountondji traced the cultural nationalist model to what he called the "progressive" European thought of the interwar years, namely, the philosophical ethnology of Father Placide Tempels, the anthropology of Claude Lévi-Strauss, and even the surrealism of André Breton (Hountondji 1976, 33–70, 156–69; 2002, 123–34). This vision of African cultures was therefore, he concluded, not so much an objective truth as an alienated discourse because it revolved around a European problematic about African cultures, and because it was essentially addressed to a European public. Hountondji argued:

> The African ethnophilosopher's discourse is not intended for Africans. It has not been produced for their benefit, and its authors understood that it would be challenged, if at all, not by Africans but by Europe alone. . . . In short, the African ethnophilosopher made himself the spokesman of All-Africa facing All-Europe. (1976, 45)

A similar observation has also been made with respect to the dynastic and imperial modes of political organization presented by nationalist dramatists and historians being "authentically" African. Scholars have pointed out that the exclusion from this vision of what anthropologists call "acephalous" African societies—precolonial polities in which power was disseminated rather than vested in the hands of a centralized authority—was driven in part by that same impulse to conform to European nineteenth-century criteria for historical achievement that comprised territorialization, empire building, centralized state authority, and a unitary conception of the nation (Ekeh 2000; Neale 1985; Okpewho 1998b; Wrigley 1971). Likewise, critics have argued that African nationalist ideology, like many anticolonial nationalisms, "remains trapped within the structures of thought from which it seeks to differentiate itself" (Gandhi 1998, 115), and consequently its "will-to-difference simply becomes another surrender to the economy of the Same" (Gandhi 1998, 118). As Peter Ekeh has observed:

> Adulation of conquerors who foundeed [sic] their hegemo-nies on the reckless and unnecessary spilling of blood is heav-ily entrenched in African historiography. Unfortunately, it is a piece of historiography that African historians willingly learnt from liberal Western historians intent on claiming for Africa the existence of its own set of conquerors. (2000, 168)

This impulse to conform creates serious problems for the postcolonial present because the activities of the rulers are not subjected to scru-tiny for "their significance in their own time and place" (Neale 1985, 12). Whatever the leaders' excesses, they are minimized by nationalist writers on the grounds that their commission was in pursuit of the only worthy goal of civilization, namely, centralized state formation. Peter Ekeh's challenge is therefore all the more relevant:

> Who wants to besmirch Egypt's reputation for its atrocities in Kushland? Many African intellectuals would prefer that we allow the holy pharaohs, who have brought so much pride to us in Africa, to rest in peace. Ancient Ghana's glory and veritable his-tory of conquests of ethnic neighbors have been appropriated by Nkrumah for his country. (2000, 147)

As a result, the new leaders end up replicating the territorialism of imperial nationalisms against which they rebelled, and in doing so negate their ideals of Pan-African unity and justice.

One such example of replication was Seydou Badian's representa-tion of Chaka, a warrior who is consecrated as a liberator of his people (the Zulu) for having freed them from "fear and famine" (1962, 112) and from being the "plaything of others" (102). But Badian conve-niently omitted other information about Chaka, who had visited "fear and famine" on other Africans, namely, the Basutho people, whose suffering is attested in history (in 1931, for example, Thomas Mofolo published a novel entitled *Chaka: A Historical Romance* in which Chaka was depicted as a southern African Faust figure and a bloody tyrant). What mattered to Badian (as indeed for Senghor in his dramatic poem *Chaka*) was Chaka's imperial achievements and not the fate of the neighboring African peoples he defeated in pursuit of those achievements. This monarchical, imperial view of the African past was denounced by intellectuals such as Hountondji, since for them the challenge facing the nationalist was to recognize his representation of Africa for just what it was—a *representation,* the product of theoretical choices and ideological positions and not of a singular and unchanging collective vision of Africans or their past. In other words, responsibility must be assumed for the authorship and paternity of discourse.

The corollary to accepting such responsibility was therefore the acknowledgment of the possibility of entertaining other discourses deriving from different theoretical options, and in turn abandoning the potentially intolerant myth of a singular African world view in matters of culture, history, or philosophy to which citizens could be forced to subscribe under threat of treason. The conceptual shift from the idea of an anonymous subject of discourse (tradition) that speaks through the sage, the ethnophilosopher, or the leader, to that of multiple and sometimes conflicting and individualized subjects of discourse, constituted one of the major intellectual events in the fight against the homogenizing ideologies of the nationalist state. This struggle for intellectual pluralism against a monolithic tradition (reminiscent in many ways of Enlightenment modernity's struggle against ecclesiastical authority) naturally had political implications. The process of asserting political rights in the face of an all-powerful state whose legitimacy derived not from a contract between "full subjects capable of self-understanding, self-consciousness, and self-representation" (Mbembe 2003, 13) but rather from the alleged ways of the ancestors (tradition) was particularly problematic. At the forefront of this struggle was "civil society," whose members, according to Chabal's definition, are

> all who may have become powerless or disenfranchised: not just villagers, fishermen, nomads, members of different age groups, village councillors or slum dwellers, but also professionals, politicians, priests and *mullahs,* intellectuals, military officers and all others who are, or feel they are without due access to the state. (1986, 15)

The post-independence state continued to speak of "development" and "national unity" long after it had abandoned these objectives, but civil society emphasized the need for economic, political, and social rights. One of the most significant manifestations of oppositionality to the postcolonial state was provided by the theatre of political critique, which drew abundantly on urban popular culture with its techniques of oblique political derision through verbal compositions such as songs, slogans, and wordplay.

Comi Toulabor (1981) explored some of the obscene and satirical linguistic devices that were used to undermine authority figures. These meanings were well known to the wider, especially urban youth, population, but less so (if at all) to the authorities, who often belonged to ethnolinguistic communities that were different from those of the satirists. For example, the Ewe-language word *amegan,* which is regularly used during official events to describe the president and his exploits and that conventionally means *illustrious* or *wise man,* also has a hidden sexual meaning—*adult phallus* or *chief's phallus.* Togolese audiences hailing the chief in public events are thus able to play on this ambiguity! Another example is the acronym of the single and only ruling party, the RPT (Rassemblement du Peuple Togolais), which Togolese oppositional popular audiences pronounce scatologically as *air pété* to suggest onomatopoeically (in Ewe) a diarrheal bowel movement or flatulence (in French, the verb *péter* means "to fart"), thus associating the post-independence state with the scent (sound?) of human waste. By holding the state up to ridicule, such corrosive popular humor, abundantly reprised in the drama, has the effect of sapping it of the respectability and moral authority necessary for the exercise of power and thus of delegitimizing it in the eyes of the population. The crisis of legitimacy of the post-independence state and the many ways in which its authority is contested by a vocal civil society (itself the site of a popular as opposed to the elite and statist consciousness of the nationalists) provide the defining parameters of the drama enacted in the post-nationalist theatre of political critique as exemplified by U Tam'si and Sony Labou Tansi.

The analysis of specific plays that begins in the next chapter will develop these ideas and observations and reveal how the theatre of the late 1970s and 1980s succeeded in demarcating itself from its nationalist predecessor. The latter was utopian (relying on the techniques of realism interspersed with folk performances), while its post-nationalist successor is dystopian (drawing on fantasy, the satirical grotesque, and derision); one privileges the "high politics" of the pre-colonial state authorities (based on foundational myths and historical legends), the other the "low politics" of civil society doing battle with a repressive postcolonial state. The contrast sharpens considerably in their respective treatment of political leadership, most notably in the plays of U Tam'si and Sony Labou Tansi where the once-mythologized warrior-king has been replaced by a figure that is to be ridiculed, having degenerated into a brutish predator, to what Jean-Michel Devésa has called "les mangeurs d'homme" (1996b) [the man eaters]. The leader's brutality was justified in the drama of nationalism for the pursuit of legitimate public ends (anticolonial resistance, for example, or, in the early post-independence phase, nation building), but no such rational argument can be made for post-nationalist theatre. Walante, the ruler in Sony Labou Tansi's *Qui a mangé Madame d'Avoine Bergotha?* proudly boasts: "Je prends mon grade du lot des monstres / aux sources de la cruauté" (1989, 33) [I come from the rank of monsters, I drink from the springs of cruelty], while Mheme, one of the members of the military in power in U Tam'si's *Le destin glorieux du Maréchal Nnikon Nniku, prince qu'on sort,* roundly declares: "Nous, notre ennemi, c'est le Civil" (1979, 41) [Our enemies are the civilians].

The theatre of political critique, in other words, can be characterized as a "theatre of cruelty" in a literal rather than in an Artaudian sense since, for Artaud, the notion of a theatre of cruelty refers to a genre of spectacle that appeals not to the audience's intellect (which he associates with the ratiocination of logocentric theatre) but to the senses:

> In a word, we believe that there are living forces in what is called poetry and that the image of a crime presented in the requisite theatrical conditions is something infinitely more terrible for the spirit than the same crime when actually committed. . . . It is in order to attack the spectator's sensibility on all sides that we advocate a revolving spectacle which, instead of making the

stage and auditorium two closed worlds, without possible communication, spreads its visual and sonorous outbursts over the entire mass of the population. (Artaud 1958, 85–86)

For our purposes, the notion of a theatre of cruelty refers to post-independence francophone theatre in which the spectacle of the suffering body (in its physical materiality) and its destruction (through torture, rape, mutilation, dismemberment, murder) are prominent features. In this theatre, we encounter what Achille Mbembe has described as a kind of "necropolitics," whereby "the ultimate expression of sovereignty resides to a large degree, in the power and the capacity to dictate who may live and who may die. Hence, to kill or to allow to live constitutes the limits of sovereignty, its fundamental attributes" (2003, 11–12). In other words, the body of the citizen and its fate have become the principal object of the exercise of power, and, accordingly, francophone dramatists have detailed the multiple ways in which that body can be destroyed, reduced in plays such as Sony Labou Tansi's *La parenthèse de sang* to *chair* (flesh), *entrailles* (entrails), and *sang* (blood). Thus, the francophone theatre of political critique depicts a world of the "generalized instrumentalization of human existence and the material destruction of human bodies and populations" (Mbembe 2003, 13).

The plays that will be examined also highlight the all-encompassing nature of the ruler's predatoriness, expressed as a compulsive hunger for power and an insatiable sexual appetite. The leader's diminished image and ignoble exploits also correspond to his diminished range of linguistic expression and tone. From the restrained to the (sometimes) spuriously sublime and rousingly defiant heroes in the theatre of nationalism, the language of post-nationalist theatre became satirical and scatological. Hierarchical relationships between ruler and ruled remained in place, but the silent and obedient subjects of the earlier theatre were replaced by the silenced and brutalized subjects of the theatre of the 1970s and 1980s, who relinquished their status as spectators to become activists. Nightmarish, surreal, and absurdist qualities characterized these plays; in *Qui a mangé Madame d'Avoine Bergotha?* Sony Labou Tansi announces that we have before us "a story of madness that quickly becomes a story of mad people" (1989, 9). Ordinary rules of rationality were displaced in favor of arbitrariness, political rights were suspended or abrogated, and the individual was violated without due process; this is a "state of exception" in which a "legal civil war [waged by totalitarian governments] . . . allows for the physical elimination not only of political adversaries but of entire categories of citizens who for some reason cannot be integrated into the political system" (Agamben 2005, 2). The world of the 1960s theatre of nationalism was at least intelligible, governed by rules of causality in which a chain of events followed a logical pattern. Even if the meaning of the historical forces and events that destroyed its many hapless monarchs remained unknown and mysterious to them, they were at least part of a knowable world. In the world of post-nationalist theatre, however, we have entered a surreal and grotesque world of excess and fantasy.

ONE

Cultural Trauma and Ritual Re-membering: Werewere Liking's *Les mains veulent dire*

The theatre of the Ivory Coast–based Cameroonian playwright Werewere Liking represents one of the most creative appropriations of indigenous performance traditions for the francophone African stage. This appropriation is not undertaken for antiquarian or aestheticist reasons, or even for reasons of nativist nostalgia, but rather for the urgent task of exploring and addressing the realities of contemporary Africa in the idiom of that continent's artistic and knowledge forms. To the extent that she turns to the indigenous cultures of Africa for both a diagnosis of, and a solution to, that continent's problems, her theatre can be seen as an example of cultural autonomy and emancipation, what Wole Soyinka has described as "the apprehension of a culture whose reference points are taken from within the culture itself" (1990, ix). Liking's *Les mains veulent dire* (1981) contains aspects of both the realities apprehended in her theatre and their mode of apprehension. To better understand these, information on the development of her theatrical career will be provided in addition to an analysis of this particular play in light of the indigenous social performance on which it is modeled. This discussion will be framed by conceptual notions of cultural trauma, amnesia, and anamnesis.

Liking's position as arguably the leading francophone dramatist of the past three decades and *the* emblematic figure of the performance-oriented theatre of the 1970s and 1980s derives from at least two facts. The first is the sheer volume and diversity of her production as well as her related and well-documented activities as theatre director, cultural activist, and entrepreneur (Miller 1996; Mielly 2002, 2003). The second is associated with the radically different function that she conceives and advocates for the theatre. Although she commenced her literary career in 1977 with poetry and has to date written five novels, it is as a theatre director and dramatist—with ten published plays and many unpublished ones—that she is best known (Conteh-Morgan and d'Almeida 2007).

Liking's dramatic career can be divided into two phases, which I will call the "holy" and the "profane." The former is characterized by works such as *La puissance d'Um* (1979a), *Une nouvelle terre* (1980), and *Les mains veulent dire* (1981), plays that are closely modeled on, and aspire to the condition of, various African sacred ceremonies, especially those of her Bassa people of Cameroon. But beyond a mere search for inspiration from these real-life experiences, she has provided, through transcription and translation, a literal stage transposition of some of them in works such as *Le rituel de guérison de Mbeng* (1979b) and *Le rituel du "Mbak" de Nsondo Sagbegue* (1979c). By the early 1990s, however, Liking had abandoned holy theatre and entered the second, or profane, period of her theatrical career. This saw her experimenting with secular performance practices: dramatized epic narratives like the *mvet* of the Beti people of Cameroon and Gabon and the Sunjata epic of the Mandingo in *Un touareg s'est marié à une pygmée* (1992b) and *Waramba, opéra mandingue* (1991b), respectively; puppetry in *Dieu Chose* (1985) and *L'enfant Mbénè* (1996a); and sung drama in *Quelque Chose-Afrique* (1996b). This period also witnessed the birth of a more socially activist Liking. No longer content with producing esoteric drama that she hoped would "initiate" her largely anonymous audience into a state of "higher consciousness," she now actively sought to intervene in the social arena:

> I create my art according to needs, like the cobbler who carries out his work for immediate use.... In the beginning, I worked in experimental theater techniques with ritual, music.... Today no one knows where to classify me in terms of an aesthetic. But it's according to the needs of the young people with whom I work. My theater is therefore a vital one; it functions according to the needs of the day. (in Mielly 2003, 54)

Liking's activism has taken two forms. The first is as a *théâtre opérationnel,* a more socially interventionist theatre, as in works such as *La veuve diyilèm* (1994b), *Singué Mura* (1990), *Quelque Chose-Afrique* (1996b), and *Héros d'eau* (1994a), in which topical issues like indigenous values and development, civil wars, and gender relations are explored. The second is her Villa Ki-Yi project—a countercultural (performing) arts center/artists' commune that she founded in Abidjan in 1985. Referring to this space as "countercultural" seems justified because it was initially conceived as a venue for the cultural and theatrical performances of the Ki-Yi Mbock troupe and as an exhibition space for her collection of African arts and crafts. But it rapidly expanded its mission to take on a more social welfare character, catering to the needs of poor or delinquent youth, some of whom were offered residencies to learn skills in the performing arts, costume designing, sculpting, and music making, with a view to improving their chances for gainful (self-)employment. In its emphasis on the crucial importance to creativity and self-sustaining development of an appreciation of the value of indigenous cultural and artistic resources, Villa Ki-Yi is indeed the social embodiment of Liking's theatrical vision. Of course, a social consciousness has never been absent from Liking's works. What changed, however, in the 1990s was that consciousness's mode of dramatic expression. It became more direct, in contrast to its earlier embedded representation in the symbolic language of myth and ritual. From a theatrical point of view, the drama of this phase was also notable for its greater use of the techniques of improvisation and collective creation, its systematic creation of texts that were not exclusively spoken, and its embrace of modern audiovisual technology and instruments (not just indigenous ones) like videos, film clips, electric guitars, and saxophones. Not insignificantly, and with consequences that will be analyzed later, this drama also became the drama of global audiences thanks to its presentation within the circuits of international world theatre festivals like the Festival International des Francophonies held annually in Limoges, France.

I hope to be clear that the phases in Liking's career referred to above should be seen more in terms of methodological adjustment and continuity rather than rupture. For if she abandoned holy drama, this was not because of a disavowal of its aims and principles, but rather because of her realization of the ineffectiveness of its methods and her conviction that its vision could be operationalized differently. Some of the earliest signs of its ineffectiveness were expressed by the actors themselves, who felt they were unable to cultivate the state of ecstasy necessary for a successful performance. For example, they insisted on impersonating characters rather than on confronting the self within, as she would have wished, believing that performing was a game played for the pleasure of others and, perhaps, for small material rewards instead of an exercise in self-transformation. In short, they were *acting* and not *worshipping*. But it was precisely the spiritually transformative quality which Liking sought for her early drama that also accounted, somewhat paradoxically, for that drama's striking originality and avant-garde status in the 1970s and 1980s.

Unlike plays by dramatists of the nationalist and early postcolonial periods, Liking's early drama does not focus on the depiction of an offstage social or political struggle set in an observable and concrete world of anticolonial or postcolonial reality. It is rather the exploration and bringing to light, for actors and audiences alike, of a space of inner truth and spiritual import that exists at a level of knowing that is deeper than that of the rational mind. Liking's search for tools to access this subconscious realm explains her rejection of the realist, French-inspired francophone theatre of her period and her fascination with religious rituals and their nonrational methods: trance, fantasy, and symbolism. One such ritual that serves as a model for *Les mains veulent dire* is the *djingo* of the Bassa people of Cameroon.

The *djingo* is a healing or, in Victor Turner's classification of a similar ceremony among the Ndembu people of Zambia, an "afflictive" ritual (1968, 13). Organized in times of individual sickness or misfortune, its purpose is to diagnose and reveal to the patient, his kin group, and his local community the causes of the affliction and to propose appropriate remedial action (herbal and/or religious) through the ritual officiant. Unlike the predominantly organic explanatory model of sickness of modern Western medicine, the "traditional" Bassa proceeds on the premise that even the most somatic of sicknesses is only the disguised presentation of unresolved conflicts or traumatic events that occurred in the past and remain unavailable to individual or group consciousness (transgression of a taboo, for example). Illness to the traditional Bassa, in other words, manifests itself as coded behavior, "an interrogation . . . a language" (Liking, Hourantier, and Schérer 1979, 15), whose semantics await deciphering and understanding, while the patient is conceived as a site of physical and psychological pathologies whose origins and force field are located beyond him, in his wider society: "family and close friends are often the actors in a drama that has chosen one of their own to express itself" (Hourantier and Schérer, 15). This view of individual illness as *social* accounts for the psychodramatic character of a healing ceremony like the *djingo* and its focus on group—as distinct from individual—therapy even when it is the individual who is manifestly ill. "Afflictive ritual," Turner observed, "is pre-eminently concerned with the health of the corporate body, with securing balance and harmony between its parts, which are groups . . . rather than individuals" (1968, 270). This approach also explains the ceremony's emphasis on public disclosure, for unless the group gains awareness of the social roots of the abnormal conduct exhibited by one of its own and purges itself of them through an act of ritual catharsis, its stricken member and thus itself will forever remain afflicted:

> Every "disharmonious" or "destructive" act requires active medi-
> ation for the restoration of the disrupted harmony. To this effect,
> ritual encourages analysis and reasoning on the part of all the
> participants. Through techniques of induction the ritual leader
> enables each participant to proceed backward to the origins of
> the problem. (Hourantier 1984, 60)

It is this therapeutic function of the *djingo* and other rites in its mold that Liking seeks to capture and that she advocates for francophone theatre in a more general sense.

I will use the word "anamnesis" to place Liking's theatre practice within the broader framework of Mircea Eliade's discussion of mythologies and of memory and forgetting in *Myth and Reality*. Just as Liking, working from Bassa origin myths, constructs in *Elle sera de jaspe et de corail* (47–53) a period *ab origine* when humanity—rescued from a devastating flood by the gods—lived wisely and creatively in their company, so Freud too (in Eliade's reading of his work; 1963, 76–78, 88–89) hypostasizes a mythical period of bliss situated in early childhood. Eliade writes: "For psychoanalysis, for example, the truly primordial is . . . earliest childhood. The child lives in a mythical, paradisal time. Psychoanalysis developed techniques capable of showing us the 'beginnings' of our personal history" (1963, 77). But in both cases, primordial bliss does not endure since a "fall" soon intervenes. In Freud's case, that fall is attributable either to an external traumatic event, such as "the primal scene" or childhood sexual molestation, or to an internal problem, such as a failed process of psychosexual development. The negative affect associated with this event is removed from consciousness through different coping mechanisms that include repression and amnesia. For Liking, on the other hand, the fall has nothing to do with a sexual event, but rather everything to do with cultural trauma.

Elaborated by analogy with psychological trauma, cultural trauma is not easily conceptualized. An idea of the difficulties involved in that task can be gained from the essays devoted to the subject in *Cultural Trauma and Collective Identity* (Alexander et al. 2004). Neil Smelser, for example, in his essay "Psychological Trauma and Cultural Trauma," advances the startling argument that, however catastrophic, "no discrete historical event or situation automatically or necessarily qualifies in itself as a cultural trauma" (2004, 35), because such an event's theoretical status as trauma would depend on a number of factors, including the health or "sociocultural context of the affected society at the time of the historical event" (36), the nature of the affect provoked in the population (36), and the imprint on the collective consciousness. "Cultural traumas," Smelser concludes, "are *for the most part* historically made, not born" (2004, 37; emphasis added). Michael Salzman and Michael Halloran adopt a diametrically opposed position in their essay "Cultural Trauma and Recovery" (1994, 231–46), since for them any singular event can in itself be traumatic irrespective of context. The theoretical status of an event as trauma resides, of course, outside the scope of this book, and whatever the differences among them, trauma theorists seem to agree on a minimal definition of the phenomenon. In the case of Salzman and Halloran, it is "a state of emotional anxiety suffered by an individual or group of individuals who have experienced severe compromise to their system of cultural meaning. Specifically [it] has severely undermined the capacity of the cultural worldview to meet the need for a world of existential meaning and value" (1994, 242). For Smelser, it can be located in

an invasive and overwhelming event that is believed to undermine or overwhelm one or several ingredients of a culture or a
culture as a whole. The Protestant Reformation qualifies as a cultural trauma because of the fundamental threat it posed to the
integrity of the Catholic worldview. The imposition of Western
values on colonial societies in the nineteenth and twentieth centuries provides additional examples. (2004, 38)

Smelser's invocation of colonial "imposition" is particularly relevant,
since this is a recurring theme in Liking's work. In her psychological
reading of it, the colonial encounter constitutes a kind of primal scene
for the peoples of Africa, the site of an originary wound equivalent
to the castration of a father figure, the etiology of the social neurosis
afflicting many of their societies. Liking's rendering of this scene in
the language of myth in *Elle sera de jaspe et de corail* is worth quoting
at some length, as she writes about humanity rescued from the flood
in her inimitable, punctuationless style:

> Ils partageaient l'ardeur le souvenir de l'ancêtre sage la renais-
> sance riche en créativité la foi de la reconstruction ardue à partir
> de soi-même ... C'était leur idéal. *Mais un jour vint l'envahisseur
> sur des chevaux et des oiseaux d'acier* ... Il les vainquit et acheta
> leur âme. L'ancêtre et l'image de la renaissance disparurent un
> jour remplacé par l'image sur le suaire ... *Et ceci a eu des reper-
> cussions jusque dans les têtes et les cœurs jusque dans les rêves et
> dans les gênes* ... L'imagination s'est atrophiée et le goût de la
> perfection semble désormais inconnu. (1983, 48–51; emphasis
> added)

> They shared the fervor the memory of the wise ancestor the
> rebirth rich in creativity the faith in the passion for arduous
> reconstruction that would begin with oneself ... That was their
> ideal. *But one day the invader came on horseback and with birds
> of steel* ... The ancestor and the image of rebirth disappeared
> one day and were replaced by the image on the shroud ... *And
> this has had repercussions all the way into* [*their*] *heads and the*[*ir*]
> *hearts into* [*their*] *dreams and* [*their*] *genes* ... Imagination has
> atrophied and the desire for perfection seems unknown from
> here on. (*It Shall be of Jasper and Coral*, 2000, 34)

Liking returns to this point more directly in an interview:

> [T]here was at some point a tremendous rupture between the
> universe inhabited by the creators of [African art] and the one
> in which we now live. This rupture [first, the slave trade and
> then colonization] was all the more serious as it was a spiritual
> one. . . . We lost contact with the divine. . . . For Africa, this led to
> enormous repercussions. . . . Our objects were emptied of their
> meaning. (in Mielly 2002)

Liking's representation of colonialism as catastrophic rupture is, of
course, commonplace in postcolonial literatures. But what is less common is the way in which Liking reframes it in existential and psycho-
spiritual terms as opposed to the usual political and economic ones.
Her reference above to the subconscious level of "dreams" and "genes"
is an indication of the extent to which, for her at least, the traumatic
violence of the colonial encounter has been repressed by the postcolony. That violence remains unavailable to its collective consciousness and exists only at the disguised level of existential meaningless-
ness and the neurotic behavior of many of its citizens. To Liking, in
other words, the existentialist category of the "absurd" is not a metaphysical feature of the human condition. It is a state of being overdetermined by concrete events in history.

While Liking acknowledges the foundational character of the
colonial encounter, it would be a misrepresentation of her position
to suggest that the encounter was wholly responsible for the social
pathologies exhibited by many postcolonial African societies. Her
work is nothing if not a sustained attempt to lay bare (in the same way
that the ritual officiant does in a *djingo* performance) the often unacknowledged dimension of individual and collective responsibility in
the crises of the postcolony, even if the distribution of the degrees of
responsibility between colonial violence and postcolonial complicity
tends to vary from one work to another.

Leela Gandhi's reading of the ambivalence at the heart of the colonial relationship may help to clarify Liking's framing of the issue of
individual and collective complicity. For if the colonial scene is one of
traumatic terror, as Gandhi has argued, it is no less a scene of seduc-
tion, of "perverse mutuality" between opposing forces, one in which
"the desire of the colonizer for the colony [is matched] by the inverse
longing of the colonized" for the culture, language, and values of the

colonizer (1998, 11). But the satisfaction of the latter longing requires a corresponding "disowning of home" (12), in other words, a devaluation of, and a distancing from, the colonized self and its heritage. It is this paradox of "hate and desire" (11), resistance to, and complicity in, the subordination/castration of the self that Liking embodies in the behavioral abnormalities (characterized by, among other traits, mimicry, beggarly dependence, and self-hatred) of allegorical characters such as Grozi and Babou in *Elle sera de jaspe et de corail* and Lem Liam Mianga in *L'amour-cent-vies* (1988a).

The solution for Liking is certainly not to be found in economic or political reform but first and foremost in psycho-spiritual healing. This she sees as an absolute prerequisite for successful socioeconomic development. Explained in the framework of her cultural practice and philosophy, the solution is to recover and re-suture what she describes in the novel of the same title, *La mémoire amputée,* namely, Africa's "amputated memory." This can be achieved by bringing to the consciousness of individuals and groups, through an act of ritual initiation, the memory and implications of the traumatic event to which they were victim *and* their unacknowledged complicity in the crisis to which it gave rise. The ability to do that is a critical step in understanding the roots of the crisis and thus in gaining mastery over it. The narrator of *Elle sera de jaspe et de corail* concludes her diary with this advice to her afflicted community:

> What we would all need
> Is a form of initiation capable of alchemy
> Our societies would once again become initiatory ones
> The Initiate would once again be
> The Great-Man who influences . . .
> Creates and participates in . . . renewal. (*It Shall Be of Jasper
>   and Coral,* 111)

Amnesia and anamnesis, forgetting and re-membering, such then is the dialectic that runs through Liking's work. Nowhere is this dramatized with greater force, as we shall now see, than in the author's *Les mains veulent dire.*

Set in a nameless valley community, the play stages the ritual healing of a woman, symbolically named La Malade (the Patient), who
suffers from psychological disorders. The decision by her family and
community to request the professional services of a ritual therapist,
the Grand Priestess Kadia, follows their failed private attempts to
help her: "Oh, High Priestess . . . We seek your advice. Through you
we implore the help of the spirit of healing" (1981, 23). The entire
play consists of the efforts by the Grand Priestess and her assistants,
notably Le Porte-Parole (the Spokesman), to induce both patient and
community to speak uninhibitedly about their neuroses. Like a modern psychotherapist, she helps them to track their origins, and thus
gain release from their stranglehold. "Why," asks the Spokesman, "has
a richly endowed mother become mad? Who is responsible?" (47).
"Dig deep; bring out all that's hidden" (49), he goads and advises the
assembly. Eager for relief from her suffering, the Patient wastes no
time in speaking out. But because of her state of mind, she comes
across as incoherent. It is to help the reader gain access to her mind
that the dramatist introduces another character, L'Enfant (the Child),
who functions as the Patient's double or alter ego. Speaking only when
in trance, the Child gives order and expression to her double's troubled
emotions, to the point sometimes of even completing her sentences.
From the statements of both characters (and also of the Spokesman),
a picture of the Patient emerges: she is a sensitive soul, a keen intelligence who has been driven to psychological breakdown by the social
contradictions of her society. A privileged member of her community,
in both material and social terms, she nonetheless experiences acute
angst and a sense of void and sterility. Speaking through the Child,
she confesses:

> I don't like this type of life, where nothing has meaning
> For me I don't like these places where my voice resonates
> and alone speaks of sterility during full moon. (28)

In a series of thinly veiled references to a wider reality in many postcolonial African societies, she alternates with her double in evoking a
corrupt and pleasure-seeking community that revels in the ostentatious consumption of what it does not produce:

The Child: We held jobs for which we were not qualified.

The Patient: We handled millions.

The Child: Made shady deals.

The Patient: Consumed champagne from Champagne, caviar from Russia, and foie gras from Périgord. (29–30)

This is a deeply fractured community where no weapon is too horrible to use on others in the frantic quest for individual success. Finally, it is a culturally confused society in which foreign values and religions like Christianity, though widely practiced, remain totally unassimilated and thus alienating, while ancient beliefs have lost all meaning:

The Child: When we accepted the rosary, we should have properly integrated and assimilated it, made it part of us and not allow[ed] it an independent existence and personality. (26)

But the Patient's ill health has more than just social causes. It can more immediately be traced to a domestic situation, that is, her skewed relationship with her husband, itself a metaphor for Africa's wider relationship with the West. For just as she has lost all autonomy and become dependent on him for her needs, identity, and sense of self-worth, so many nations in Africa have lost all agency in their relations with metropolitan nations:

The Child: It's always got [to] be someone else to tell me that I am beautiful and intelligent, to tell me what I'm worth.

The High Priestess: It's the same for all the weak of the world. . . . A powerful person has to give them value. . . . Who presides over the fate of the economies of developing countries, if not the developed ones? They control our needs. . . . we accept the assistance they care to give; tanks in place of medicines . . . and we sing the praises of cooperation. (54)

References in the play to "aid agreements" and unfinished development projects (1981, 40–41) are instances of how Liking embeds contemporary, topical sociopolitical realities into what could easily be dismissed as a retrograde ceremonial practice of no particular relevance to modern Africa. In this regard, her very choice of an indigenous performance idiom as the model for her theatre, and not the imported dialogue drama of texts, is the enactment at the level of form of the central issue explored in her play, namely, the need for individuals (and, by extension, postcolonial nations) to reconnect with, and to use their often devalued cultural and other resources as a springboard for, individual creativity and national development. For unless they retrieve these resources, adapt them to modern circumstances as necessary, and make them the cornerstone of their artistic and development projects, these nations will, like the Patient, continue to suffer from cultural disorientation and dependence on others for a sense of self. Underpinning Liking's theatrical vision is the idea that change can only be meaningful if it is inscribed within a context of cultural continuity. Restoring that broken continuity—the condition of any act of self-directed development (personal or collective)—is the aim of her theatre.

Having said this, *Les mains veulent dire* does not merely seek to utilize the cathartic and thus restorative functions of healing rituals. It also attempts to recapture their theatricality, which is a constant source of fascination for the playwright. One of the most noticeable formalities in *Les mains veulent dire* is the play's nonlinear plot structure. A helpful way to imagine the structure of this play's action, which unfolds in four phases, is to think of it in terms of the order of worship of a (possibly revivalist) church service. The opening phase combines both a processional and preparatory dimension during which an unspecified number of female and male officiants and three players of sacred drum music take their place in what, for want of a better word, approximates a chancel but without the railings. An important task of the last of the female officiants to arrive is to cleanse the performance space of malevolent spirits and to invest it with sacredness. Coming after this act of consecration is the Patient (the raison d'être of the ceremony) and, finally, the principal officiant who, in meticulously choreographed movements, dances her way to the "chancel." This is followed by the play/ceremony during which the Priestess tries to get from the Patient and members of her family a preliminary idea of the nature and cause of her illness. To the gathering of kin and friends constituting the ritual assembly, she emphasizes the importance of mutual dependence and tries to create the right atmosphere for generalized confession. In the third phase, a kind of call to confession, Kadia and her assistant, the Spokesman, invite the celebrants to interrogate their consciences and acknowledge their roles in the degraded state of their community, as it has manifested in the insanity of one of their own. But this phase turns out to be the most acrimonious in the proceedings as the entire congregation, with the exception of the Patient, resists the Priestess's gentle prodding for self-examination:

> Husband: It's not my problem, I'm not responsible for it.
> (1981, 33)
>
> Another Woman: I've got nothing to blame myself [for], nothing to do with it. (34)
>
> The Woman: As for me, it's not my problem; it's not my job to solve it. (38)

In his discussion of coping mechanisms in situations of cultural trauma, Smelser lists "blame and scapegoating" as being among the most recurrent. He writes:

> At the psychological level this mechanism is an obvious one. It involves both displacement and projection—assigning responsibility and blame on others for unwanted internal and external intrusions, especially if these intrusions evoke the possibility of self-blame or guilt. . . . Who is at fault? Some hated group in our midst. . . . Conspirators? A foreign power? (2004, 52)

Such a reaction is exactly what one sees unfold in *Les mains veulent dire.* Even when the severe problems affecting the community are raised (for example, absence of hospitals, unpaved roads; 1981, 40–41), the residents' first impulse, as the Spokesman notes sarcastically, is to turn outward for excuses: "It's the fault of the colonizer, right?" (40). As for the Patient, they feel nothing but deep resentment for her for daring to be idealistic: "I am not hungry, I am thirsty" (55). They view her illness as an unacceptable indictment of their crassly materialistic society, hence their reference to her as "a public danger" (30).

However, the community's resistance does not last indefinitely. Under the influence of various trance-inducing techniques by the Grand Priestess, who invites them to listen to their hearts, it begins to crumble. The turning point in this process is reached when one of the women participants, in a symbolic gesture of self-cleansing that becomes contagious, removes her outer garment and tosses it into the fire with the admission that it had too long concealed unspeakable things (43). The fourth and final episode concludes in an atmosphere of the restoration of health to patient and community.

Les mains veulent dire, it is clear, avoids the causal relationship between events in which the movement of the action is based on the rational explanation of the motives of, or the statements made by, characters. Here, the action consists instead of individuals who, under sustained exposure to sensory stimuli, slide in and out of psychological states of ecstasy, rapture, and frenzy. To refer to psychological states is to touch on the most visible trace of the model religious ceremony on which *Les mains veulent dire* is built. It also highlights the latter's alternative, avant-gardist theatrical nature in relation to the dominant drama inherited from the French.

Classic francophone African plays like Seydou Badian's *La mort de Chaka* or even Cheikh Ndao's *L'exil d'Albouri* essentially rely on language, or more specifically speech, to communicate. Their target is the intellect and their aim the promotion of nationalist sentiment. Their techniques of choice are discursive reasoning and demonstration. Alternative works like *Les mains veulent dire,* on the other hand, depend very little on speech which, when used at all, tends to be poetic, incantatory, and invocative. They seek instead to act on the senses, the "organism," as Artaud would put it. Their target is the unconscious, and their preferred communicative media are nonrational, that is, symbols, rhythms, fantasy, music, hieratic movements, and so on. To quote Turner in his analysis of ritual symbolism, these various media function as "'storage units' of meaning" (1968, 1), in other words, as "languages" in their own right whose semantics (at least for the people whose culture is being evoked) "are understood at preconscious or even unconscious levels" (8).

Let us examine a few examples of the way these media are used in the play, beginning with the symbolism of space. It is not just a measurable, physical reality in which people evolve. As the play's first producer, Hourantier, explains in great detail (Hourantier and Liking 1987, 86), every section within the semicircle in which the ceremony is performed (facing it is another semicircle for the celebrants) is pregnant with meaning. The north end, for example, is reserved for spirituality, for the gods, symbolized by a mask. The west, with its basket of clothes, represents the subconscious and the need for self-awareness. The south, with its two sticks of wood symbolizing fire, represents purification; and finally the east, with its gourd containing kaolin (a symbol of purity), is the place of healing. Specific actions call for specific areas. Thus, in order to summon her healing powers at various moments of the play, it is to the north that the Priestess turns. Also, in a symbolic demonstration of her purpose, she enters the acting space from the west, the area of obscurity (of the unconscious), and then progressively moves eastward, the region of light and healing.

Like space, colors also constitute a network of meanings. The white clothing of the Priestess and the children, according to the stage directions (1981, 17–21), signifies purity and spirituality; black, the color of the women, represents mourning. The red clothing of the men and the Patient (she additionally wraps a piece of black cloth around her head) represents life and violence, and the tricolors of the musicians, creativity. Even the musical instruments, of which there are three types—the so-called talking drum, the crier drum, and the sacred drum (the *nken*)—acquire a layer of meaning beyond the purely utilitarian. They function as characters endowed with the power of speech. To the Priestess's first question to the Patient, "What ails you my daughter?" (23), it is a drum that provides the initial elements of an answer, translated into speech for the non-initiate to read, "You suffer, she suffers, the cross, faithless joy" (23). Elsewhere, they guide the thoughts of the celebrants, induce emotional states in them at various moments of the action, and comment on their reactions to the point of even accusing them, in the speech of the talking drum, of "dissimulation-discrimination" (35). It is the synesthetic fusion of these various elements of color and sound, symbol, music, and movement that accounts for the play's emotional impact in performance and its novelty in the francophone repertoire.

Two

The Dramatist as Epic Performer: Eugène Dervain's *Saran, ou La reine scélérate*

I f one considers the quality and number of plays on which it is modeled, religious ritual was perhaps the most visible indigenous performance idiom on the francophone stage of the 1970s and 1980s. But it is only one of several such idioms to have been so appropriated. In this chapter, our attention shifts to the use of epic performance as material for a literary theatre in French in one of the most significant plays in that tradition, *Saran, ou La reine scélérate* (1968) by the Martinican Eugène Dervain, who acquired Ivorian citizenship.

Strictly speaking, this play falls outside the time period considered in this book. The justification for its inclusion is its importance as a precursor to the performance-based drama and epic-based theatrical works of the next decades and the ways in which it serves as an early embodiment of the later theatre's aspirations and practices. Oral epic traditions constitute one of the earliest sources of theatrical creation in francophone Africa. But while *Saran, ou La reine scélérate* shares with these plays a common source of inspiration in epic traditions, it stands in sharp contrast to them in its handling and conception of the function of epic drama.

Defined as "an extended narrative on a historical topic, delivered in public performance, most often with musical accompaniment" (Belcher 1999, xiv), the oral epic functions as an archive of a people's historical memory, one that enshrines in songs and fantastical deeds the major events of their history, including their myths of origin and wars of conquest or liberation, while also celebrating their social and political institutions. The tone of the narrative is heroic and the qualities exalted, even if by counterexample, are courage, justice, and self-sacrifice. This archival and instructional aspect of oral epic traditions seems to have most attracted the attention of francophone dramatists of the early post-independence period. It was advocated by leading drama critics of the day, such as Bakary Traoré, for whom francophone African theatre "will either be epic theatre or nothing" (1958, 10). In his introduction to Cheik Ndao's *L'exil d'Albouri* (1973), he lists the following criteria as essential to the nature of African theatre: "Furthering recognition of African values . . . promoting fidelity to them" (10). These criteria are manifest in such plays as Sory Konaké's *Le grand destin de Soundjata* (1973) and Massa Makan Diabaté's *Une si belle leçon de patience* (1973) which, through the stage dramatization of the careers of Sunjata and Babemba of Kénédougou, respectively, recreate moments of a grand historical past and, consistent with Traoré's prescriptions, contribute to the recognition of African civilizations and values. In short, what is of interest to Konaké and Diabaté in the epic is its status as chronicle or historical resource.

Eugène Dervain, on the other hand, firmly rejects such a use of it. His approach to epic material is more artistic than political or historical. This is not to suggest that he shows no interest in the historical events in epic narratives. When he does, however, it is not to approach such events as ends in themselves. It is rather to extract from them episodes and characters that make for gripping drama rather than rousing ideological exhortation or historical display. Additionally, he uses the historical material in epics as a mere backdrop against which to engage in a reflection on larger moral and philosophical meanings, and (much like Corneille and Racine did with Roman and ancient Greek history) to provide majesty and nobility to dramatic action. In short, epic traditions for Dervain are meant to furnish only the raw materials for the creation of a modern French-language African drama. It is precisely this objective that the narrator enunciates in the prologue to *Saran, ou La reine scélérate*:

> The troupe that is performing tonight requested that an
> African play be written for it, and the author did like the
>   Classics.
> He turned to legend, and in place of Ismene, Antigone or even
>   Creon grappling with ancient Greek problems

You'll be watching instead Saran, a queen in love with a hand-
    some prince. [guitar music]
This is only a first attempt, but our legends are rich
    And in them, we have our Cid, Ruy Blas, Curiacee
Douga and Saran characters. (13–14)

Just as French dramatists exploited the myths and legends of Greek
and Roman antiquity, so African playwrights have turned to their
epic narrative and performance traditions to invent a modern theatre. *Saran, ou La reine scélérate* is such an attempt, one which, as we
shall see is further infused with intertextual allusions to other French
influences, such as Jean Giraudoux's *La guerre de Troie n'aura pas lieu*
(1935).

The immediate source material for the play, its *avant-texte,* as it
were, is the Bambara epic of Ségou. The published version used in this
study is the one narrated and performed by Kabine Sissoko and collected and translated into French by Lilyan Kesteloot in collaboration
with Amadou Hampaté Ba and Jean-Baptiste Traoré (1972; Conrad
1990; Dumestre 1979). Divided into twelve songs, the epic narrates
the rise and fall of the last of the great empires of the western Sudan,
the Bambara empire of Ségou, which at its height counted 100,000
soldiers and covered an area of 6 million square kilometers (Kesteloot
1972, 4–6). Founded around 1710 by Mamari Biton Koulibaly, it
flourished until 1861 when it fell to the Toucouleur empire of El-Hadj
Omar, which in turn was defeated by the troops of the French generals Louis Archinard and Joseph Simon Galliéni in 1890. Song 11,
on which *Saran, ou La reine scélérate* is specifically based, is a tale
of passionate love, poisonous treachery, and destructive warfare. The
action unfolds in 1807, shortly before the end of the reign of Monzon
Diarra, monarch of the kingdom of Ségou. It narrates the events of
a conflict between Diarra's son and heir to the Ségou throne, Prince
Da Monzon, and Douga, ruler of the neighboring kingdom of Koré,
a conflict triggered by the defection to the latter of the former's griot.
But the tale also sings of Douga's betrayal by his queen, his defeat and
suicide, and, finally, the murder of that queen, Saran, by the victori-
ous troops.

Unlike epic-oriented dramatists like Konaké, who may have been attracted to such a tale because of its heroics, the politics of the situation, or even the morality of its actors, Dervain was drawn to it by something quite different, specifically the tragic view of life embodied by the seventeen-year-old Saran. This view is scarcely brought out by the singer of the tale, whose emphases tend toward the moralistic. In the epic, Saran is a minor character who appears only a third of the way through and is presented basically as a traitor to be reviled. Douga's fate commands the compassion of the singer, for it is his grave efforts to preserve the integrity of his country from the hegemonic ambitions of the ruler of Ségou that are thwarted by his unworthy and treacherous queen, presented as a symbol of Bambara woman. Absent from the play, on the other hand, are the sexist and moralistic overtones of the epic. In the play, not only is Saran the central character, but her subjectivity is elaborately explored and events are viewed from her perspective. What emerges is not an evil woman but a victim, first of all, of a social system that forces her at a very young age into marriage with an aging ruler—"Douga picked me as one would a pink cola nut, and said: 'That's the one I want!'" (1968, 39)—and, partly as a consequence of that event, her romantic longing for happiness acquires the force of fate.

No less crucial to the events in *Saran, ou La reine scélérate* is Saran's favorite griot, Tiécoura Danté. He, in a sense, sparks the entire tragedy when, on a visit to the court of Douga before his defection, he captivates the young queen's mind with enchanting tales of chivalry about the court of Ségou, its glamour, and its prince, Da Monzon. Saran, "the bird in the gilded cage" as she describes herself (1968, 16, 24, 40), feeds on the sensual romance of the tale and falls in love with the image of the dashing eighteen-year-old hero long before meeting him. So, when she finally catches a glimpse of him in her husband's court during last-minute negotiations to avert war, the reader is not surprised that she literally loses control of herself. Events unfold from this point on with a tragic inevitability:

> Today, no one, no power will be able to restrain me. I've just discovered my true destiny. I've seen Da: I have only one desire, one wish, to follow him wherever he goes . . . to hold him in my arms, to submit to his will. (1968, 33)

In the hands of Dervain, the Bambara epic has been transformed into a tragedy of destructive passion. But to highlight this dimension, the playwright effects certain changes in the epic material. Not only does he develop characters and situations more fully, he changes the order of events. An example of such a change occurs in act 3, scene 16, and concerns the circumstances of Saran's death. In the epic, Da Monzon's soldiers put her to death only after he refuses to be persuaded that, having betrayed her husband, she is equally capable of betraying him in the future. In the play, on the other hand, overzealous soldiers are instructed to kill all captives and mistakenly kill her. The irony of a man who inadvertently orders the death of the woman for whom he has been fighting in part lends a sense of futility to the entire enterprise. A distraught prince poignantly expresses this sense of the absurdity of war:

> Saran is dead! This campaign has all been in vain. . . . I've gained nothing from it. I waged war for a griot that will not even return to Ségou. All we've done is destroy and plunder. Is this the picture of the rest of my life? Succeeding my father to the throne, I'll wage other battles. . . . Will they be as futile as this one? (1968, 70)

In this speech, it is not difficult to discern Dervain's critique of the warrior ethic of feudal societies and its associated notions of honor and pride. This is the connection to Giraudoux's *La guerre de Troie n'aura pas lieu*. In both plays, a wounded national pride (Greek in the abduction of Helen and Segovian in the defection of Tiécoura) and the attempt to restore it lead to war. But the war in question is not one of glorification but rather is a source of devastation where "the conquerors and conquered mix their tears and grief in the same sterile and tenacious hatred" (Dervain 1968, 60). In the context of the various conflicts in Africa that Dervain had in mind at the time of the play (such as the war of Biafran secession from the Nigerian Federation), war is also shown to be a cause of balkanization and weakness that can only lead to foreign intervention:

> Oh Africa, Oh Fatherland, Oh Bambara Kingdoms! In how many years, towards which balkanization, towards which catastrophe are all these little wars by little rulers leading us? . . . When they

finally raise their heads, it will be to see the white shadow of
white helmets and boots. (1968, 60–61)

Echoes of the Giraudoux play go beyond the condemnation of war
in general and are suggested by another change in the order of events
in the epic.

Fearing that Tiécoura's action will lead to war, Douga, like Hector,
makes frantic attempts to appease the irate Da Monzon. He invites the
latter to peace talks. The meeting takes place, but Da Monzon refuses
to lift his ultimatum. Douga requests a three-day period of reflection
in the hope that mature counsel will prevail, and this is granted. He
then asks for a further seven-day delay, and this is also accepted. It
seems war can be averted, the inevitable avoided. In the end, however, the Bambara war can no more than the Trojan war be avoided.
What both plays bring out is a sense of tragic inevitability, the idea
that men and their passions are only a conduit through which an evil
destiny insinuates itself into human affairs and wreaks havoc on them.
Tiécoura reflects, before his suicide, on the *machine infernale* that he
set in motion:

> All of a sudden events are following the course I had foreseen. I
> found myself caught up in this affair in spite of myself. Whether
> I only served as an excuse is but of momentary importance. . . .
> The threads of the tragedy have been wound. The die was cast
> long ago. We can now only let the wind of disaster howl past.
> . . . I'm going to take leave of this absurd world, where nothing
> protects or guides man against his own folly. (1968, 64)

The human folly to which Tiécoura refers is not just misconceived,
the product of ancient notions of honor, of his patron's fatal passion,
or of Da Monzon's inflexible will. It is also linked with dreams of territorial expansion and hegemony, embodied by Da Monzon's father.
For while having his honor avenged is an important explanation for
war, what is equally important is the desire to annex a prosperous
neighbor and thus control an important trade route: "Monzon laisse
partir Tiécoura, mais il en prendra prétexte pour investir cette cité,
la piller, la détruire et s'assurer la maîtrise de la route" (20) [Monzon
allows Tiécoura to leave, but he'll use that as a pretext to invade, pil-
lage, and destroy the city and ensure his control over the trade routes].

The confluence of these factors, endowed with the stature of a transcendental force of fate, in the end consumes the actors in the drama. Tiécoura's realization of his role as an unwitting accomplice of fate is all the more tragic because he, like Saran, hints at it early in the play with rich dramatic irony:

> Tiécoura: As you can see, I'm already composing the tune that'll make you famous for generations of Bambaras to come.
>
> Saran: You talk well, Tiécoura . . . but deep down I sense and fear a great misfortune. (1968, 30)

Saran will indeed be known to posterity, but more for her notoriety as the *reine scélérate* (wicked queen) than for anything else.

So far, we have seen how Dervain modeled his dramatic practice on a certain reading of the French tradition, even echoing elements of a specific French play in his own. But unlike the French dramatists to whom he makes explicit or covert references, he does more than just exploit the thematic and affective resources offered by the epic. He also attempts to transform into literary drama its formal characteristics, including its performance dimension. In short, he tries to textualize epic orality, an effort that accounts for the experimental nature of the play and its formal self-consciousness. An inspired instance of such an effort (in addition to the prologue, in which the events to be dramatized are first narrated to the accompaniment of an *ngoni* string instrument) is act 1, scene 12. Using the technique of the *mise-en-abîme,* the playwright has Tiécoura engage in an (oral) performance within the larger (written) play of a few verses of the epic on which the play is based and which it dramatizes. Tiécoura is thus doubly an actor: within his internal mini-performance, where he plays several roles, and in the larger play. Saran occasionally takes on an extra role, such as when she finds herself in Tiécoura's absence acting the role of a performing griot to console herself, while her confidante Kounadi improvises as her musical accompanist (1968, 24).

Oral performances, Isidore Okpewho reminds us, take place in "a lively human environment" (1979, 190), since audiences are constantly intervening in the performance, either to applaud or criticize the narrator, comment on the action, ask rhetorical questions, and even urge the narrator to race through episodes that they deem uninteresting or painful. This interactive quality is captured in Tiécoura's act. Saran, his audience of one, not only applauds him, "You are a marvelous storyteller . . . I'll never tire of listening to you" (1968, 29), but like a real spectator in a live performance, she also influences the pacing of the performance by her suggestions of which episodes should be abbreviated or completely left out. "You always go too far back into the past by at least 50 years" (27), she complains exasperatedly, threatening to indispose the narrator and thus to derail the entire session. But also like a narrator in a "real" event, Tiécoura engages his patron in dialogue: "What should I narrate for you?" (29). He also improvises praises—"you are full of talent, Princess. . . . I can see that your destiny is prodigious" (29)—and links, albeit in a tragically ironic way, the contents of the epic poem to present and future events in her life, and thus to the larger play. But in spite of his efforts in *Saran, ou La reine scélérate* to capture aspects of the poetics of the epic in performance, Dervain's play remains primarily a work of literature. His interest is not merely in re-citing, in writing a sequence of events known to the entire community in the manner of his oral counterpart. It is in providing a unique response to, a personal interpretation of, those events, bringing out their implicit significance. Such an interest means, of course, developing the text of the play (its characters, language, structure, symbolism, dramatic devices) in a way that is not given to the oral narrator, whose originality lies mainly in his manner of performance of a preexisting text. This leads inevitably to making literature out of the oral version. The conclusion to this analysis of *Saran, ou La reine scélérate* will be devoted to a brief consideration of the dramatic technique that informs this literary project.

Dervain's dramatic technique reveals itself in the way he creates for his play a compelling narrative line that is rich in imponderables and suspense. The action itself consists of a main plot—Da Monzon's war against Douga—and a subplot, the love of Douga's wife, Saran, for Da Monzon. The plots run parallel to each other, with an uncertain outcome built into each of them. Thus, although he is determined to wage war, there is every indication that Da Monzon may be defeated (and he is aware of this), given Douga's vastly superior military and magical powers. Similarly, everything points to the fact that Da Monzon will remain for Saran nothing more than a knight of chivalry in an epic poem. How then does the dramatist link the two actions into a coherent whole? A hint as to how this link will be established is given in act 2, scene 1, when, at a planning session with his soldiers, Da (self-consciously acting the playwright) recalls the motif of spousal betrayal in another West African epic: the Sunjata epic in which Nana Triban reveals the war secrets of her husband, Soumangourou Kanté, thereby ensuring his defeat. At this point, no indication is given that a Nana Triban will come his way. Douga himself, however, ironically provides the occasion for this to happen. In his anxiety to avoid war, he commits the fatal error of inviting Da Monzon to his court, thus providing Saran with the opportunity to catch a glimpse of him. From this point on, the two plots become intertwined as Da Monzon explains to Saran, who by now has scaled her palace walls to meet him: "If I do not conquer Koré, I will certainly die.... I'm not afraid of death, but I'll also lose you, Saran! You therefore make my victory all the more necessary" (1968, 48).

But just when the reader feels that one of the plots will have a successful outcome, a new twist is introduced that leads to the destruction (psychological in the case of Da Monzon) of all the parties in the drama. It is Dervain's skillful handling of both plots—making them arise, far more than in the epic, from the characters and their reactions to their circumstances—that lends dramatic intensity to his play and sustains the interest of the reader or viewer.

THREE

The Power and the Pleasures of Dramatized Narrative: Bernard Zadi Zaourou's *La guerre des femmes*

First performed in 1989 at the Festival International des Francophonies in Limoges in a production by the author himself, and used later that year as part of a set of student exercises at the École Nationale de Théâtre in Canada, Zaourou's *La guerre des femmes* (1985) broadly derives from an ancient art form of the Bété people of central and southwest Ivory Coast, known as the *didiga*. *Didiga* refers both to the art form and to the theatrical troupe that he founded in 1980 in order to experiment with and translate the former's aesthetic principles on the modern stage.

Didiga is the name given to hunter narratives, a species of oral literature that relates the multiple adventures in the wild of the hunter, a Bété cultural hero. The guardian and protector of human society from the beasts of the wild and an important economic agent, the hunter-hero of *didiga* tales, Djergbeugbeu, is known through various praises: "the Initiate among initiates . . . the one who knows but whose knowledge is not a sword raised against society . . . the one who is at the service of everyone. . . . In short . . . the man par excellence" (Zaourou 1985, 128). As a celebrated figure of society, the hero naturally provokes destructive envy and enmity. His rivals and foes resort to multiple stratagems to destroy him, including disguises as wild and dangerous animals. He, in turn, enjoys the magical protection of his mother, who always manages to materialize with victory-enabling potions at crucial moments in his struggles. The reference here to supernaturalism identifies an important feature of *didiga* art, namely, its fantastical and fabulous character. The tales are bathed in an atmosphere of epic encounters and surreal happenings, where hunter and hunted enchantedly whisk themselves in and out of existence, adopt the shape of objects, or transform themselves into one of the natural elements. Rules of rationality are suspended in *didiga* tales, which explains why the genre is also commonly known as "the art of the unimaginable."

But it is perhaps its deployment of "a coded musical language" (Zaourou 1985, 130), decipherable only by initiates, that is the *didiga's* distinguishing quality. Central to this language is its speaker, who is not a human being but a musical instrument, the *dôdô*—a bow-shaped instrument in whose form Zaourou sees the displaced veneration of the Bété hunter's bow, the latter's "poetic and symbolic projection" (1985, 130). Endowed with human characteristics, Zaourou explains, this instrument displays mood swings. It is particularly susceptible to envy, admits of no competition from lesser instruments, and jealously demands the total attention of the audience. It carries first and last names, and like a stage actor it engages in dialogue with the narrator. Such then is the indigenous narrative form that has served as a model for Zaourou's theatrical creation. To say this, however, is not to imply— and he is emphatic on this point—that Zaourou submits slavishly to the *didiga,* documenting it in ethnological fashion and mechanically transposing it to the stage. As the artistic director and producer of the Didiga Troupe, he has clearly outlined the guiding principles:

> To seek inspiration from tradition rather than imposing it on contemporary society. . . . To understand that artistic creation is not an ethno-sociological activity, and to show proof of initiative in concrete ways—a quality without which there can be neither art nor creator. To avoid being prisoner of an ancient ideology served by our ancient arts. (1985, 132)

To do otherwise, he argues, is to run the risk of emptying ancient cultural practices of all dynamism and relevance and of reducing them to quaint pieces (even for local African audiences) fit only for the museum of ethnological curiosities. The challenge, as he sees it, is to create works that are not held in thrall to tradition and yet are tethered to it in important ways.

La guerre des femmes is one of his experiments in this direction, and the play derives from the *didiga* in a number of important ways. The first is in its conception of the protagonist and her career. Scheherazade, the heroine in *La guerre des femmes,* emerges, like her ancient counterpart, as the protector of society in general, but in this instance of women in particular. She is variously described, in praise-name fashion, as the "sun of deliverance," the "sun of the future," and the one who "will be the liberator of women from the yoke of their oppression" (1985, 19). Also, like her traditional male counterpart, her life career describes an epic struggle with a rampaging human beast, the sultan Shariar, who literally preys on his country's womenfolk, having had a thousand of them decapitated before her arrival in his court. A woman of courage and determination, she is also assisted in her fight, like Djergbeugbeu of the hunter tales, by her mother, or more accurately in her case, by the mythical mother of all women, Mamy Wata. A water spirit widely known in many coastal West and Central African cultures (Drewal 2008), she is depicted in popular paintings and lore as occasionally seated on a marine rock combing her long flowing hair. When Scheherazade appeals for help, Mamy Wata magically responds and provides her with a life-saving strata-gem. The action of the play partly takes place in a fabulous and surreal world in which humans and animals communicate, where meetings between humans (Scheherazade) and genies (Mamy Wata) are held in the watery abode of the latter, and in which goddesses (Mahié) take human and spirit form at will. The action also constantly moves between mythical and historical time.

But while *La guerre des femmes* is continuous with an ancient narrative art in significant ways, that art form does not exhaust its sources. Just as Zaourou refuses to be limited by strict fidelity to indig-enous idioms, so he refuses to restrict his artistic sources to African folk traditions. His aim, he explains is "[t]o take advantage of the mix-ing of peoples which characterizes our age, and not to hesitate to bor-row from other cultures, African and non-African alike, what is best in their art to enrich our own imagination, and create works that do not speak uniquely to an African sensibility" (1985, 132).

Unlike Eugène Dervain, who, as we already observed, sometimes turns to French seventeenth- and twentieth-century tragic theatre, or Werewere Liking, whose work exhibits strong parallels with French modernist playwrights even though she repudiates the implications of their influence, Zaourou turns to a rare source in francophone theatre in the guise of the Arab storytelling tradition, as exemplified most powerfully by *The Thousand and One Nights*. The outer, framing tale in this collection narrates, it will be recalled, the story of a sultan named Shariar who, as revenge for the deceit and sexual infidelities of his wife, declares what amounts to a murderous war on all women. He decides to take a new bride everyday, and to have her killed after spending the night with her. Moved to pity and despair by this state of affairs, Scheherazade, one of the daughters of the sultan's viziers, decides to marry the sultan against her father's will in order to put an end to his mad campaign. Her ploy is to narrate a tale for him every evening for a thousand nights. She will, however, make sure to always break it off at dawn, at a point sufficiently suspenseful for the king to want more and thus postpone her execution. Fedwa Malti-Douglas has transposed this narrative strategy into the terrain of sexuality in the Arab Islamic context and compared it to the process of arousing and sustaining sexual desire in a partner while continuously deferring its consummation. While such a dynamic might be considered exploitative, Malti-Douglas suggests that it could be interpreted as the "classical female pattern of extended and continuous desire and pleasure . . . that permits the forging of relationships, and [is] nonexploitative" (1999, 22). Whatever the symbolic interpretations of Scheherazade's narrative technique, the fact remains that it is legitimate in its context and achieves its desired objective, for the sultan is so entertained by the fertile imagination of his bride and potential victim that he spares her life.

It is this storytelling device that Zaourou borrows for his version of Scheherazade. Almost every other aspect of the original tale is modified, most notably the forced marriage to the sultan in Zaourou's version. Likewise, whereas the storytelling ruse is the fruit of Scheherazade's inventiveness (even if she relies on her sister Dinarzade's cooperation for its successful execution), in *La guerre des femmes* it is Mamy Wata who suggests it to the African princess in response to her appeal. But these and many other modifications are deliberate. By casting an image of a princess who, unlike her mature and wily Arabian counterpart, is ingenuous and helpless, thrust into the arms of a practiced and hardened killer, and saddled with what seems like an impossible mission (restoring his sanity), Zaourou lends deeper intensity to her fate and elicits in the reader/spectator, initially at least, a greater sense of fear and pity. His heroine's achievement is all the more dramatic because of the seemingly insurmountable odds ranged against her.

But perhaps the most significant modification in *La guerre des femmes* lies in its enframed stories. While the playwright borrows the plot device, his stories have everything to do with African myth and legend, and nothing to do with such "Oriental" tales. Fragments of African legend are also incorporated into the play, the most elaborate being the Bété myth concerning the origins of gender inequality, which provides the drama's structuring element. Central to the Mahié narrative, as this origin myth is also known, is the issue of male violence. Situated in primordial time, the myth tells of an age when men and women lived essentially separate lives, in complete ignorance of each other. "Essentially" because among the women lived a lone male (Zouzou) who, having been created with them, was also ignorant of the existence of any other human type. This golden age comes to an end when a male hunter accidentally discovers the existence of what turns out, to his astonishment, to be a new and beautiful species of humanity. Rumor of its existence quickly spreads in the male settlement. The women's hidden location is rapidly found out, and it is not long after that the battle of the sexes breaks out. The women remain invincible, but then Zouzou is accidentally captured. Tortured and hypnotized, his resistance weakens, and he ends up divulging to the enemy the war secrets of the women's camp. Angry at what she sees as (male) treachery, Mahié, the female troop commander, has him promptly executed upon his return to base. She also orders that hostilities be pursued, but her troops, by now war-weary and inconsolable by what they see as the unjust execution of one of their own, revolt against Mahié. As a result, she goes into exile and transmutes into the water spirit, Mamy Wata, while they sue for peace. The mutual discovery of the pleasures of sex come next, and soon the warring parties are married. However, far from fulfilling the hope of a partnership of equals and ushering in a new golden age as the women had expected, marriage, as Mahié had feared, simply institutionalizes their defeat and thus becomes the new expression of the battle of the sexes.

It is the task of dramatizing this legend and making its meanings relevant to contemporary society that Bernard Zadi Zaourou sets himself in *La guerre des femmes*. At the beginning of the play, the dramatist presents a man, in every way a contemporary scholar, nervously rehearsing a public lecture that he is to deliver the next day on the subject of gender inequality in modern society:

> Ladies and gentlemen,
> I've been invited to give a talk on the relationships between men and women in modern society. Well, I'll not be beating about the bush! My duty, as I see it, is to state things as they are, unvarnished. (1985, 12)

The man is so absorbed in his lecture/rehearsal that he almost forgets his promise to take his wife to the theatre that evening to watch a play titled, as it turns out, *La guerre des femmes*. Now, by self-reflexively linking the topic of his modern character's lecture to the myth-based subject of the play that the lecturer-husband and his wife are going to watch, Zaourou highlights the parallels between ancient legend and the modern situation, and the relevance of the former to the latter. Also, by structurally containing or embedding the legend—which belongs to an oral storytelling performance tradition—within a modern theatre form, he not only establishes continuity between the two performance modes. He also gives a concrete example of how the former can fruitfully be adapted and textualized to form the basis of a modern, scripted, francophone drama.

Like the first movement of the play, the last is also set, as the stage directions indicate, in the contemporary world of "cars . . . phones, trains, jazz and reggae music" (1985, 57). In other words, the action of the play begins in the world of identifiable historical time (twentieth-century urban Africa), plunges shortly thereafter into the fabulous and atemporal world of legend, and reemerges months later at its original point of departure. The attentive reader/spectator will observe in this circular sequence of theatrical events the tripartite structure of an initiatory tale: first is the moment of separation of the initiate from the social world (the initiate here is a group consisting of the husband and wife duo, the sultan Shariar, and the reader/spectator); then comes the initiate's experience of liminality in an in-between realm of the fantastic (represented in the play by the world of Mahié, Mamy Wata, and talking animals); and, finally, the initiate's reincorporation into the modern world (of cars, phones, reggae music, and so on). Although there is a return to the social world, it is a return with a difference. The innocent initiate has now been reborn a wise, reflective initiate. We will later consider the issue of this mature wisdom. For now, however, we should return to the core movement or mythic section of the play, the one encased between the first and last sections of *La guerre des femmes.*

This section itself is in two distinct but interrelated parts. The first (tableaux I–V), the outer framing tale, functions as a scene of exposition that introduces the two sets of protagonists—the sultan Shariar and his vizier, on the one hand, and Scheherazade and her protector, Mamy Wata, on the other—and provides the information necessary for an understanding of the play. Its action is in the main dramatized, although on one occasion it is narrated by a *diseur* (1985, 15), a narrator/commentator of the tales. The second part, and the main substance of the play itself, is the enframed or inner tale that Scheherazade finally persuades the sultan to listen to. Here, the action alternates between narration and dramatization. The narrator of the tale, who also functions as its stage director and producer, is in fact Scheherazade, and her (internal) audience of one is the sultan. In a staging of the play, the princess/narrator and the sultan could both be seated on one level of a split stage, where one level depicts the palace and the other is occupied by the internal "actors," with the spotlight switching rapidly from "palace" to "performance space" and back. Alternatively, one could resort to the technique of a film or video screening of the dramatized action, with the narrator/princess serving as announcer and commentator of that action, and the sultan both her audience and interlocutor.

It is no accident that narration should occupy an important place in the enframed story because it is an instrument of power on which the narrator's life and those of her community of sisters literally hinge. Scheherazade exploits it to create suspense and to control and shape the events of the legend, inflecting them deftly in directions that reveal parallels between the fiction of legend and the reality of her plight, all in a bid to placate the sultan's murderous fury by both instructing and entertaining him. We thus see Scheherazade making pointed remarks when, for example, the sultan discovers to his astonishment that the leader of the female troops, Mahié, is a woman—"woman is not born a slave to man" (Zaourou 1985, 40)—or when he cowardly confesses that he would not have personally volunteered to be part of the group of men seeking to locate the women's camp: "Cowardice has always been a characteristic of the powerful" (38).

However, the sultan is not a passive listener; neither is he too numbed by brutality to be unaware that the enframed Mahié legend, and Scheherazade's use of and exchanges with him on it, are in fact a commentary on *his* real-life conduct with women as this is depicted in the play's outer story frame. Drawn into an absorbingly narrated and dramatized legend, and yet stung by the princess/narrator's interpretive gloss on it, plus the legend's depiction of female valor, which challenges all his assumptions about women, Shariar the ruler—as opposed to Shariar the spectator—does react, at times with curiosity and confusion, at others with childlike excitement and enthusiasm, and even with sympathy when Zouzou, having been wounded and captured, is finally executed.

But beyond mere reactions, Shariar allows himself to be drawn into argument with the princess/narrator, which is precisely what she hoped would happen. By engaging in dialogue and debate with her, he brings himself to Scheherazade's level, and thereby loses the aura of brutal superiority that had hitherto characterized their relationship. Worse, the princess has by now aroused his sexualized narrative desire so intensely—always holding out the pleasurable promise of its satisfaction, but never actually fulfilling it—that she feels secure enough to begin to manipulate him. Through irony and sarcasm, she is able to turn virtually all his reactions and arguments against him. Thus, when he excoriates Zouzou for being a traitor to male potency, she uses that same unfair observation as proof of male treachery, a trait he hitherto saw as purely female. When he hears about the women's courage in battle, he unconsciously betrays admiration tinged with fear of women, and Scheherazade replies that he is a "liar" (1985, 37) and that if he really feared women, he would not be exterminating so many of them. Shariar tries to regain the initiative and his composure by occasionally issuing warnings and veiled threats: "Watch it! Watch it! Watch it!" (41); "Hey! You said what? Are you telling me a story or judging me? Be careful, my generosity has limits" (44);

and "What are you insinuating[?]" (64). But Scheherazade is not impressed. Persuaded of the pleasures of her narrative and conscious of its humanizing impact on Shariar, she conflates with ever more daring the fiction of legend and the reality of female life in Shariar's court and the modern world. Legendary and historical time, fiction and reality, the outer framing story and the embedded tale all merge in tableau XVI when, in reply to Shariar's question "Do you think my good people and women of Arabia are unhappy?" (58), the narrator/princess replies: "Love, justice, equality . . . I'm looking for all that in the new order that you, men, have created. . . . Ah, yes! Marriage has become a chronic illness. What's the cure for it?" (58). This remark is immediately followed by two examples of what Scheherazade sees as institutionalized inequality: a civil wedding ceremony in which the marriage vows stipulate the submission of wife to husband (60), and its religious equivalent, where the very topical issue of the ordination of women into the Catholic priesthood is raised through the officiating clergy, a self-ordained Roman Catholic woman priest (61). She proudly modifies, to applause and consternation from the female and male congregants, respectively, the standard opening line of the prayer to now read: "In the name of the Father, *Mother*, Son, and Holy Ghost" (62; emphasis added).

But the sultan did not have to wait for such an open actualization of the legend to understand the purpose of Scheherazade's storytelling. Long before the ceremonies described above, he explains to the narrator how the beautiful Souad had betrayed him (1985, 59). This understanding is followed, after those ceremonies, by what can only be termed a moment of epiphany and a plea for forgiveness:

> I beg you Scheherazade. You see, you arrived and the day shone like a ray in the abyss of my despair. Stay here, very close to me, and you'll see. Stay and you'll see that everything will change. Everything, everything! Including all the couples in *your* kingdom. (1985, 65; emphasis added)

The reversal of roles could not be more complete. Shariar, the tyrant, has become a meek supplicant while the death-row bride is now his master; she has succeeded in saving her own life and that of her community, winning a kingdom along the way. It is not the least of the ironies in this play that the ruse and cunning of which the lecturer jokingly accuses women in the opening tableau (labeled tableau 0), and which Shariar levies against her with deadly consequences, is confirmed in the narrative exploits of Scheherazade. He might still think her his captive (witness his occasional threats), but he has long since become hers.

References above to "understanding" and "epiphany" naturally bring one to the enactment of what the dramatist sees as the all-important initiatory function of literature and the artist. This occurs through a religious, ceremonial quality where the initiate/inductee is a human being and the master of ceremonies/inductor a spirit figure (in tableau II, for example, Scheherazade is taken to Mamy Wata's watery shrine to be taught the mystical language of signs and female self-liberation; and later Mahié initiates Gôbo and her women into the knowledge and power of sex). Even the sultan's epiphanous understanding of the genesis of gender inequality can be said to take an initiatory character as Mamy Wata suddenly appears in the final moments to assist Scheherazade, to whom alone she is visible, sealing both that understanding/healing and the grand reconciliation with Scheherazade and society in which it results.

This pedagogical or initiatory aspect of narrative (literature), secularized and stripped of all mysticism, corresponds to Zaourou's definition of the role of the African writer. Like the Arabia of legend, the modern African postcolony has its fair share of rulers whose exercise of power is as arbitrary and deadly as that of any sultan, and countries are held captive like Scheherazade and the women of Arabia to their whims. In the same way that Scheherazade is able through narrative art to lead her tyrant to a mature understanding of the roots of the conflict between the sexes, of which he is both victim and dangerous accomplice, so too can the writer in modern African societies seek to educate and humanize arbitrary power by speaking truth to it. Of course, not all writers are as adept or as successful as Scheherazade, and storytelling itself in Africa has proved to be a dangerous activity: many writers have been jailed and persecuted in postcolonial times. For Zaourou, the Arabian princess, and her African successor, this is a risk worth taking.

FOUR

Theatre as Writing and Voice: Patrick Chamoiseau's *Manman Dlo contre la fée Carabosse*

lthough Patrick Chamoiseau is mostly associated with fiction, his earliest attempts at writing were for the stage, including *Manman Dlo contre la fée Carabosse* (1977). Earlier, in 1975, he had adapted Sophocles' *Antigone*, performed in Martinique by Luc Saint-Eloy's Théâtre de l'Air Nouveau (Bérard 2008). Published in 1982, *Manman Dlo contre la fée Carabosse* introduces many of the techniques and themes that would blossom in his later works and cultural theorizing, a programmatic expression of his ideal of a new francophone Caribbean theatre. In its creolized French, which "turns and loops dizzily and wanders off on a journey" (Chamoiseau 1982, 75), as one of the characters complains, the play's didacticism, cultivation of fantasy, polyphony, and distancing techniques clearly advertise *Manman Dlo contre la fée Carabosse*'s continuity with the folktale.

Among the themes that are more elaborately developed in his later work are those of domination and resistance, cultural Otherness and imperializing universalism, urban development and ecological degradation, and, not least, the dialectic of speech (orality) and writing (literacy). The last theme finds expression in the modernist, self-reflexive framing of the play in which its fictional storyteller *and* its author cannot take part in its performance because of their upcoming tribunal for the "crime" of reducing speech to writing and thus, in the eyes of the trial judges and custodians of the culture of orality, of betraying the former's very essence. The storyteller's defense is that by freezing speech into writing—which he concedes deprives it of its dynamism—he paradoxically contributes to its preservation by ushering it into the new world: "The Theatre is both Writing and voice; it makes it possible for the Children of the Word to enter a new world without leaving theirs" (Chamoiseau 1982, 5). The challenge therefore, as the storyteller sees it, is not to reject writing but to learn to write speech or orality. The ways in which this task is accomplished in *Manman Dlo contre la fée Carabosse* will be examined later. For now, let us briefly consider the key issue explored in the play, namely, the colonial encounter.

In the francophone Caribbean context, this encounter is at the center of such nationalist drama as Aimé Césaire's *La tragédie du roi Christophe* (1963) and *A Tempest* (1969), and Edouard Glissant's *Monsieur Toussaint* (1961). Where, of course, Chamoiseau departs from that drama is both in the form and language in which he allegorizes the encounter and in the characters he uses to embody it. The folktale has now replaced heroic drama, and instead of Prospero and Caliban or Toussaint Louverture and General Charles Victor Emmanuel Leclerc, one now has Carabosse (the evil, hunchback fairy of European origin) and Manman Dlo (*manman* and *dlo* are Martinican Creole for "mother" and "water," thus literally "Mother of the Waters"), the title of an aquatic deity of African lore (herself a synthesis of the European mermaid and African water spirits). But while Chamoiseau breaks with the nationalist tradition of Caribbean playwriting in terms of form, the nature of characters, and language, he does not in terms of the spirit and temper that animate his play. This makes his play discursively atypical of his literary production, as Michael Dash has convincingly explained, even if it is not (and this is a point to which we shall return) quite the aberration that Dash takes it "mercifully" to be (1998, 139). In terms of atypicality, however, it is true that unlike such later works as *Chronique des sept misères* (1986) and *Texaco* (1997), which explore what Dash has termed social relations of "adaptation and contact" (1998, 139), of complicity with and subversion of the dominant system, *Manman Dlo contre la fée Carabosse* stages a situation of implacable opposition to that system. The aquatic spirit and embodiment of that opposition, Manman Dlo, is not a human by-product of adaptation and contact with the system like Marie-Sophie Esternome of *Texaco* and Pipi Soleil of *Chronique des sept misères* are. Neither does she feel condemned like them to accept it as an immutable given that leaves the sole option for survival within its interstitial spaces to be *débrouillardise* (individual knowhow and resourcefulness). Her action, on the contrary, is pursued from *outside* the system in the clearly delineated terrain of river and forest. In this respect, she is not the typical hero of Caribbean folktales who hustles his way in life through wit and cunning and is solely preoccupied with his own survival. Because he operates within the terrain of the enemy, he is reduced to acting by indirection, relying on little smart moves rather than on a grand strategy.

It is easy to understand why *Manman Dlo contre la fée Carabosse* has been compared specifically to Césaire's *A Tempest* (Silenieks 1994b). Both texts, of course, stage rebellious figures whose resentment of the colonial order is only matched by their radical desire to overthrow it, and the action of their characters is sustained and not improvisational, part of the collective struggle of a preconstituted community whose existence predates the arrival of that order. But perhaps the strongest parallel between the works is in their representation of the colonial enterprise as an unsustainable model concerned with the exercise of power and the pursuit of economic gain. Carabosse, the symbol of this enterprise, is in this respect aligned not just with dukes and courtiers like Prospero and Gonzalo, but also with the lowly, antimonarchist, republican mariners Stephano and Trinculo. Similarly, Chamoiseau's Carabosse has hardly swooped down into new, foreign territory with its "vast murmur of flowers and birds" (1982, 11) than she is already staking ownership to it. "All that is ours," she tells her dismayed servant Broom (11), and threatens shortly thereafter to use the magic of her superior technology to reduce her indigenous fairy counterparts to the rank of "devoted slaves" (18). Echoing Prospero's self-proclaimed role as a musical conductor charged with bringing harmony to what was only cacophony, Carabosse recalls her "philanthropical duty to control this chaos, to carry this world on [her] shoulders" (25). But it is not long before Broom reveals the true meaning of Carabosse's cultural project for the natives, thus exposing her philanthropic duty as a mere pretext for domination:

> To separate the native from his skin,
> history, and culture; to remove his hat
> and fill the empty space with Hellenic culture!
> A gentle, shock-free form of depersonalization

With Greece as his Ideal
he will celebrate being our slave. (78)

Through Carabosse's actions, Chamoiseau suggests a co-substantiality between the colonial project and domination, a point confirmed by Carabosse herself when, in her answer to Broom's bewilderment at her knack of staking arbitrary claim over foreign territory, she replies almost fatalistically:

It is inherent in my spirit
I leave home
Land somewhere
And everything in front of me
Is mine. (1982, 10–11)

Beyond political imposition, *Manman Dlo contre la fée Carabosse* explores through the mode of caricature and satire an issue that would become central to Chamoiseau's later work, namely, cultural dispossession. Carabosse's Greco-Latin culture, whose universalist assumptions and archaic assimilationist policy account for the rejection of what Glissant has referred to as the *divers* (difference; 1996), is lampooned by Chamoiseau; the *divers,* on the other hand, emphasizes networks and relations with discrete particularities (cultural, ethnic, national, and so on) as well as transverse connections. "To nourish its claims to the universal," Glissant observes, "the Same needs the flesh of the world. The Other is its temptation; the Other not as draft agreement, but as material to sublimate" (1992, 190).

Manman Dlo contre la fée Carabosse is a dramatic expression of this sublimation, which occurs, when necessary, through violence. "Everything that is not my spitting image will be struck down by my power" (28), declares Carabosse, who reconceptualizes the notion of the human, culturally and even phenotypically, to fit only Greco-Latin culture and its custodians. She peremptorily excludes her indigenous counterparts from the category of the human on the grounds that they do not possess such attributes as her "nose" and "skin color" (68) and that their artistic products—"masks and sculpture"—are unlike those of her culture (69).

In a satirical reductio ad absurdum of her position, Chamoiseau has Carabosse even banish the indigenous population from human-kind because they possess "taste" and "commonsense" (1982, 22), or use methods and technologies which, though different from hers, achieve rigorously identical objectives. Broom's awed admiration for a native who flies without a broom, unlike Broom's mistress, and his description of this feat as "classy" (76), draws an angry response from the latter: "They master no technology / Come on, my friend Broom/ drop this admiring look" (76). It is no coincidence, given Carabosse's radical universalism, that her preferred form of communication with the servants would be the language of declarations: "We'll take possession of this country / Control the rivers / Domesticate the winds" (16–17); of imperatives: "stop squirming" (10), "write, my friend write" (23); of edicts and proclamations:

How can you accept that people
answer back at Greco-Latin
magical culture when it *issues orders?*
Its language is *magisterial monologue.* (61; emphasis added)

But such "magisterial monologue" is also, for Chamoiseau, the language of silence and silencing, the silencing of the Other who is eliminated from the circuit of communicative exchange and thus destroyed. The effectiveness of silence as a weapon of control explains why, after subjugating her enemies by paralyzing their speech organs, Carabosse's first political act is to institute a regime of silence. Speech promotes dialogue and thus life. Silence is monological and thus authoritarian, hence its description by Manman Dlo as "Silence-the-Killer, the friend of death" (1982, 50). Its oppressive force also explains why the revolt against Carabosse should take the form of a claim to speech, which is associated with dance, music, and the vital, whereas silence is equated with Carabosse's unequal treaties, arbitrary legal codes, and specious logic—in short, with the scriptural.

The references to domesticating land and rivers lead, naturally, to a consideration of the significance of the final aspect of the colonial enterprise explored in *Manman Dlo contre la fée Carabosse*, namely, its project of modernization of both the human and natural worlds.

"Imperialism after all," observes Edward Said, "is an act of geographical violence through which virtually every space in the world is explored, charted, and finally brought under control" (1990, 77). As a mechanism that "universally commodifies all space" (Said 1994, 225), it gains proximity to Carabosse's desire:

> To domesticate the winds
> Classify plants . . .
>> Dissect the leaves
> Systematically survey everything . . .
>> and control
> every bird—big and small
>> every butterfly
> every ant
>> everything that crawls, walks and runs. (Chamoiseau 1982, 17)

Imperialism takes an even more frenzied turn in Carabosse's determination to subjugate nature ("We'll imprison this Nature"; 103) and to grind it into the powder of its chemical components: "We'll break nature down / into its smallest chemical parts" (102).

Not surprisingly, environmental imbalance and fierce native insurrection are the consequence of this frenzy, a revolt that takes the form of what Richard Watts has labeled "a reclamation of water" (2003, 900) with particular reference to Chamoiseau's *Biblique des derniers gestes* (Chamoiseau 1982, 35). The eponymous character, Manman Dlo, queen of the Lézarde River, reclaims more than just water. In her psychologically and culturally symbolic search with her daughter Algoline for the deceased Papa Zombi's testament on resistance—an orphic search conducted across forest, river, and ravines—she is effectively reclaiming and re-identifying with the geographic locality from which Carabosse displaced them, simultaneously reconnecting with the repressed sources of her self. Unlike Carabosse who, in her predilection for factories and industrial urbanization ("pestilential architecture," in the storyteller's words; 104), symbolizes a modernity gone mad, Manman Dlo emerges as the symbol of a "spiritually-charged environmentalism" (Watts 2003, 905) that regenerates polluted and drought-stricken rivers and brings succor to injured marine life. Manman Dlo's final victory over Carabosse, whose technology fails ultimately in the face of the purifying forces of water unleashed by Manman Dlo, therefore marks the triumph of spirituality over materialism.

The Manichaean distinction between a destructive modernity (Carabosse) and a beneficent nature (Manman Dlo) has led Michael Dash to dismiss Chamoiseau's play as a "naïve exercise in wishful thinking . . . a fanciful modernist fantasy" (1998, 139). Although a little hasty, this judgment is not totally inaccurate. It would even seem to be borne out by the river goddess's adamant refusal to grant her daughter Algoline's request to mix and play with her terrestrial as opposed to marine counterparts:

> Algoline: Why, why always remain in hiding / live alone?
> Again yesterday, I saw many children in the woods / . . .
> I wanted to go play / chat / and run around with them.

> Manman Dlo: We must remain pure in this forest which is
> deteriorating. If you get to mix with every one there /
> you will become like them / and will never again / never
> be pure. (33)

Manman Dlo's symbolic advice, beyond its ostensible references to children and playing, sounds like a plea for cultural purity against *métissage,* in favor of the preservation of an essential self. The product of mixing, she warns her daughter with the example among others of the blackbird's "unnatural" marriage to the hummingbird (38–39), can only be a monstrosity. By associating with such creatures, she foretells ominously, Algoline risks advancing sideways like "a head-less crab" (38) instead of walking straight. In other words, she risks becoming a physical and, no doubt, a cultural monstrosity.

However, to conclude that Chamoiseau's introduction of Manman Dlo's insurgency against Carabosse and subsequent advice to her daughter constitutes, as Dash suggests, "wishful thinking" is to be indifferent to the complexity of the situation and to ignore the deep tension that is staged in her dialogue with her daughter on purity and mixing. Chamoiseau's heroine does *not* reject modernity, which she realizes can be emancipatory but only if it is not an external impo-sition or a force of fate that should be helplessly suffered. It is precisely because of its inseparability from violence and imposition in her context and its denial of agency to her community that Manman Dlo resists and rejects modernity. But this rejection is provisional and tactical, a position confirmed at the end of the play when she offers her war trophy (the defeated Carabosse's magic wand) to Algoline with powerful words:

> This wand contains / all her centuries of experience / It was her Memory and Technology. . . . All the while remaining my daughter . . . and without repudiating water and vegetation / You will assimilate this wand / integrate it into your natural harmony / And without it swallowing you / swallow it / And from today, I give you permission to assimilate everything, to know everything. . . . Learn all that there is to know / and outstrip me / outstrip us. (139)

What initially looked like a futile nationalist quest for cultural purity on Manman Dlo's part turns out to be a mere strategy of resistance that gives way, after the recovery of her autonomy, to a critical embrace of the modern. For Manman Dlo, Carabosse may have been defeated, but her knowledge and science must become integral to the identity of her newly independent/decolonized community. This is an identity, however, that is not unanchored and free-floating (as it will turn out to be in Chamoiseau's later works), but rather an identity that is rooted, even while remaining open to the new influences. *Manman Dlo contre la fée Carabosse* is thus a transitional play that straddles the space between the roots/nationalist ideology of the negritude of the 1960s and the rootless/post-nationalist movement of Caribbeanness of the late 1970s and beyond. Where the play unambiguously belongs to the latter period, however, is in its form, which is largely derived from the oral folktale genre. It is to a consideration of its appropriation in the play that the rest of this chapter will be devoted.

Although Chamoiseau continuously emphasizes the need to produce works in the tradition of the "master of the word," his relationship with that master and his tradition of "Creole orality" (1994, 153) are far from being straightforward. Chamoiseau uses the expression "creative mystery" (1994, 157) to refer to it, thus suggesting that it is not a simple question of mechanically transposing folktales and their performances onto the stage, but rather of choosing and recontextual-izing specific elements in the new reality of writing. In other words, it is a question of creating a new artistic product that carries the imprint of an individual talent. He writes:

> The question, in point of fact, is not to move from orality to writ-ing as one would from one country to another; it is to envisage an artistic creation that is capable of mobilizing the totality that is given to us . . . the genius of speech and the genius of writing . . . their points of convergence but also of divergence. (1994, 158)

The importance of creating a "*new* artistic product" is already evident, as Bérard has observed (2005, 91–105), in the play's subtitle: *théâtre conté* (folktale-derived theatre) as opposed to *conte théâtralisé* (theat-ricalized folktale). The former genre seeks inspiration from the folk-tale and is not bound by it, whereas the latter is the mere transposition of the tale onto the modern stage. Equally significant is the fact that while Chamoiseau uses well-known animal characters from indig-enous lore—Ti-boute-le-colibri (the hummingbird), Baye-nerfs-le-crikette (the cricket), Siroko-le-merle (the blackbird), and even the water fairy—the story in which they figure is from his creative imagi-nation and not part of the indigenous repertoire (Bérard 2005, 92). But, perhaps, the most central element that he uses as a basis for his play is the figure of the storyteller, the *conteur*. *Manman Dlo contre la fée Carabosse* establishes continuity with the latter in several areas, the first of which is narrative function. Traditionally a narrator and an actor, the *conteur* presents events and characters but also embod-ies those characters and dramatizes their roles. In *Manman Dlo con-tre la fée Carabosse,* however, this role changes somewhat since the *conteur* functions almost exclusively as a narrator, a kind of modern Caribbean equivalent of the ancient chorus. He becomes part of the action only once, when he decides to play the role of Papa Zombi, who happens to be absent when Manman Dlo calls on him in his forest abode for assistance against the invader Carabosse (1982, 84–96). The only other time he is onstage during a dramatic enactment is when he provides, almost like a war correspondent, a live report on the mili-tary engagement between Carabosse and Zita's three daughters (1982,

58–62). These examples apart, the *conteur*'s function in the rest of the play is to introduce the principal actors, narrate and comment on the events in which they will be involved, and focus the attention of the audience on specific characters or episodes. This, for example, is how he presents Manman Dlo:

> Oh little children, my sweet little ones
> We're going to discover
> Manman Dlo
> My children, it is Manman Dlo who creates waves
> to disperse plankton
> So little fish can eat. (1982, 27)

With his interventions occurring between major dramatized episodes—"let's stop the talking and instead go discover Manman Dlo in action" (1982, 30)—he not only demarcates the action into clearly delineated acts and scenes but also performs the role of an internal director, switching the action from the narrative to the dramatic mode, controlling the pacing of events, introducing musical interludes, and substituting for absent actors.

Reference to musical interludes brings us to an important function that the *conteur* appropriates in the play, that of host or presenter. In this capacity, he does not merely narrate events to a passive audience but interacts with the latter and elicits its participation. The interaction in *Manman Dlo contre la fée Carabosse* takes place on two levels. The first is between the *conteur* and the members of his group, including his assistant, Marianne, whom he sometimes admonishes for her tearful responses to certain episodes (1982, 27) or otherwise chides for failing to teach the children in her care the community's traditions of orality (8), and his musical accompanist, the master drummer, the timing of whose musical interventions he carefully regulates (7, 26). The second level is between the *conteur* and his audience, which consists mostly of children (*ti-manmaye*) and a few adults (*gwan mounes*). As far as the audience is concerned, contact takes many forms of which the consecrated call-and-response formula *crii/craa* and *misticri/misticra*, which opens and punctuates a storytelling session, is perhaps the best known. But the *conteur* also resorts to other techniques. When he is not addressing questions to the children ("Who can claim not to know a story about Manman Dlo?" 7), he is apostrophizing them ("my sweet little children"; 28), inviting them to applaud (30) or shed a tear or two (27), advising them on rules of good conduct (8), or, consistent with the pedagogical vocation of folktales, teaching them about the origins of certain cultural practices.

Chamoiseau's desire to explain to the audience the historical origins of their cultural obsession with things French, symbolized by Carabosse, the fairy of "castles and golden carriages" (1982, 8), and their corresponding indifference to the indigenous Manman Dlo of "oak trees and mango trees" (8) is the impulse behind his play. It also accounts for its etiological character:

> Don't forget either / that if Carabosse . . . / is better known to you than Manman Dlo . . . / it's because / one day riding her mechanical broom / she landed in this place, chased from her fir trees / by I don't know what desire! / The fact remains that once here, she belted out her bizarre classical music-sounding laugh / which sent a chill down Little-Mano-the-hummingbird's spine, and sent Screeeeech-the-mongoose fleeing. (1982, 8)

It is Chamoiseau's hope that the dramatization of this piece of allegorical history will lead his young audience to a liberating understanding of the roots of their skewed cultural tastes and to a corresponding desire to redress the imbalance by rediscovering the repressed in their traditions. But beyond his immediate circle of spectators, the storyteller also elicits the active participation of his invisible audience of readers whose verdict, on the charge against him of betraying orality by putting it down on paper, he solicits.

Among the narrative, as opposed to performance, techniques that the storyteller borrows from the folktale is the use of multiple voices. While the *conteur* is witness to most of the events in his tale, and therefore is their principal narrative voice, his narrative is sometimes the product of multiple perspectives. Reported statements such as the following abound in the rendering of the evil fairy's "bewitching enterprise" (26), statements that lend a quality of truthfulness to his narration of events:

Siroko-the-blackbird . . . spoke to explain that . . . It's Ti-boute-
the-Hummingbird . . . Who reported it to me He got it from
Golette-the-bamboo. (26–30)

But perhaps the most important element of Caribbean authenticity and culture in *Manman Dlo contre la fée Carabosse,* and the medium
of expression of its folktales, is the Creole language itself. "Antillean
existence," Chamoiseau writes, "can only be expressed in Creole or
Creolized French" (1994, 189). As a language in its own right, Creole
is mostly used in the play for the names of animal and spirit characters
and in exchanges between the narrator and his assistants/audience.
On occasion, characters code-switch into Creole from French, and
it is also the language of the songs intoned by Marianne (1982, 29)
and of *timtims* (riddles), such as the one Manman Dlo has to solve
before being let into Zita's home (1982, 49). But it is important to note
that Creole is deployed in the play as an integral component of the
French language of the indigenous characters and that the creolization of their French occurs at all levels: lexical with such words as *zouc*
(merriment), *caye* (rock), *pié-mangot* (mango tree), *oulélé* (disaster),
zouelles (streets); syntactic with "Si Carabosse . . . est mieux debout
dans votre tête que" (literally, "If Carabosse stands better in your head
than . . .") or "c'est la question . . . que j'étais justement en train de
poser à mon corps" (109) [That's the very question that I was . . .
asking my body]; and stylistic with the use of repetition like in "un
silence lourd, lourd, lourd" (26) [a heavy, heavy, heavy silence] or
"bonsoir de bonsoir / trois bonsoirs" (85) [good night once, twice,
three times]. The reciprocal influence on French is noticeable, as that
language aspires to the condition of Creole orality with a profusion
of exclamations (*pff, popopo, hé! hé! hé*); onomatopoeic sounds like
heug heug heug to convey Zita's daughters' death rattle; idiophones
like *avaler glouque* to suggest the sound of greedy swallowing or "Je
retomberai . . . tchuaaaaa" (36) to convey the splatter of a heavy down-
pour; and, as Stéphanie Bérard has pointed out, a near absence of
punctuation to communicate the rhythms and "velocity of speech"
(2005, 98).

One final quality worth mentioning about the Creole folktale
as appropriated by Chamoiseau is its non-illusionism. *Manman*

Dlo contre la fée Carabosse is nothing if not a self-conscious artistic product in which the narrator constantly draws attention to the fictional status of the work and disrupts any spectatorial impulse to identification with its action or characters. The narrator continuously reminds his audience of the conventions of the genre that regulate his performance. Thus, to justify the amount of time he has spent on Carabosse's first night in her new environment, he feels obliged to remind his audience: "[the night] was long / loooong for in Folktales / a night lasts centuries, as you know" (80). When one remembers that storytelling, like modern theatrical performances, usually takes place at night, then it is clear that the "loooong night" in question is not just that of the action, but also of his performance. As was observed earlier, Chamoiseau seeks as much to root his theatre in indigenous practices as to recreate them in the light of contemporary realities. Besides his recourse to writing, the transformation that most stands out relates to his recontextualization of the folktale for the modern stage. This has involved certain changes to the model, including the redistribution of theatrical roles, and his modifications of such traditional functions as singing and dancing have redefined the distance between actors and spectators (Bérard 2005, 100–101).

But it is in the elaborate staging, suggested both in the narrator's descriptions of scenes and actions and in the stage directions, that Chamoiseau has effected the greatest transformation in his oral material, recreating onstage the qualities of fantasy, horror, and magic that have enchanted generations of folktale-performance audiences. But because these performances rely almost exclusively on language and are enacted on a bare stage with few props and no setting, the spectacle they evoke is a matter for the imagination rather than the eyes. The play calls, for example, for elaborate costumes (possibly masks) to represent its various characters (birds, fish, gnomes, deities, and so on) and for stage sets to indicate such places as Zita's oak tree abode and Manman Dlo's aquatic grotto. Other stage effects, necessitated by Carabosse's many (literally) flying trips across the new land, call for an actor with the skills of a trapeze artist who can swoop on and off the stage, astride her human broom. The three epic battle scenes, though, reveal the production's most dramatic effects. The stage directions describe one of these scenes as "a powerful spectacle of lights" (60), and along with sound effects, these battles are highly choreographed. Given that the acting space is enveloped in near darkness—both as a temporal indication of the moment of battle and as a symbol of the tragedy that has befallen the native habitants of the land—the flashes of light and sound become the audience's only means of gauging the course of the battle. In the stage directions for the Carabosse–Papa Zombi encounter (97), for example, bright flashes of red and white light and an explosion of fireworks against a background of rolling thunder signal that Carabosse is on the attack, and possibly on the ascendancy. In this instance, light and fire are her instruments of war, whereas a head-splitting din of drum music, which Papa Zombi can command at will, as he can violet light from the moon, serves as an indication that he is enjoying military success at that specific time.

According to Chamoiseau, the Creole writer must endeavor, like his traditional storytelling counterpart, to become "a lone individual . . . bound to a circle of crushed souls that expect enchantment . . . and entertainment from him" (1994, 157). The question of whether Chamoiseau's contemporary audience is made up of "crushed souls" might be a matter for some debate. But what is indisputable is the delight that a magical spectacle like *Manman Dlo contre la fée Carabosse* provides to their imaginations.

FIVE

Tradition Instrumentalized: Elie Stephenson's *O Mayouri*

The poet and playwright Elie Stephenson was born in Cayenne, French Guyana, in 1944. Comparisons have frequently been made between his work and that of the acclaimed and influential Guyanese writer Léon-Gontran Damas (Jack 1996, 127). Although Stephenson has not received the kind of critical attention his Guadeloupean and Martinican counterparts have, he is widely considered to be an important poet and playwright (Favre 2004). Numerous volumes of poetry—notably *Une flèche pour un pays à l'encan* (1975) and *Catacombe de Soleil* (1979)—augment a distinguished bibliography of plays, including *Les Voyageurs* (1974a), *Un rien de pays* (1976), and *Les Délinters* (1978). First performed in 1975 (and written a year prior to that), Elie Stephenson's play *O Mayouri* (considered here in the French translation by Marguerite Fauquenoy), though in many ways quite different from Patrick Chamoiseau's *Manman Dlo contre la fée Carabosse*, also belongs to the post-Césairean new wave of francophone Caribbean dramaturgy. While, as has been observed, the dialogue between the indigenous characters in *Manman Dlo contre la fée Carabosse* is conducted essentially in creolized French and only occasionally in Creole proper (of course, French in all its registers is the language of the foreign characters), *O Mayouri* is written almost entirely in Creole. What French exists in it is more a reflection of the linguistic relationship of power in Guyana than it is a concession, as seems to be the case in *Manman Dlo contre la fée Carabosse* to the non-creolophone reader/spectator.

The officially peripheralized language of the private sphere in Guyana, as indeed in the other French departments of the Caribbean, Creole is the sole language available to almost all of *O Mayouri*'s major characters, except the mayor, Frederic, Fanny, and, to a more limited extent, Camille. As Marguerite Fauquenoy has pointed out in her analysis of the linguistic dimension of the play, Creole is the language of domesticity and of the social/ceremonial, of friendship but also of dispute, in short the language of social life. French, on the other hand, is the language of power and officialdom appropriately represented by a nameless official known only by his title, the mayor. He speaks to his constituents exclusively in French, even when they occasionally address him in Creole. For him to do otherwise would be to bridge the social gap between him and them, a gap he has every interest in maintaining. His relationship with his constituents, in other words, is strictly hierarchical. French to him functions almost like a police officer's truncheon: "Shut up fool! Elections are imminent, I must destroy your worker cooperative" (1988, 89), he bellows at Frederic.

But the superior social values that attach to French are not just the privilege of figures of authority. They are so much a part of the unconscious of the wider community that even Frederic and Fanny, the apostles of cultural autonomy, ironically find themselves (especially Fanny) unreflexively switching from Creole to French in the belief that it is a more refined medium of communication between man and woman, and one particularly suited to the expression of love:

> Frederic: I wonder why we always speak to a woman in French
> as if to do so in Creole were a sign of impoliteness.
>
> Fanny: I don't know why, I've never given it [a] thought.
>
> Frederic: Admit that we are a hundred percent assimilated.
> (Stephenson 1988, 47)

Of course, as their love for each other and their commitment to social change deepen, the incidence of French in their conversations correspondingly lessens even if it does not entirely disappear.

Like in *Manman Dlo*, the use of Creole in *O Mayouri* is more than an act of linguistic realism. Contrary to Bridget Jones's statement that "the defense of Creole in French Guyana is not linked to any specific political option" (1994, 393), it is indeed one of cultural and, by extension, political assertion. The play, it should be recalled, was written in 1974, the period of independentist agitation in the francophone Caribbean. The Guyanese critic Biringanine Ndagano advances two reasons to explain this movement. First, there was the creation in 1968 of the Ariane space station in Kourou and the expropriation of land and the population resettlement that occurred in its wake. Second, and perhaps even more important, was the 1974 economic development plan (later abandoned), which provided for the massive resettlement of French metropolitan and other Latin American nationals in Guyana. These measures galvanized the articulate section of the local population (the entire population at the time was estimated at 150,000), which felt threatened and in danger of even greater marginalization in their own country. "What is now called . . . 'Guyanese identity' had never been more forcefully asserted," writes Ndagano (1994, 55), and the Creole language became its principal mode of expression: "Creole was asserted everywhere: in the media, schools, meetings, and in music. It would seem that people were even led to believe that the simple fact of speaking, learning, and writing Creole solved the problems of the Creoles" (55).

O Mayouri can thus be seen as a theatrical manifestation of the spirit of this era. But while the play asserts a Creole identity through language, that identity is by no means the same as that manifested in *Manman Dlo* and, by extension, in Chamoiseau's Martinique. Creole identity in the context of Martinique refers to a common culture and language that are shared by, and the product of, the mixing of the various cultures and complex ethnic and racial groups that make up the island's population, but it certainly does not refer to any single racial or population group. The same, however, cannot be said for Guyana, where the major population groupings—whites, Creoles, Amerindians, and the so-called Africans or, in Guyanese Creole, *bushinenge* (Maroons who sought refuge from slavery deep in the forest)—lead separate existences in their self-enclosed communities and where the idea of a common culture is virtually nonexistent. Guyana, Ndagano quotes a local mayor as saying, "is made up of different peoples living alongside, but never together with, one another" (1994, 37). In this context, Creole identity refers to the identity of a specific population group, namely, the black and mulatto descendants of slaves, even if it tends to pass itself off as the identity of an emerging, alternative nation: "On these ethnic bases, Guyanese identity is off to a bad start . . . for when a Creole says 'we Guyanese,' he actually means, 'we Creoles'" (Ndagano 1994, 41).

Another manifestation of the spirit of the 1970s, besides the use of Creole, is the play's recourse, like in *Manman Dlo*, to local Guyanese performance traditions and idioms (although not folktales, as in Chamoiseau's play) like the *grajé* (Stephenson 1988, 33, 103) and the *cassé-co* (Stephenson 1988, 37, 45, 53), which are dance forms, the former with slow, waltz-like steps and the latter with more vigorous "body-breaking" movements (hence the Creole expression *cassé-co* from the French *casser corps* [body breaking]) and the *mayouri*. However, these similarities between *O Mayouri* and *Manman Dlo* should not obscure fundamental differences between the two plays. One of these differences is Stephenson's predominant concern with socioeconomic problems rather than with issues of cultural identity. Although he does not minimize the importance of the latter, they are more Antillean than Guyanese for him and certainly of less critical importance to his territory than such socioeconomic problems as youth unemployment, massive emigration to France, economic stagnation, and dependency, subjects that he explores in his plays.

To Stephenson, the mere culturalist act of writing in Creole or indeed of using local artistic forms to explore these problems cannot necessarily solve them: "As far as the use of Creole to resolve our problems is concerned, I am skeptical. The question can be asked whether the debate on Creole does not prevent us from debating the real questions, which are political, economic, or social" (in Ndagano 1994, 56). On the contrary, and this may not be unexpected for the economist Stephenson, it is only by addressing these problems and thus creating a supporting material infrastructure for the practice of its arts, culture, and language that Creole culture can regain the vitality and function it enjoyed during slavery as an instrument of resistance (56). To do otherwise would be to indulge in pure Creole folklorizing.

The desire to avoid such a pitfall explains the difference between *Manman Dlo* and *O Mayouri* in terms of form. Chamoiseau's play uses the folktale as a structuring device and incorporates other Creole idioms, like riddling, and arts, like music. *O Mayouri,* on the other hand, is realist drama. Although it uses rural Creole art forms, these do not structure the play but rather constitute interludes in a development that derives strictly from dialogue drama. They are at best devices for the creation of the appropriate festive atmosphere necessary for the communication of a reformist and modernizing agenda. The welcoming party for Frederic, for example (act 3, scene 1), is nothing but a social gathering where guests debate the prodigal son's ideas for reform. The influence of Haitian novelist Jacques Roumain (*Gouverneurs de la rosée,* 1944), who posits certain beliefs in vodou though not the actual intervention of spirits in village life, can be felt, though *O Mayouri* bears only limited traces of supernaturalist elements or, for that matter, of the poetic magic of *Manman Dlo.* Its language is consistently secular, instrumental, and prosaic, and the world it evokes is not the enchanted universe of fairies nor the animal world of folktales. What we have in Stephenson's work is a real-world rural environment of poverty, failed crops ("empty farms and stunted manioc"; 1988, 17), petty rivalries and jealousies, and despotic public officials. Even when a member of the wake-keeping audience evokes the possibility of dark, supernatural forces in Frederic's death—"An evil spell, a curse has been cast on this young man" (115)—Camille is quick to debunk that idea with the very secular problems of human "stupidity, wickedness, and ignorance" (115) against which, precisely, Frederic was fighting.

However, Stephenson's play is not directed at French or elite Guyanese audiences whose recognition or admiration of its cultural forms it seeks. It rather addresses a rural, Creole Guyanese audience, which is invited to cast a critical look at its attitudes and beliefs and urged to find solutions to its plight. In other words, *O Mayouri* draws on elements of Creole performance culture not to celebrate them as ends in themselves (that would be to indulge in the culturalism of Chamoiseau), but instead to instrumentalize them in the service of social and economic development. No better example of such instrumentalization can be given than the *mayouri* of the play's title. Known as a *coumbite* in Haiti and also widely practiced in rural Africa—Camara Laye's farming scene in *L'enfant noir* (1953) constitutes one of its most memorable evocations—the French Guyanese *mayouri* is an association of peasants that operates on the principle of mutual aid whereby an association member is assured of the combined labor of fellow farmers for such labor-intensive tasks as land clearing and harvesting. A *mayouri* is a festive event enlivened with abundant supplies of *tafia* (alcohol) and the sounds of drummers and musicians, who are enlisted to supply exhorting work songs to set the rhythm of the laboring farmhands. With modernization, the decline of peasant agriculture, and the concomitant exodus of farmers to the city, the *mayouri* has all but disappeared in Guyana. But it is this event, conceived both as social performance and as metaphor, that gives its title to, and is celebrated in, the play. The play's development climaxes in the *mayouri*'s stage recreation (act 5, scene 1), but that is not what matters to Stephenson. The social values, such as group solidarity and mutual help, are the central objectives of the event. Thus, endowing an ancient social practice with new, development-oriented meanings, actualizing and instrumentalizing it, in other words, is Frederic's goal. This point is clarified to his father, who is worried that he is about to embark on a futile and expensive adventure: "Nous ne ferons pas un mayouri comme autrefois," Frederic reassures him, "nous lui don-nerons un autre sens" (59) [We'll not be organizing a *mayouri* like in days gone by; we'll give it a different meaning]. Ironically, Frederic's undertaking does prove expensive in the end, although not in the sense envisaged by his father.

O Mayouri revolves around multiple sets of characters, each of which represents a specific world view. The first set—Frederic's parents, Melanie and Gaga—is the human symbol of a community mired in poverty and hopelessness, a community in which the population has been reduced to the level of helpless spectators in a life of misery. They are resigned, especially Melanie, to a plight that they accept as part of the divine order: "There are people who are on earth to live in happiness, and others who are there solely to suffer!" (13). Although Gaga resolutely rejects this attitude, even rebelling against the idea of a beneficent God, his rebellion remains mostly rhetorical, never translating into acts of personal or collective empowerment. Indeed, he dismisses them as exercises in futility: "drop this idea of farming . . . it's much too difficult" (21), he tells his son. Gaga's rural Guyanese community is one in which traditional solidarity has been replaced by narrow individualism and where the young are consumed by dreams of migrating to the capital, Cayenne, or to France.

In contrast to the fatalistic attitude of his parents, Frederic is con-vinced of the possibility of effecting social change. He is strong and intrepid and, although warned by Fanny of the danger to his life from vested interests, prepared to sacrifice himself for the good of his society, a society he dreams of regenerating through increased agricultural production and the restoration of its lost sense of community:

> We want to bring about change here, give life to the commune.
> . . . Life will again be beautiful . . . [it] will again be good. . . .
> When we see everywhere all the produce of these farms, and
> can go fishing and hunting together, we'll then be able to live in
> brotherhood. (Stephenson 1988, 49–53)

Frederic eschews institutional political action, which he sees as the realm of the corrupt, and in any case as ineffectual for his community in the absence of a unified social movement and collective organization at the grassroots level, of which such action is the expression. This view explains his focus on the *mayouri,* whose spirit and values he wishes to revive and reinscribe in the minds of the population.

Between the fatalism of the poor and Frederic's idealism lie powerful economic and political interests, represented by the mayor, the peasants' class enemy, and more personal and petty enemies like Sonson, Frederic's eventual murderer. The mayor thrives on the peasants' ignorance and lack of economic independence, hence the vehemence of his opposition to Frederic's attempt to organize and empower them: "I am the master and mayor here, young man! . . . I must watch over the interests of my constituents. . . . I understand the situation of these people, know their needs, and know what needs to be done" (85). It is interesting to note that the mayor in *O Mayouri* is not Chamoiseau's foreign evil fairy hounding a hapless, indigenous population, but rather he is part of that population even though his economic and political interests overlap with those of the evil fairy, of which he is the local neocolonial representative. In other words, Stephenson introduces a class dimension into his analysis of Creole society, emphasizing the fact that, dominated as it might be by France, such domination is differentially experienced depending on the subject's class situation within Creole society.

Analyses of the conflict between Frederic and the mayor are often presented as one between noble idealism and vengeful selfishness. While there is little doubt about the negative portrayal of the mayor and his social class in this play, it would be hard to defend the position that Frederic does not emerge unscathed either. Through him, Stephenson ponders not just a certain fateful unrealism of political utopias (Frederic's vision lacks an adequate politics and thus self-destructs), but also the paradox of intellectual vanguardism on which they rest for their realization. Developing Michel Serres's 1973 analysis of this paradox as it applies to Manuel in *Gouverneurs de la rosée,* Celia Britton has argued that Manuel assumes a religiously inflected role once he has succeeded in convincing the villagers to abandon God (2006). One could also extend this analysis to Frederic, who encourages the peasants to self-organize and to rely on their collective force, but he never ceases to adopt and play the role of organizer in their affairs. Having spent a decade in France and having fought in Algeria, he sees himself as uniquely positioned to lead his benighted people to the secular salvation of material independence. Opposition to his views and methods can only be the result of misguided ignorance, and as his comments to Fanny confirm, he is convinced that he will eventually be supported: "They'll end up understanding one day" (Stephenson 1988, 107).

Although self-serving, accusations that Frederic wants to direct everyone are not inaccurate. One of the critiques levied against political vanguardism is that when it does not degenerate into intolerance of those who do not "understand" and who are not willing to subordinate themselves to the views of the avant-garde leadership, it self-destructs. Frederic does not get to the point of authoritarianism since he is destroyed before his revolution is complete. While his murder can be seen as the tragic death of a noble vision, it could also be an indication of the dramatist's ambivalence toward utopianism, an ambivalence theatrically "resolved" by the hero's murder.

SIX

Militariat Grotesqueries and Tragic Lament: Tchicaya U Tam'si's *Le destin glorieux du Maréchal Nnikon Nniku, prince qu'on sort* and *Le bal de Ndinga*

In his book *Coups from Below: Armed Subalterns and State Power in West Africa,* the political scientist Jimmy Kandeh examines one of the most important manifestations of the crisis of the post-colonial state, namely, the recurrent intervention in politics of that substratum of the military he characterizes as the "militariat." This category shares points of commonality with the proletariat as "the subaltern ranks . . . who occupy a class position in the army that is analogous to the working class in society" (Kandeh 2004, 1). Some African heads of state, such as Eyadema in Togo (1963), Mobutu in Zaire (1965), Bokassa in the Central African Republic (1966), Kérékou in Benin (1972), and Sankara in Burkina Faso (1983), Kandeh argues, are the products of a social universe of severe "material deprivation, social alienation, thuggery [and] criminality" (2004, 3). This makes their intervention in politics, essentially as a manifestation of interclass conflict and intense hostility toward a ruling elite (civilian and professional military) whose enrichment they perceive as having occurred at their expense, qualitatively different from earlier interventions by the officer classes, for whom the usurpation of power was the expression of intra-ethnopolitical elite competition and conflicts.

The militariat generally lack a "social consciousness" (Kandeh 2004, 3), as well as the intellectual skills, organizational expertise, and military discipline necessary for governance. Their exercise of power, when they erupt into politics, is not in the service of any coherent agenda (as is the case, at least rhetorically, for the professional soldiery) and disintegrates into pure violence. The regimes they put into place are completely unmindful of distinctions between public and private resources; exercising predation and lawlessness, theirs is a pathological world that was theorized in the late twentieth century by political scientists (Chabal 1992; Bayart 1989), though dramatized as far back as 1979 by Tchicaya U Tam'si in his dystopian play *Le destin glorieux du Maréchal Nnikon Nniku, prince qu'on sort* (Kadima-Nzuji 1980; N'Da 1980).

The action takes place in an imaginary African country (Mutulufwa) where a coup d'état has just occurred, resulting in the overthrow of President Ebolobo's civilian government. Corporal Nnikon Nniku is brought to power and quickly proclaims himself field marshal (in Mutulufwa, military titles are kept in a basket and literally handed out like candies), but shortly thereafter he is overthrown by another member of the Mutulufwa militariat, Private Sheshe, a man with the unfortunate habit of urinating on himself when under pressure! Incontinence thus replaces cowardice (Nnikon the field marshal seeks refuge under a table at the first gunshot) in what becomes an endless ballet of coups and terror in the dysfunctional Republic of Mutulufwa, which after all means "of those destined to die" in Lingala (Kadima-Nzuji 1980).

Although specific references to various well-known symbols of political leadership (panther-skin caps and leopard-spotted battle fatigues) anchor the play in the Central and East African region of the continent, the immediate geographic and sociopolitical frame of reference is transcended in order to embody postcolonial civilian or professional military dictatorships. The new rulers in Mutulufwa belong to their nation's military underclass, but their behavior, like that of their real-life counterparts, is indistinguishable from that of the ruling elites. The latter, in Kandeh's discussion of West African regimes, use the poor soldiery

> as instruments of oppression ... to reproduce relations of [elite] domination in society. . . . Enforcing state power seldom serves the interests of the militariat as a substratum but it nonetheless draws its personnel closer to the corridors of power. The violent usurpation of the power they are routinely called upon to enforce occurs largely in response to bad governance and the degeneracy of the political classes. (2004, 4–5)

This interrelationship between an elite that depends on and exploits the military underclass and the latter's aspirations to elite privilege and domination is captured in a dialogue in *Le destin glorieux du Maréchal Nnikon Nniku, prince qu'on sort* between Sheshe and Mheme concerning the impending coup against their country's leaders:

> Sheshe: It's all going badly in our country because it has been sold for peanuts to the Baincus and the Noichis. And our bosses have stuffed their pockets as much as they have stuffed our brains with trash. But it'll all be over in a few hours.
>
> Mheme: Calm down.
>
> Sheshe: We obey and obey, do nothing but obey! We play at being galley wardens, that is when we are not sent off to fight their wars. (U Tam'si 1979, 16–17)

It is hardly surprising in light of this type of resentment that Ebolobo is overthrown at the first opportunity. But far from being an improvement on Ebolobo's rule, Nnikon Nniku's simply transforms Mutulufwa into a living hell where all normal values and expectations are inverted. The most striking example of such mad inversion is Nnikon's "generous and sublime" program of government (U Tam'si 1979, 90), which is inspired by the new leader's ideology, known as "Nnikonnicunism," and whose central agenda concerns social and political retrogression appropriately titled *régressivité* and *régressité*—measures accompanied by the abolition and criminalization of all work (77, 82), the closing down of factories and the scrapping of industrialization projects (85), the reduction of the nation's economic output (91), and finally the deepening of poverty (78). In a proud declaration of his government's achievements, Nnikon Nniku exults:

> Our revolution has advanced the revolution of the free world! . . . We applied ourselves to deepening our poverty, making it ever more severe. Our per capita income, when we came to power, was close to that of the less rich of the richer nations. Today, our GNP is declining to zero. [cheers] And that is victory, great victory. (U Tam'si 1979, 91)

Another feature of Nnikon Nniku's rule is its recourse to gratuitous violence and terror, as the state has abdicated its most basic function of providing security and protection for its citizens. Its new mission is to hold them captive and prey on them (it is surely no coincidence that the play opens and closes with a prison scene). As Mheme declares, "Power? We have it. Corporal Nnikon Nniku seized it for us. We'll keep it to make the civilians march along or to the court-martial" (41). They now devote their time to the torture of innocent civilians (including children), to mutilating "unsubmissive" women, and to rampant killings. Embodying this terror, of course, is the leader, who boasts in a public speech, "We've brutally liquidated all those who supported the old order" (90), and whose earliest and most profound desire is that "every one, whether they eat, sleep, shit or screw, laugh or die . . . at my will" (57).

Most citizens of this imaginary country cower in fear, but some emerge as symbols of resistance (for example, the characters Lheki and Nnyira), adopt the tactics of their enemies, and organize an underground resistance movement that leads to a popular uprising, which in turn provokes a coup d'état that ends Nnikon Nniku's regime. This underscores U Tam'si's faith in civil society, but also reveals a degree of pessimism concerning the possibility of enacting positive change in this fictional country and, by extension, contemporary Africa. Given Tchicaya U Tam'si's dystopian vision of contemporary African politics with its excesses and nightmarish or surreal leaders, it is understandable that critics have pointed to a literary kinship between him and the nineteenth-century French dramatist Alfred Jarry, the author of *Ubu roi* (1896). Both plays feature usurping rulers who kill their predecessors and establish grim tyrannies characterized by mutilation and punishment. Likewise, they not only provoke civil strife but are also ultimately toppled. But it is perhaps at the level of the idiom of representation rather than narrative particulars or the substance of representation that Nnikon Nniku's Ubuesque dimension is most obvious. This shared idiom is the grotesque or, more precisely, the satirical grotesque with its indulgence in verbal bingeing, scatological humor, and riotous laughter. The qualifier "satirical" serves here to distinguish this aesthetic category from the "fantastic grotesque" or from "fantastic caricature," as the eighteenth-century German critic Christoph Martin Wieland labeled it (in Kayser 1968, 30), although it is in a sense related through the common use of fantasy, exaggeration, and unnaturalness. Unlike the fantastic grotesque, however, which creates a world that has no connection with reality, a purely "subjective" world born of a "wild imagination" rather than of imitation (Kayser 1968, 30–31; Thompson 1972), the satirical grotesque remains tethered to the real and even proceeds from it. In other words, the satirical grotesque does not so much invent a monstrous and extravagant reality (as disapproving theorists of classicism and realism claim) as bring out, like caricature, the monstrous and extravagant in reality. It is a realism for a new age, for an age in which, like in many contemporary (francophone) African sociopolitical formations, the real has become so unnatural, so dreamlike that it can only be adequately apprehended by means of an aesthetics of the unnatural and the absurd, in short by the satirical grotesque. The dissolution of the natural into the monstrous is what accounts for the feelings of horror provoked by this aesthetic category. But horror is only one pole of the reaction, alongside laughter. As its name implies, the satirical grotesque also seeks to ridicule through such additional techniques as parody, irony, and political derision, devices of which Tchicaya U Tam'si makes extensive use in *Le destin glorieux du Maréchal Nnikon Nniku, prince qu'on sort*.

The play's very title reveals its raging satirical thrust. As foreshadowed in his ignominious royal title, *prince qu'on sort* (literally, a prince ousted, but also a prince consort, or a prince and company), Nnikon Nniku's destiny is anything but princely or glorious. But more than his title, it is perhaps his obscene-sounding name, Nnikon Nniku (whose significance he appears too stupid to have recognized), that reveals the playwright's aggressively satiric and Ubuesque intent; in spite of the homophonic disclaimer *ni* before his first and last names, Tchicaya U Tam'si's protagonist's name juxtaposes the French *con* (that is, an "idiot" or "prick," which would probably be more apt in this context, but this word is also an offensive reference to female genitalia) with *cul* (an ass). The ridicule is compounded by his claim to leadership on the sole ground that his "name sounds better than his fellow conspirators" (1979, 24). The phonic qualities of *Ubu* in the name *Nniku* are worth highlighting, given that both names not only rhyme, they also link their bearers with their respective *culs* (Beaumont 1987, 38). Tchicaya U Tam'si's protagonist insists on this link when he emphasizes that the correct pronunciation of his last name is "Nniku" as in *c-u-l* and not "Nnikiou" with an "iou," as a foreign diplomat tactfully does (1979, 77).

Both Ubu and Nnikon Nniku are inextricably connected with toilets. Ubu tends to lose control of his bowel movements and is also quick to brandish a lavatory brush in anger, while Nnikon Nniku was formerly a latrine cleaner, a fact that probably explains his obsession with having his country's farmers use human waste as manure: "Nnikon Nniku declares: I'll fight shit with shit" (37). Finally, just as Ubu is given the name "le gros P.U." (act 1, scene 3), ostensibly using his initials (his full name is Père Ubu) but phonically a reference to his hygiene (*le gros pue*, where the French verb *puer* means to "stink"), so Tchicaya U Tam'si's antihero is accused of being a "bête puante" (55, 56, 97, 105) [stinking beast] in a not-so-oblique reference to his brutal politics and his past profession. U Tam'si's use of grotesque names is, like Jarry's, not limited to the central protagonist: Père Ubu's fellow plotter Bordure, whose name rhymes with *ordure* (trash) may signify the sphincter (the French also use the reference *le sphincter* like the English; Beaumont 1987, 38), and Nnikon Nniku's minister of defense is named Nkha Nkha Dou (the infantile term for "poo" in French is *caca*) and his "backside stinks of excrement" (U Tam'si 1979, 62).

But perhaps the aspect of Nnikon Nniku's character that the dramatist most harshly critiques is his desire for total control and absolute power over his subjects, evoking what Achille Mbembe has argued constitutes a central feature of the *commandement* in the postcolony (2001). Ironically, this obsession with absolute power allied with his gross superstition renders Nnikon Nniku vulnerable to the first diviner/swindler who claims to be able to secure total control for him. In one of the play's most farcical and bizarre, yet quite satisfying, scenes (act 2, scene 10), we see Nnikon Nniku, the leader who claims to have "twelve meters of intelligence" (57), being manipulated with childlike ease by a former victim of his regime's depredations, now disguised as a diviner. The latter recommends the most hideous and improbable of measures to Nnikon Nniku, measures ostensibly designed to secure his power, but in reality calculated to humiliate him and foment opposition to his rule. These include the requirement that he impose on every minister and high official of state as a condition of service in the government an act of auto-mutilation of the eye as a sign of "blind" loyalty, and that he in turn take a public bath in slug slime to acquire the necessary slipperiness, physical and metaphorical, to elude his enemies!

Nnikon Nniku's ancestralism comes in for severe censure. Embodied in the ideological concoction termed "Nnikonnicunism," the doctrine's central tenet involves the cult of the ancestor-leader which, he argues, is consistent with "authentic tradition" (90). Using absurd reasoning, double entendres, humor, and wild caricature, Tchicaya U Tam'si mocks and parodies this and many other political ideologies of a return to sources that have been assumed by various postcolonial African leaders, most notably Mobutu as the exponent of *authenticité*. Tchicaya U Tam'si does not take issue with the multiple ways in which knowledge systems, values, and political traditions could legitimately be incorporated into projects of national self-renewal. It is rather the demagogic use of these phenomena made by rulers intent on obscuring leadership failures, class inequalities, and foreign domination to which he objects. Paulin Hountondji cogently makes this point in his observations on the exaltation of black cultures by cultural nationalists, and he gives the example of Senghor:

> Hypertrophy of cultural nationalism serves to compensate for the hypotrophy of political nationalism. [It] emphasize[s] only the cultural aspect of foreign domination at the expense of other aspects, the economic and political in particular. Worse still, these cultural problems are themselves strangely simplified as culture is reduced to folklore, its most obvious and superficial aspect. (1996, 160–61)

Nnikon Nniku is a fictional example of such demagoguery since for him "tradition," as exemplified by the stage set, decor, and *mise-en-scène* of his coronation ceremony, is no more than an assemblage of amulets, shrieking dancers in bright plumage, wild erotic dances executed to the rhythms of ankle bells and "boudoum-boudoum"-sounding drums, fire-eating sorcerers, and warriors in varying degrees of trance sporting nose-piercing bones, namely, the kind of commercialized folklore beloved by tourists. Far from being a vision of cultural "authenticity," Nnikon Nniku's is an alienated vision that reproduces the most stubborn stereotypes of Africa.

Tchicaya U Tam'si's most ferocious attack is reserved for what could be described as his protagonist's debauchery. "The Supreme Guide, number one national procreator" (1979, 71), spends a lot of state time being massaged by prepubescent girls supplied to him by a state agency. At the high point of these ceremonies, he is called upon by his priest/diviner to perform the "dance of the inseminating serpent" (71), after which he is magically fortified with the reptile's seminal life force. Also, the ceremonial masks used in the proceedings are dabbed with body fluids, including, of course, semen. A global resonance is accorded to the play and to the central issue of dictatorship given that, much like other strong-armed rulers who have their Red Book (Mao in China) or Green Book (Khadafi in Libya), Nnikon Nniku has his own Grey Book. However, his is different to the extent that, unlike other leaders, his does not outline a vision of politics and society but rather consists of sayings such as "Woe betide he who resists sex. He loses the will to be" (47).

Readers of Nnikon Nniku might be tempted to dismiss this recourse to the scatological and the phallic as a distracting and gratuitous display of filth (Kadima-Nzuji 1980). Jacques Chevrier was severe in his evaluation of a similar style found in Sony Labou Tansi's novel *L'État honteux* (1981a):

> I ask Sony Labou Tansi to forgive my impertinence, but I find that his last novel wallows in the genre "excrement-and-pee for informed adults!" Throughout *L'État honteux*'s one hundred and fifty-seven pages one reads about nothing but defecation, and fornication matched, it's true, with scenes of rape, torture, and other forms of punishment which fortunately spice up a narrative whose abundant scatological references end up being boring. (in Anyinefa 1990, 154)

One may of course agree with Chevrier's assessment, but to attribute the use of this language to gratuitousness is to fundamentally misconceive of its function and the dramatist's intentions, particularly since such measures were extensively used by the most innovative and groundbreaking francophone sub-Saharan African authors of the 1970s and 1980s (Moudileno 2006; Thomas 2002). These stylistic devices in systems of domination, of which the African postcolony is a classic example, are characterized, as Mbembe has shown in his book *On the Postcolony*, by vulgar excess, disproportion, and obscenity. The obscenity in question is not a moral category, but rather an aesthetic construct that denotes a lack of restraint or proportion as a reflection of the display of disproportionate violence against even the mildest dissent or the unrestrained pursuit of pleasures of the flesh by the authorities.

Tchicaya U Tam'si is engaged in a double act, illustrating through the example of his protagonist a larger social and political phenomenon, but to the extent that he carnivalizes political authority he also derides that authority, exposing it as a huge theatre of buffoonery and puppets. Nnikon and his colleagues are bespattered with filth, a real-life technique one should not forget was utilized by resistant popular culture against real-life leaders as a way of undermining and neutralizing their authority (Mbembe 2001, 2003; Thomas 2002). As such, these gestures emerge as statements of liberty, as affirmations of courage over fear, of life over death.

A notable shift of emphasis occurred between the plays of the 1960s and those of the 1970s in terms of the representation of the sovereign ruler, the "founder" of the nation. Yet, nationalist and post-nationalist traditions of political drama share a common preoccupation in terms of their concern with political leadership either as a force for good that can be celebrated or as an ill to be reviled. Having said this, it needs to be emphasized that the post-nationalist theatre of political critique is not exhausted by leader-centered plays, however satirical they may be. There also exists a stream within the late 1970s and 1980s tradition that explores the political condition of the postcolony from the subjectivity of the ordinary citizen, whose function is not merely to bring into relief the depredations of the leader, but rather to stand as the central dramatic consciousness through which events are filtered and judged. Spectators now witness the impact and effect of public policies on private lives rather than the conception and execution of those policies. Exceeding the status of victim, the citizen is now also an agent, who makes decisions and struggles within the system. Horror, the satirical and the grotesque, the fantastic and the carnivalesque, are now replaced by citizen-centered humor, the tragic, the lyrical, and the confessional as the dominant artistic resources and principal modes of representation. Leader-centered theatre cultivated the art of exaggeration and extravagance in which the exterior world was aggressive and destructive, while the alternative now fosters the art of restraint and suggestiveness, in other words, theatrical minimalism accompanied by the intense exploration of interiority. The discussion that follows will examine this practice with particular reference to Tchicaya U Tam'si's play *Le bal de Ndinga* (1987).

I will begin by noting that *Le bal de Ndinga* is among the most successful French-language plays from Africa ever written, having been produced in Haiti, Guyana, Quebec, Congo-Brazzaville, and Paris, where it ran continuously to packed audiences for over a year in a production by Gabriel Garran of the Théâtre International de Langue Française (Pont-Hubert 1990, 101–109). Exploiting, as will be shown in more detail later, the practices of the song lament, the dramatized narrative, and the cinematic technique of the flashback, this short but emotionally intense play narrates the life of a poor Congolese hotel cleaner appropriately named Modeste Ndinga. The action takes place on the eve of the former Belgian Congo's independence and unfolds over a three-month period from April to Independence Day on June 30, 1960.

Overwhelmed by a life of suffering and humiliation, particularly at the hands of his Belgian employer, Van Bilsen, Modeste Ndinga spends most of his wakeful moments daydreaming about political independence. When the long-awaited day finally arrives, Ndinga joins a crowd at a political rally in the public square to celebrate. A few moments into the celebration, a stampede breaks out and revelers flee in all directions, except for Ndinga who, alone in the square, is absorbed in a joyful dance of freedom, the cha-cha. Suddenly, he collapses and dies "anonyme au bal de l'Espoir" (U Tam'si 1987, 185) [anonymously in the ball of Hope], the victim, according to official radio news bulletins, of an unknown gunman. *Le bal de Ndinga* is an unmistakably allegorical play in which Tchicaya U Tam'si both celebrates the dream of independence and mourns its defeat, and through the play's central character he conveys the sense of a certain stillborn quality to independence: "Ndinga has a premonition that the word independence carries deep within it a sense of the most painful feeling that a soul can ever withstand" (1987, 181).

The choice of Ndinga, an antihero in all regards, as the central character in this play is itself further evidence of the changes in form and vision that occurred by the 1980s in francophone African theatre. Unlike the figure of Patrice Lumumba in Aimé Césaire's *Une saison au Congo* (1967), whose heroic resistance elates and inspires admiration, Ndinga elicits only pity and has nothing of the stature and moral nobility of Césaire's hero. He submits to, but does not initiate, action, which in part explains the static nature of the play. Ndinga is not only on the economic margins of society, but with his many ailments, his physical health is marginal as well: "He limped . . . usually walked like someone with a hernia between the legs" (169). His death is a non-event (the radio announcement does not even give him a name), and he is like the floor cloth of his cleaning job, "Even his blood is a dirty rag" (185). Participating in a "ball of Hope" that turns into a ball of death, Ndinga's unfulfilled dreams symbolize the broken aspirations of an entire post-nationalist generation. Orphaned at a very young age, he is forced to abandon school, then in early adolescence he joins the rural-to-urban exodus in search of a better life: "We hung on to the promises of the city as we had to tree branches" (179). These urban promises turn out to be a mirage, but return to the countryside is no longer an option since it has lost "its protector gods" (179), and the resulting disillusionment is realigned on dreams of political independence.

Tchicaya U Tam'si demonstrates compassion for Ndinga's shattered life while nevertheless attributing partial blame for his tragic outcome; the play is therefore at once a celebration of, and a critical reflection on, a certain popular understanding of independence. For, as the narrator observes, "if you are hit by the twisted arrows of adversity, then folly must have played its part" (1987, 183). More than just symbolizing an era of political freedom for his country, independence was going to offer him the promise of "an increase in the significance of life" (176) and the end of work, "[n]ever having to wash endless corridors of hotel floor" (172). These changes would also be accompanied by the end of "fratricidal quarrels" (172) and a redistribution of wealth: "everything would belong to him as much as to others" (176).

Ndinga's hopes and aspirations were, of course, shared by those who embraced and adhered to the principles of the anticolonial struggle: "Henceforth we'll no longer hear threats; gone, all those kicks. Thank God, it'll all be over. Gone, the arbitrary arrests, the humiliation inflicted for the pleasure of laughing at the suffering of the poor African" (U Tam'si 1987, 177). In an intensely erotic evocation of independence, Ndinga schedules his conquest of the hotel sex worker Sabine (heretofore beyond his financial means) for June 30, equating independence with a reaffirmation and recovery of the Congolese virility that had been temporarily emasculated by Belgian colonial rule: "I'll bang her all night. I'll bang her until she cries out: Stop! Stop! And promises to go out and proclaim to the world that 'yes, yes indeed, Ndinga is a man, a true male!'" (176).

Ndinga, carried away by song and dance, loses his ability to assess the significance of social and political developments, in turn underestimating the treacherous forces conspiring to destroy him and, by extension, the young Congolese nation. Through two symbolic characters, Ndinga's Belgian employer (Van Bilsen) and his accomplice in the local army and bourgeoisie (Sergeant Outouboma), Tchicaya U Tam'si sketches a wider, international, and neocolonial dimension to the crisis of Congolese (and African) independence. Van Bilsen represents the former imperial power whose determination to manage the autonomy of the young nation is confirmed by such statements as "there will always be servants" (173) and "Congo will always need us, Independence or not" (173). In a tragic foreshadowing of the role Van Bilsen will play, he orders a drink called *mort subite* (sudden death) shortly after delivering ominous warnings to one of his employees: "Beware, beware! Don't let politicians' sweet talk lead you astray. I'll punish any sign of insolence from you, clear?" (175). Later, Ndinga calls him, with tragic prescience, "Judas or Pontius Pilate" (177), a description that turns out to be apt when Outouboma, acting on the pretext of controlling the riotous, Independence Day revelers, gives orders to his troops to open fire. Ndinga's ensuing death confirms the tragic outcome of the nationalist struggle and dashes the short-lived hopes that liberation would introduce a civil society.

Le bal de Ndinga's success can be partially attributed to the originality of the dramatic form and influences selected by Tchicaya U Tam'si to convey his vision. Some critics have suggested influences from sources as varied as Bertolt Brecht's epic theatre, Arthur Adamov's theatre of the absurd, and even Ariane Mnouchkine's ludic theatre (Jouanny 1996, 132). However, more immediate sources of Tchicaya U Tam'si's eclectic drama can be found in an indigenous African art form known as the "lament" or the threnody. Among many African peoples, the death of a loved one is not an occasion for private sorrow, stoically borne in the solitude of the home. It is a public, staged affair in which wailed songs and spoken expressions of raw grief (by family, friends, and even hired professional mourners) alternate with a more detached narrative recall and assessment of the life of the deceased. In an observation about the Akan that is valid for many African societies, Kwabena Nketia writes, "Grief and sorrow may be personal and private; nevertheless, Akan society expects that on the occasion of a funeral they should be expressed publicly through the singing of a dirge" (1969, 8). It is this art of the dirge or the lament, of coming to terms with loss by expressing it in song and openly acting out the emotions of grief occasioned by it that partly serves as a model for *Le bal de Ndinga*. "Ndinga" in Kikongo also means "voice," and this definition can be extended to "lamentation"; the "ball" then emerges as the site of the lamentation, of grief, and of penitence.

Unlike nationalist writers like Senghor, who saw himself as the *dyali,* or the praise singer, of his people and their aspirations, or the Senegalese dramatist Cheikh Ndao, who claimed the role of forger of the nationalist myths, the post-nationalist Tchicaya U Tam'si conceived of his role as the professional mourner of his people's lost illusions. Like in a traditional lament, the time scheme in *Le bal de Ndinga* alternates between the present and the past. The curtain rises on a present of loss and confusion during which Jean-Pierre Mpendje, distraught and in despair, tries to make sense of the nightmare of the moment. The immediacy of his pain and anguish is conveyed by the present tense in his account of the mad rush for safety he had to make with his friend once the shooting started: "We ran in all directions.

... I make fun of him. I forget fear. ... I run behind a flame tree where I seek cover. ... I curse the foolishness that keeps him standing unprotected right in the middle of the field" (U Tam'si 1987, 169–70). With him onstage is the deceased's niece Angélique Koba who, with a group of neighborhood mourners, chants their sorrow in Kikongo in solo and chorus with a call-and-response pattern:

> Where has Ndinga gone?
> Oh, poor child!
> Oh, unlucky child!
> Oh Ndinga, dear father! Ndinga, dear father.
> He's lying there his nose in the grass, what should I tell his
>   mother's sister? I, his poor niece, overwhelmed by his
>   death. (170–71)

The choice of the style of mourning implemented by the dramatist here is very important for, in keeping with his character's modest social status, the sung expressions of sorrow in his honor are keyed in a low literary register. They have none of the restraint and formality that Nketia (1969, 119–30) sees as characteristic of the dirge, and they make no attempt to associate Ndinga with some famous ancestor. Instead, the spectator is treated to spontaneous expressions in everyday language and to pathos coupled with references to the misfortune of the deceased. The significance of these opening moments of the performance, in other words, is not the depth of their content, but rather their ability to create mood and atmosphere through the qualities of voice and the melodies of the mourners. The opening wails soon give way to narrative recall when the narrator, in a sudden shift in time frame, provides different snapshots of the deceased's immediate and distant past. That past is presented in dramatic mode and also in narrative mode during which Jean-Pierre Mpendje enacts, rather like a traditional narrator/performer in a kind of one-man show, the multiple roles he describes. Then, the various characters hitherto only described—Van Bilsen, Outouboma, and the dead Ndinga—suddenly materialize onstage as full-fledged actors interacting with one another and with the narrator, who has now turned into a full actor. In this dynamic, the illusion of a play, of dramatized action unfolding in the present, is deliberately and constantly undercut as Jean-Pierre Mpendje moves in and out of roles, thereby preventing the spectator from identifying too closely with the action and the characters.

Unfortunately, Tchicaya U Tam'si died in April 1988, just a few months before the premiere of *Le bal de Ndinga*. Not the least of his achievements in this play was his ability to avoid maudlin sentimentality in spite of the profoundly tragic fate of his antiheroes. Instead, he was able to force people to think about the complicity of the post-colony in its fate, the very kind of introverted analysis of which Ndinga was incapable, but which could have spared him so much suffering.

SEVEN

From the Grotesque to the Fantastic: Sony Labou Tansi's *Qui a mangé Madame d'Avoine Bergotha?*

M arcel Sony, born in 1947, altered his name to Sony Labou Tansi when he started writing as a way of indicating his profound admiration for Tchicaya U Tam'si. However, the latter's plays, though characterized by exaggeration and extravagance, nevertheless depict a recognizable world organized within a realistic framework, while the reader/spectator of Sony Labou Tansi's work will soon realize that this dimension has been evacuated and replaced by a space of fantasy, one that enjoys "no pretensions to a connection with reality" (Thompson 1972, 23). In *Qui a mangé Madame d'Avoine Bergotha?* first performed in Brazzaville, the capital of the Republic of Congo in 1989 (in a co-production by the author and the late French director Jean-Pierre Klein), Sony Labou Tansi dramatizes the antics of Philippe-George Walante (also known as Jean-Leopold Walante), the ruler of the imaginary tropical island of Bergotha. Determined to assert his island's independence vis-à-vis foreign ideologies and influence, he proclaims: "We refuse to be independent along the lines of some crazy crooks who would give us a national anthem, a hammer, and a sickle" (1989, 32). In a position reminiscent of the one Mobutu took against Patrice Lumumba for his alleged communist sympathies, Walante proclaims the need for a sovereignty built on the nation's cultural traditions, "following the deepest essence of its customs" (31). Enunciated in these terms, such a policy sounds reasonable; its actual implementation, however, triggers a process of rapid political degeneration. Walante's first measures consist in abolishing the constitution, banishing all but a handful of men from Bergotha, and then proclaiming himself the island nation's "inseminator-in-chief." He subsequently organizes a series of festivals which enforce mass copulation in order to increase the population in anticipation of potential threats of external aggression.

The relationship between reality and the illogical actions and decisions made by the regime is constantly placed under pressure in *Qui a mangé Madame d'Avoine Bergotha?* In a bid to secure a blessing from the visiting pope, Jean-Désiré I, for his future marriage to an as-yet-unknown bride, Walante sequesters the pope in Bergotha and appoints his cousin Watney Windsor as his replacement in the Vatican. When Walante does actually find a bride, Micheline d'Avoine, a burlesque twist further complicates the situation when he discovers after their wedding that she is a man in drag, namely, Yongo-Loutard. Angry at having being fooled and at the growing rebellion he sees against his rule, he orders a mass execution, including that of his own daughter Messadeck and her lover, Madison (who also happens to be Walante's nephew). The play ends with Walante overwhelmed with remorse and aimlessly drifting in the streets of what an unknown female interlocutor and fellow somnambulist tells him is the country of the dead:

> Walante: I here drag with me the tattered ribbons of my con-
> science. I've lost count of the days that whirl and disap-
> pear into the vortex of my delirium. The blood in my
> veins has dried up; my memory is shattered. . . .
>
> Woman: How did you manage to cross the frontier?
>
> Walante: Which frontier, Madam?
>
> Woman: You are in the land of the dead. (124)

This play is an exercise in fantasy which nevertheless succeeds in achieving propositional value. As Eileen Julien has persuasively argued, recourse to the fantastic in Sony Labou Tansi's novel *La vie et demie* (1979) "allows us to see the 'real' world from outside its parameters. It is thus the density of form, its atypicality that, *because it alienates* the real world it evokes, makes that world all the more visible" (1992, 139). An analogous distancing function of fantasy is at work in *Qui a mangé Madame d'Avoine Bergotha?* whereby Sony Labou Tansi does not so much document the contemporary reality from within its space as suggest it from the outside through the indirect and aesthetically alienating form of the fable. "Where do you want me to speak from if not from the outside?" (1979, 9), Sony Labou Tansi famously asks in his prefatory note to *La vie et demie*. The contemporary reality we encounter in *Qui a mangé Madame d'Avoine Bergotha?* is a repressive one in which "independence" is but an empty word rammed down people's throats (1989, 16) when it is not asserted by other means such as peeing on them (14).

The play cannot, however, be reduced only to its political vision. Sony Labou Tansi produced a large corpus of committed works, but he was also concerned with aesthetic innovation, insisting on the quality of art as "invention" and the role of the artist as "fabricator": "I do not teach, I invent. . . . To those in search of an engaged writer, I propose an engaging writer" (*La vie et demie*, 9). *Qui a mangé Madame d'Avoine Bergotha?* is arguably the play in which one finds the most systematic treatment of these positions. Obviously a burlesque satire of the post-colonial order, *Qui a mangé Madame d'Avoine Bergotha?* is above all a playful experiment with a variety of theatrical traditions serving as intertextual referents.

The first indication of artistic self-consciousness occurs in the opening scene, titled "Porte Cassée" (Broken Door), in which the Maître du Marathon warns his friends, "Be ready to breathe in the new cuisine" (Tansi 1989, 11), and wonders with them, "Who will be cooked tonight?" (11). The reference to "cuisine" is, obviously, not to the literal act of cooking. It is, rather, to the art of concoction in the sense of "cooking up" a scheme or narrative emplotment. Thus, when he talks of "[t]he new cuisine of the Mad Elders, Walante and Touma" (11), the Maître du Marathon is referring to the scheming of their country's most important personalities, equated here with burlesque theatre.

The impression that Bergotha's ordinary citizens are about to watch a "play" whose performance they will not tolerate indefinitely, however, is reinforced toward the end of the opening scene when Commandant Macoute warns his fellow audience members: "I was brought up in the cult of Sophocles and others. Don't imagine this play will last a lifetime" (Tansi 1989, 12). Peasant B's yelp of joy shortly thereafter, "a magnificent evening awaits us" (18), coincides, as the stage directions indicate, with the arrival onstage of some of the members of the cast and the opening of the internal play: "Touma arrives leading a group of policemen" (18). Touma's imperious announcement at the end of the second of the two opening scenes, "Here Begins the Republic" (18), is accompanied by the strains of a satirical national "anthem of the bulls" and acts as a framing device that signals the beginning of the play.

Sony Labou Tansi is, of course, the author of the published play, but Touma, in the tradition of the Presenter in Senouvo Agbota Zinsou's *On joue la comédie,* is the scriptwriter and producer of the internal play. Touma, however, does not manage to extricate himself from the convoluted and potentially dangerous situations in which he places himself, for he weaves a plot so complex that he ends up getting tangled in it. As the leader's trusted counselor and confidant, he cannot be seen to be orchestrating a plan to eliminate the rampaging Walante from the political scene, so Touma enlists the assistance of a number of people whom he largely succeeds in manipulating. These include Walante himself, Yongo-Loutard, and Messadeck, with whom Yongo-Loutard is intensely in love, a love of which Messadeck is completely unaware, being in love herself with Madison. Touma weaves a different story for each of these characters and allocates them a specific task. For Yongo-Loutard, for example, he proposes (allegedly on Messadeck's "request") that he disguise himself as a woman by wearing a silk skirt and adopting a woman's name, Micheline d'Avoine Bergotha, and that he enter Walante's compound to introduce himself through song to Messadeck. Touma's ultimate but improbable calculation (the only way, Touma reasons, to secure Yongo-Loutard's participation in his elaborate scheme) is that Walante will see the "woman" and fall in love with her as he is readily wont to do with women, and that she in turn will temper his brutality and, if necessary, rid their country of him. Touma's advice to Yongo-Loutard—"I'll bet you my soul that if *well acted* this sequence will not leave him indifferent to your charm" (Tansi 1989, 69; emphasis added)—is additional proof, if any were needed, of Touma's self-perception as a theatre director.

In a wonderful piece of tragic-comic quid pro quo, Yongo-Loutard, who by now is serenading Messadeck outside her window (Sony Labou Tansi's 1992 play *La résurrection rouge et blanche de Roméo et Juliette* is, of course, an adaptation of Shakespeare's *Romeo and Juliet*), is threatened with arrest by an angry Messadeck awakened from her sleep. He is, in the end, arrested, though not on Messadeck's orders, but on her father's, who is equally irate at the late-night intrusion into his residence. To keep his entire scheme from collapsing, Touma rushes to Messadeck and justifies his actions on the grounds that they were concocted to save her lover, Madison, whose life was threatened by her mad father. The stratagem works for a while before Walante ultimately takes murderous revenge, but it is the permanence of the danger of exposure and Touma's frantic efforts to keep the lie alive—"If only my lies would work" (Tansi 1989, 23); and "If only my Master remains fooled to the end" (24)—that give a quality of melodrama to the play.

Touma shares points of commonality with the (West) African dramatic tradition of the trickster. I will return to Touma's status as a trickster character shortly, but let us first consider the other influences on his construction that have been, and can be, proposed. The first is that of the *atalaku* (a Kikongo word which means "look at me and follow my example"), a popular composite figure of urban Congolese *soukous* music (Nkanga 1995), whose own inspiration has been traced to rites of healing, local musical practices, and the theatre of political and cultural cheerleading. According to Bob White, the *atalaku* is more of a dancer than a musician, who leads and coordinates the various choreographed dance routines that accompany vocal or instrumental music sessions during a live performance, showcasing individual, especially female, dancers using "suggestive language that frames the dancer's presence as an object of male desire" (2004, 203–204). Additionally, the *atalaku* mediates between the various musician-singers and the audience/public: he exhorts the musician-singers through a variety of techniques to outperform one another and themselves on the dance floor, and he encourages the audience to offer financial gifts to the performers and, of course, to him as their clownish entertainer. These techniques, drawn from a "bag of performative tricks," include "shouts," "various other vocal gymnastics," and coded commentary, sometimes lewd, sometimes satirical, directed at individuals, state officials, or topical issues of society and politics, the objective being to whip the audience into an emotional high (White 2004, 203).

The "Scène Horizontale" in *Qui a mangé Madame d'Avoine Bergotha?* is a moment of devastating parody and grotesquerie. Although it might not seem to refer to the practice of animation, which "ultimately created certain reflexes and attitudes in relation to situations that people experience every day" (Kapalanga 1989, 20) and was so beloved of authoritarian states such as Mobutu's, closer examination reveals the degree to which the scene is at the very least evocative of it. The reader/spectator is treated to the now customary parade involving the leader and state dignitaries: "Walante arrives floating in gold, diamonds, and ermine" (Tansi 1989, 38). They are accompanied by displays of garlands, flags, and banners (37), formations of uniformed male and female dancers attired in red and pink, respectively (37), the *animateur*, or "lead conductor" (Touma), and the frenzy and slogans promoting the national project and the all-powerful leader. In this scene, however, animation is reduced to an absurd and even animal sport. The setting is a slaughterhouse (37), and Touma as the *atalaku/animateur* has become a veterinary doctor whose responsibility is to examine the participants and to determine their physical fitness in comparison to cows and bulls. Above all, the entire performance has been emptied of what little entertainment or political value it may have in real life. Typically, it is staged either in honor of a visiting dignitary or as propaganda in favor of the national development plan. In this instance, though, Sony Labou Tansi has reduced it to a dehumanizing and coerced act of public copulation, a "planned insemination" (38) with the enlisted participants belching out such slogans as "Long live the founding father of the bulls" (38) and "Long live supreme insemination" (42).

A more important function performed by Touma, however, is that of trickster. But to refer to him as a "trickster" is not to evoke some unconscious influence of traditional lore on Sony Labou Tansi but rather to point to a deliberate selection on his part of a figure linked with Africa's verbal arts, yet one whose trickstering function is here vested with new meaning. Touma-as-trickster expresses Sony Labou Tansi's disenchanted vision of postcolonial politics as sordid theatre, full of scheming, lies, and betrayals, little else but "machinations," "cunning," and "shady deals" (Tansi 1989, 22). Naturally, these prove costly, sometimes deadly, to both the tricksters and the tricked alike.

Another important but insufficiently studied intertextual refer-ent for *Qui a mangé Madame d'Avoine Bergotha?* is Aimé Césaire's *La tragédie du roi Christophe* (1963), a play Sony Labou Tansi knew extremely well, having produced it in Congo (Devésa 1996a, 175). In what follows, I will pay detailed attention to the intertextual relation-ship between the two.

Césaire's recourse to culinary metaphors—"But I've explained that Christophe was a *cook*, that is a clever politician" (1963, 15; emphasis added), explains the Presenter—and his views of politics as a (cockfighting) performance (12) are both present in Sony Labou Tansi's play. There are, of course, numerous such echoes and allu-sions, characterizations and techniques, that point to a more deliber-ate and concrete influence of Césaire. An immediate example that comes to mind is the Haiti-Africa parallel that Césaire establishes in his play: "Poor Africa! I mean poor Haiti. It is the same thing, by the way. There, tribes, languages. Here, Negroes, Mulattoes" (1963, 49). Haiti's historical experience with independence is reformulated as a warning to freshly independent African nations. Not only is the impression given from the opening lines that the play's setting could be Haiti, "Haiti, you smell of anger" (11), but the name of one of Sony Labou Tansi's characters, Commandant Macoute, is immedi-ately reminiscent of the feared Tonton Macoute (Milice de Volontaires de la Sécurité Nationale, MVSN), the paramilitary security police that worked for Haitian president-for-life François "Papa Doc" Duvalier (1957–1971). This point is made explicitly by Peasant A when he com-pares Walante's police to that force: "They search stomachs and turn intestines inside out as did the *macoutes* in Haiti" (55). There is also the scene of the forced weddings in *La tragédie du roi Christophe* (act 2, scene 4), slightly adapted in the "Scène Horizontale" in *Qui a mangé Madame d'Avoine Bergotha?* with the clown Hugonin, just like Touma, certifying in almost identical terms the fitness of the female partici-pants and auctioning them off to males: "Awarded, to you!" (89), says the former; "Auctioned, fit for service" (Tansi 1989, 37).

To mention Hugonin is, of course, to refer to an important model in the crafting of the composite figure of Touma. In addition to the latter's many other roles, his "accumulation of functions" (Tansi 1989, 89), he is also, in the way Hugonin is to Christophe, Walante's court jester. In this capacity, he both entertains and flatters him (85, 94), keeps him informed about goings-on in the land (47–53), and speaks truths to him that no one else dares. However, and this constitutes a fundamental point of departure, Touma rises up in revolt against Walante's tyranny, thus accelerating the latter's downfall and, of course, his own too:

> Touma: I've decided to bite you the best way I could. . . .
> Consider me a madman, a traitor, or a monster, if you
> will; but I had to craft a language that could strike right
> into you, to give a name to the hell you created. (114)

But perhaps *La tragédie du roi Christophe*'s most significant presence in Sony Labou Tansi's play is at the level of dramatic structure. Césaire's play is built on alternating sequences of popular scenes that feature Haiti's peasants, market women, and rafters, and elite scenes dramatizing the power struggles within the ruling group. The popular scenes provide a pause in the dramatic action, interludes when the people, excluded from power and yet the object of its multiple exactions, have the opportunity to reflect, sometimes critically, on their fate and their country's.

This structure of alternating popular and elite scenes embodies the clearest debt of *Qui a mangé Madame d'Avoine Bergotha?* to *La tragédie du roi Christophe*, highlighting the gulf between the rulers and the ruled, whereby the latter are portrayed as outsiders, mere spectators of their country's destiny. The commentaries made during these popular scenes provide insights into the workings of power. Césaire's mournful observations on the economic and security plight of the ordinary citizen in post-revolutionary Haiti, cited below, are echoed in the words of Sony Labou Tansi's Peasant A in the Bergotha postcolony:

> Second Peasant: But I say to myself, this: if we drove the whites
> into the sea, it was to own this, our land, ourselves, not
> to labor on the land of others, not even blacks. . . . The
> drum hardly starts beating than they jump all over us. To
> think that there is no more liberty for the gods than for
> men. (Césaire 1963, 74–75)

Peasant A: Walante throws away 37% of the budget on phone
tapping and surveillance. . . . He makes us drink the juice
of a police [force] that is forever brutal. . . . What's the
function of independence if not to piss on the poor peasant and her husband. (Tansi 1989, 13–14)

Finally, a function common to the popular scenes in both plays is the
creation of dramatic tension through the anticipation of the plays'
tragic denouements. Long before the uprisings that will put an end
to the tyrannical rules of Christophe and Walante, the reader is fore-
warned through the respective peasants' sense of foreboding:

Second Peasant: Something is not right . . . not right. . . . There
is something rotten in this kingdom. (Césaire 1963,
110–11)

Peasant C: There's a smell of burning, believe me. Somewhere,
the Republic is on fire. But who lit a fire under the
Republic's bottom, go figure? One thing is clear: there's
gonna be work for the executioners. (Tansi 1989, 56)

In his outburst at Walante quoted earlier, Touma talks of "craft[ing]
a language" (114) appropriate to the task of naming his leader's evil
deeds. Elsewhere in the play, prior to their falling out, he advises
Walante on how to best address the nation: "My Lord! It's important
that the words thrown at the people come not from the dictionary, but
from the heart" (29). Indeed, the extracts provided of Walante's radio
address can be seen as a self-conscious exercise in style. Sony Labou
Tansi's insistence on the need to create a space of linguistic liberty
within the French language which would allow for experimentation
and accordingly stamp the language with stylistic uniqueness—"a
language is meant to name and not to silence or obstruct" (in Bohui
2003, 17)—has long been considered to be one of the defining characteristics of his art (Thomas 2002).

Not surprisingly, French theatre director Jean-Paul Delore opted
in his production of Sony Labou Tansi's *La parenthèse de sang* (1981b)
to limit the entire staging of the play not to its characters, themes, and
dramatic action, but rather solely to its language. As Sylvie Chalaye
has observed:

To approach Sony's theatre not through staging, but through its language, through his theatre's resonant dimension, the resonant material that he uses, the words that he bangs together and shakes up the better to wake up French, that is the real challenge of the choice made by Jean-Paul Delore. (Chalaye 2006)

One could easily envisage a production of *Qui a mangé Madame d'Avoine Bergotha?* that would also focus on the play's language. These linguistic practices include numerous neologisms, such as *pognoniser* (to spend money; 14), which adapts the French term *pognon,* which is slang for money; a playful vocabulary; and metaphors. Sony Labou Tansi frequently derives his vocabulary principally from the culinary realm, "cooking" up new words and phrases like "le mal est si beau quand on le mange cru" (1989, 35) [evil is so beautiful when it's consumed raw] and "J'espère que vous n'allez pas ... me faire boire quatre heures de parlotte sans sel" (29) [I hope you're not going to make me drink four hours of saltless words]. The peasants constantly complain about "all the evil that independence is stuffing down our throats" (16).

A close reading of Sony Labou Tansi's texts will reveal that the movement of his thought is from the abstract to the concrete, hardly ever from the concrete to the abstract. Consider the following examples from *Qui a mangé Madame d'Avoine Bergotha?:* "une morsure d'Histoire" (11) [history's bite], "dépecer la magouille" (13) [to skin corruption alive], and "avoir les doigts sur l'insoutenable" (49) [to have one's fingers on the unbearable]. In each of these examples, it is an abstraction—"history" compared to a snake or an animal, "corruption" to an animal, and the unbearable and the unthinkable to a gun's trigger—that is provided. Sony Labou Tansi's mastery of language, imaginative reach, and playfulness have transformed both a language he once described as a "langue frigide" (Ngal 1982, 134) [frigid language] and the coordinates and potentialities of francophone theatre.

EIGHT

Exile and the Failure of the Nation; or, Diasporic Subjectivity from Below: Simone Schwarz-Bart's *Ton beau capitaine*

The critique of the nationalist state was an important feature of francophone African theatre during the 1970s and 1980s. As we have seen, this phenomenon was deployed with equal satirical verve in the francophone Caribbean in such plays as Daniel Boukman's *Les négriers* (1972) and *Ventres pleins, ventres creux* (1973) and Elie Stephenson's *O Mayouri* (1974), and in the collective experimental theatre production of *Kimafoutiésa* (1976) by Joby Bernabé and Rosy Varesse. The post-nationalist plays of Tchicaya U Tam'si and Sony Labou Tansi adapted/adopted a broad range of theatrical devices in order to distance their corpus from the referentialist dimension of the earlier generation and to address the growing disenchantment with contemporary postcolonial society. Analogous circumstances were to be found in the Caribbean, a geographic space increasingly adversely impacted by the rapidly shifting coordinates of the global economy, changes that were exacerbating socioeconomic disparities and that were of growing concern to activists, politicians, and authors such as Simone Schwarz-Bart, who turned her attention to these matters in her groundbreaking play *Ton beau capitaine* (1987).

Of course, to the extent that France's West Atlantic territories are not, unlike francophone African countries, former colonies that achieved independence, but rather colonies that became integral regions of the former colonial power with departmentalization in 1946, it might seem inappropriate to talk of a critique of the nationalist state in connection with their dramatists. There may be no local examples to challenge the reputations of Mobutu, Bokassa, or for that matter Duvalier, yet profound similarities are to be found in Caribbean and African dramatists' responses to their respective post-1946 and post-1960s political conditions. While the legal and political arrangements for which nationalists fought might be different, the objectives pursued by these arrangements essentially involved analogous claims for freedom, rights, and economic development. Indeed, for Aimé Césaire, the leading francophone Caribbean nationalist of the period, the legal and political name given to a territory's status mattered little as long as that status was consistent with the pursuit of democratic objectives. Thus, for him, if the fact of becoming French signified the acquisition of permanent citizenship rights for hitherto enslaved and colonized Caribbean people in the same way that independence guaranteed similar rights for colonized francophone Africans, then the question of (an) independent state(s) was secondary.

But in both francophone Africa and the francophone Caribbean, the nationalist promise of decolonization, whatever form that decolonization took, progressively gave way, especially among intellectuals and artists, to what Aijaz Ahmad evoked in the context of the Indian partition as a "nationalism of mourning" (1992, 119). The impressive material progress registered in the francophone Caribbean in terms of infrastructure development, higher wages, social security, improved health, and higher educational standards was offset *not* by political instability, tyrannical government, and growing economic asymmetry between the wealthy and the poor as in the (francophone) African postcolony, but rather by economic dependency (Anselin 1995). This alignment with metropolitan France resulted in the mass migration of Caribbean people to France, a process encouraged and organized until 1981 by state agencies, notably the Bureau pour le Développement des Migrations dans les Départements d'Outre-Mer (BUMIDOM). Thus, a degree of material progress and French citizenship rights may have been obtained, but the opportunity costs of these remain highly problematic: physical deracination and cultural and psychological exile.

Migration patterns contributed to a mood of deep ambivalence or even outright disillusionment with departmentalization, in the same way that political authoritarianism and economic immiseration did in the African postcolony. Given these circumstances, it is hardly surprising that the evidentiary modes provided by migration and exile should loom so large in francophone Caribbean drama: in *Les négriers*, Boukman frames sponsored Caribbean migration to France as a modern variation of the slave trade, and in *Kimafoutiésa* (the title means "What kind of craziness is this?"), the character Bumi & Dom (an obvious reference to the aforementioned agency, BUMIDOM) exhorts the newly arrived Creole-speaking migrant workers to "forget the land, flesh, and soul of your country" (Bernabé and Varesse 1976, 31–32) and to accept their new working conditions. In turn, Schwarz-Bart's *Ton beau capitaine* offers a poignant and lyrical treatment of migration and exile.

Ton beau capitaine is centered on a husband and wife who are separated by exile and who communicate only through "cassette letters." Their predicament is dramatized, in particular the husband's (Wilnor Baptiste), whose hopes and dreams of a comfortable retirement in his native Haiti, after years of toil in sugarcane fields in Guadeloupe, do not come to fruition. Wilnor Baptiste learns from his wife (Marie-Ange) that she is expecting a baby fathered by the intermediary who occasionally delivers the messages, and his former security, which resided in the belief that he was the "captain" of his life, wife, and home, is transformed into a crisis of anguished self-doubt. However, he surmounts this crisis thanks to a revelation (in the religious sense of the word) that is mysteriously made possible by his wife, whose infidelity he now forgives:

> Wilnor: Marie-Ange . . . When I read your cassette, for an
> instant, one brief instant, I almost doubted you. . . .
> Fortunately, I've always been appreciated by those in
> heaven. . . . And here I was believing without believing,
> doubting and not doubting, when all of a sudden I heard
> your voice right here at my house . . . and suddenly I saw
> the light: it came to me. It may have been a kind of ges-
> ture, an act of mercy from Saint Anthony of Padua. . . . I
> saw the light, bright and clear: oh yes, as though I had an
> electric bulb in the middle of my throat. . . . Now I see, I
> know, I understand. (Schwarz-Bart 1987, 54)

We shall return to the significance of Wilnor's religious experience. At this juncture, the question of the displacement of the migrant experience from a Guadeloupean to a Haitian subject may seem perplexing.

The relative age of modern Haitian migration, a phenomenon that goes back to the 1920s as illustrated by Jacques Roumain's novel *Gouverneurs de la rosée* (1944), may be a contributing factor. But of course, Haitian migrants are disproportionately represented in almost all the Caribbean islands: estimates in Guadeloupe alone are 24,000 out of a population of some 300,000 (Brodwin 2003, 384). The precariousness of their legal status, difficult emigration circumstances, and vulnerability to various exploitative practices can explain the interest Schwarz-Bart had for the plight and condition of Haitian migrants in particular. In fact, as Judith Miller has noted, this condition takes on a larger allegorical significance because it unfolds in the context of metaphors involving ships and captains against a historical background that connects with the original traumatic dispersion of African populations by the slave trade (1995, 155). Of course, by figuring Haiti in *Ton beau capitaine,* Schwarz-Bart adds her name to a long and illustrious Caribbean dramatic tradition in which Haiti has featured prominently: Aimé Césaire's *La tragédie du roi Christophe* (1963), Edouard Glissant's *Monsieur Toussaint* (1961), Vincent Placoly's *Dessalines; ou, La passion de l'indépendance* (1983), Elie Stephenson's *O Mayouri* (1974), and Maryse Condé's *An tan revolisyon* (1989). Naturally, the image of Haiti has not remained static in francophone Caribbean theatre. In the 1960s, Haiti was associated with heroic nationalism because of the 1791–1804 revolution, but by the 1980s it had become a metaphor for disillusionment. *Ton beau capitaine* can thus be seen as a dramatic instantiation of that disillusionment, a subversion via the modes of elegy, the tragic, and even the comic of the predominant epic grandeur of *La tragédie du roi Christophe* and, by extension, the theatre of anticolonial nationalism.

La tragédie du roi Christophe stages the creation of a nation and as such is a play about the construction and cementing of the unity of a people, their home (the national community), and rootedness:

> Christophe: Stone, I am looking for stone! Cement, I'm looking for cement! All this scrap heap, Oh! How can it be raised upright! Upright in the face of the world. . . . the time has come for us to put an end to our quarrels to build this country and unite this people. (Césaire 1963, 46)

On the other hand, *Ton beau capitaine* dramatizes the fracturing of that community/home and concentrates on the uprootedness and dispersal of its people that ensue. Where images of solidity and permanence predominate in *La tragédie du roi Christophe,* displacement and errancy more accurately describe *Ton beau capitaine.* King Christophe is repelled by all that is watery and viscous, attracted instead to stone as the symbol of the essential solid reality of nation and culture. A sharp contrast thus emerges in Schwarz-Bart's introduction of the transnational Haitian nomad, who is constantly on the move in search of substantial solidity and who spends a considerable amount of time on water and, not uncommonly, drowns in it. Marie-Ange informs her husband:

> Marie-Ange: Good news from all our exiled ones around the world: Grenada, the Dominican Republic, Puerto-Rico. . . . Yet, unfortunately . . . Oh God, I can't avoid telling you that your friend Petrus has . . . drowned. He was lost at sea and vanished along with thirty other souls who were trying to reach America on a raft. (Schwarz-Bart 1987, 14)

While *Ton beau capitaine* stages the non-homeyness born of displacement and deterritorialization, the play does not indulge in any kind of postmodern celebration of this condition. Wilnor and his fellow migrant workers from Haiti are no more attracted to leaky rafts and water than are the nationalist Christophe and his elite warring generals. Wilnor longs for nothing better than to live within the unambiguously delineated, bounded territory of his nation, to which he hopes to return. However, as a member of his society's underclass, his options are limited and his biography rejoins those of many other postcolonial subjects for whom the experience of displacement and dislocation is an abiding trope.

Wilnor, a member of the global migrant working class, gains proximity to what Edward Said has alluded to in a poignant description of this group as "refugees without urbanity, with only rations and agency numbers" (1983, 50), workers who toil in agricultural fields and in factories. As such, Wilnor's circumstances differ considerably from those of postcolonial émigré intellectuals, as do of course their attitudes toward exile. In the postmodern/post-nationalist disposition of writers and theorists such as Edouard Glissant, Patrick Chamoiseau, Edward Said, Homi Bhabha, and Salman Rushdie (among many others, of course), exile is characterized in both physical and metaphorical senses. To Glissant and Chamoiseau, nomadism and Caribbeanness are even coterminous, and the former is crucial to the process of creative creolization, liberating the individual from tyranny, from the parochial and singular root identities fostered by anticolonial nationalism. But for dispossessed and powerless migrants like Wilnor, exile corresponds to a psychological *and* material burden whereby non-homeyness is the site of unproductive anguish, exploitation, and humiliation. The homeland, on the other hand, is not the totalizing construct repressive of difference that postcolonial postmoderns take it to be, an imaginary entity to be transcended in the name of translocal and happy hybridities. For Wilnor, the nation defines the ground of his being, and return is by no means a futile endeavor but instead an essential reality to whose protective female embrace (symbolized by his wife) he yearns to return. Wilnor fails in this endeavor, however, unable to complete the circular journey back to Haiti, but nevertheless he learns a lesson along the way.

Critics are divided when it comes to determining the broader message of Schwarz-Bart's play (see Gyssels 2003; Larrier 1990; Miller 1995; McKinney 1992). Miller, influenced by feminist criticism, argues that Wilnor arrives at a liberating understanding of the "banal horrors" experienced by women in conditions of patriarchy, including sexual blackmail, clandestine and botched abortions, and situations in which the husband "travels away . . . [and] has the right to 'act'" while his wife "waits and is condemned to wait" (Miller 1995, 151). Wilnor thus comes to appreciate the "legitimacy of [his wife's] desire and the needs of her body" (152), a discovery that frees him from the "masculine nightmare" (153) or "the old 'macho'" behavior (Gyssels 2003, 238) linked to his consumerist and materialist priorities. He no longer conceives of her as a mere extension of his being, another "possession" of his like the tape recorder that plays her voice. For Kitzie McKinney, Wilnor is a man who advances from "a naïve reader" of his condition to a reader "in full possession of the meanings of signs" (1992, 453).

These compelling and perceptive readings contribute to our understanding of the aims and objectives of the play, but there is an additional dimension beyond the domestic problems faced by the Wilnor–Marie-Ange couple that deserves attention. *Ton beau capitaine* is also a "national allegory" in the way that Fredric Jameson has employed the idea to discuss works from the postcolonial world which, although "seemingly private and invested with a properly libidinal dynamic, necessarily project a political dimension . . . [in which] the story of the private individual destiny is always an allegory of the embattled situation of the public third world culture and society" (1986, 69). The bitter wisdom that Wilnor obscurely acquires is similar to the Glissantian recognition of the exile's impossibility of returning to the wholesomeness of nation, a realization which Véronique Mercier also reaches in Maryse Condé's *Hérémakhonon* (1976). Wilnor's awareness of departure and errantry, as opposed to return and permanence, as integral components of his life extends metonymically to the wandering of Antillean and New World descendants of the African diaspora, and his transformative lesson takes the quality of a religious initiation, a "spiritual illumination" (Gyssels 2003, 229).

Miller hints at this initiatory dimension of the play in her reference to its structure "tend[ing] toward the ritualistic" (1995, 150), a position that can be substantiated by Wilnor's invocation in his moment of epiphany of "ceux d'en haut" (Schwarz-Bart 1987, 54) [those who live on high], namely, his protector gods from the Haitian pantheon: Anthony of Padua (who recovers stolen property and grants wishes), Legba (the Cerberus-like guardian of the infernal abode of the gods), Damballa Ouedo (the serpent god of mercy and grace whose arrival is signaled by a whistling sound), and Erzulie Freda Dahomey (the coquettish goddess of love and erotic desire). Viewed as a form of religious experience, the play takes on new meaning, and Marie-Ange (literally, Mary the Guardian Angel) assumes a different function in its symbolic economy. More than a wife in a drama involving long-distance love, erotic desire, and infidelity, she is also the priestess (a *houngan*/master of ceremonies) who initiates her husband into the truth of their common fate: "You over there and me here, you here and me over there, it's all the same," she tells him (Schwarz-Bart 1987, 13).

The state of dislocation and unbelonging, the uncomfortable strangeness (*unheimlich*) which Wilnor thought only temporary and conquerable with wealth, turns out to be much more intractable. This is confirmed by the nightmare he has in which he sees himself holding on tightly to his pot of savings, as if to an anchor, to avoid being swept away even farther into unknown, distant lands: "I'm afraid that one fine morning I'll no longer be able to find the way back" (Schwarz-Bart 1987, 50). The hope of return animates his life, and the realization to which he arrives—that departure and wandering are built into his fate—allows him to see that his nomadism does not flow from individual fault (which would be reparable by an act of the will) but rather from a metaphysical force. Wilnor's awareness of this serves to explain why his reflections on separation and the resulting frustrations and temptations transition from the particular and the individual (that is, from psychology and ethics) to the general and human (allegory and philosophy):

> Wilnor: Ah yes, that's how it is when separation sets in. When boats drift apart, when airplanes begin to roar, their engines full blast; a man's body cries for a woman's body, a woman's body cries out for a man's and that's what the Good Lord wishes. Separation is a vast ocean and more than one person has drowned in it. (Schwarz-Bart 1987, 41)

The shock of the discovery that Marie-Ange is in a sense as much a victim as he is of an overdetermined black diasporic condition with roots in the Middle Passage, but *also* of a female condition adversely impacted by patriarchal structures, accounts for Wilnor's willingness to pardon her. Suddenly, her infidelity seems insignificant and an ethics of understanding and solidarity replaces the will to dominate and take revenge.

Marie-Ange's role as a priestess brings Wilnor to an understanding of their shared (racial) and differential (gender) plight. Although she is often portrayed as the dutiful and submissive wife, Marie-Ange is on close reading the real captain in this drama. Wilnor may have initially conceived of his position as dominant in their relationship— "No doubt about it, a woman truly needs a man," he says confidently

(Schwarz-Bart 1987, 16)—but in reality she is the active agent and Wilnor the reactive one. Even though she describes him as the "handsome captain" of her life and compares herself to a sailing vessel that longs to carry him, her "lord and master," to undreamed-of lands of erotic pleasure—but also of human dignity—such behavior and pronouncement, rather than being indicators of her submissiveness, are in fact mere psychological ploys to assist her husband in confronting reality. She thus initially indulges and reassures his fantasies of wealth and male superiority. Having learned through a traveler of Wilnor's precarious health and material circumstances—narratives that contradict his own versions of events—she prefers not to confront him directly with this knowledge since this would be tantamount to unmasking her "captain" and could potentially induce him to harden his position. Instead, Marie-Ange resorts to a number of tricks, subtly letting him realize through repeated questioning and voice inflection that she is aware of his situation: "Wilnor, how are you. Tell me, *really, how are you?*" (13). In order to give him time to adjust to this new dynamic and thus prevent retrenchment on his part, a humiliating confession, or continued (self)-deception, she dismisses the traveler's tales about him as perhaps nothing but a joke: "Perhaps he was saying that just for laughs" (15).

Marie-Ange's quiet strategy proves effective, in spite of the indirection of her methods, but Wilnor, rather than admitting to his circumstances, resorts to discrediting her by affecting an attitude of superiority: "A woman really needs a man. I no sooner leave than even her dreams go haywire" (Schwarz-Bart 1987, 16). The stage directions confirm that her observations have been registered, since he immediately goes to the mirror to put on a shirt and tie, symbolic acts that reveal him shoring up his shaken self-confidence or, in theatrical terms, adjusting the mask that has just slipped from his face. During the rest of the play, the hitherto self-effacing Marie-Ange becomes more assertive, assuming the role of teacher of Wilnor—indicative of this role reversal is her use of imperatives—and Wilnor, correspondingly, slides into a crisis of self-confidence:

> The Voice: Do you understand, Wilnor? [The man is bewildered] Do you understand? Wilnor, I know you . . . stop

shaking your head and figure it out. Take time to think.
... This is earth, Wilnor, and on earth everything is
whirlwind and smoke. (28–29)

After a last angry and desperate refusal to consider their domestic
drama within the larger context of a fate-driven tragedy of displacement, Wilnor finally agrees, like an initiate who has gone through
anguish and suffering, to the truth of exile earlier articulated by his
wife: "Ah, separation is a big ocean, which muddles everything: it
shakes things up like a cupful of dice" (55). To refer to Wilnor's trial
by ordeal is not to suggest that Marie-Ange willfully inflicts the pain
of infidelity on him to teach him a lesson. What she does, however, is
to extract from her bitter experience a usable lesson for Wilnor.

While *Ton beau capitaine*'s feminism lies in its uses of a socially
transgressive act (female adultery) to focus attention on gender relations in patriarchy (Miller 1995), it also resides in the reversal of
the traditional trope found in francophone Caribbean and African
literature of woman as "mediatrix," as James Arnold uses the term,
"between [the] alienated self and fullness of being" of the male quest-
ing hero (in Haigh 1993, 6). The passive role of the woman as the site
to which the "warrior" returns to achieve self-realization and whole-
ness is problematized, even rejected, in *Ton beau capitaine*. Wilnor
longs for but is ultimately refused what Samantha Haigh describes as
the means "through which he can represent his relation to origins"
(1993, 19), to the Haitian homeland. Marie-Ange's affirmation and
subsequent rejection of her passive role may introduce a degree of
ambiguity, but this contradiction is only an apparent one, since she
affirms it the better to subvert it as she assumes the more active role
of initiator of her husband to the liberating awareness of the futility
of his (mock-heroic) quest for a return to the fullness of origins.

Ton beau capitaine is compelling for its vision, but perhaps even
more so for its dramatic treatment of the topos of exile and the way
the play also speaks to the reader/spectator at a deeply emotional and
affective level through the sustained exploitation of the poetics of literary minimalism. Minimalism's roots have been traced to a variety
of European writers, including Samuel Beckett and the Russian dramatist and short-story writer Anton Chekhov (Hallett 1999, 23–41),

singled out in this context because of their influence on Schwarz-Bart (Montantin 2003, 185; Upton 1997, 248). Cynthia Hallett has identified a number of features characteristic of works of literary minimalism. The most pertinent to *Ton beau capitaine* concerns minimalism's predilection for "non-heroic characters that resemble everyday people doing everyday things" (1999, 25), for individuals who tend to be inarticulate and to live in troubled relationships. Minimalism also has recourse to techniques of formal sobriety and austerity, privileging an aesthetic of compactness and contraction (Hallett 1999, 25) that extends to the setting and plot, which are "condensed . . . to the singular and symbolic" (Hallett 1999, 25).

Minimalism's use of the lean and spare and its narrative brevity (the texts tend to be short) should in no way suggest a poverty of artistic vision. If anything, the opposite is true. Minimal means are deployed to maximum effect through a network of metaphoric and symbolic associations, whose net effect is to make an audience feel that the text implies far more than it says. A third and final trait of minimalism worth highlighting is a certain conviction about the inexpressibility in language of the fullness and complexity of experience, or in Hallett's formulation, "the recognition that words are useless, for most things are unsayable" (1999, 25). This economy is particularly important to *Ton beau capitaine,* a play that is essentially static and storyless and yet a work of great dramatic intensity. To achieve this effect, Schwarz-Bart excises all that is superfluous in order to focus on the bare essentials. Unlike *La tragédie du roi Christophe,* whose action unfolds in palaces, cathedrals, and battlefields, *Ton beau capitaine* is concentrated in a Creole shack. The narrowness of this abode (Wilnor stumbles over something each time he moves) coupled with the starkness of its furnishings (there is only one of each item: a stool, a machete, a shirt and tie, etc.) and the fact that the action takes place at night are not only visual images of Wilnor's misery and loneliness but serve to create a sense of claustrophobia. The spectator gasps to be let out of the narrow confines in which s/he and Wilnor have been imprisoned, but is left with little choice but to focus on the suffering character. Language itself provides the greatest emotional intensity: the text avoids wordiness, and what little is uttered is done haltingly. Marie-Ange is no orator, and her speech is neither ornamental nor flowing, but rather punctuated by eloquent silences, sighs, shifts in tone (from the ceremonial to the ordinary to the accelerated), sobs, and moments of breathlessness. Listening to her gives one the impression that words are inadequate to express her complex and complicated emotions in which intense erotic desire, guilt, *and* innocence (note her contradictory and yet not wholly implausible explanations for stumbling into adultery) are combined, echoing in many regards Wilnor's frustrated hopes, sense of betrayal, and ultimate forgiveness.

Wilnor's and Marie-Ange's intuitive recognition of the untranslatability and unsayability of certain emotions explains the use they make of their indigenous culture's total communicative resources. In her stage directions, Schwarz-Bart writes:

> An imaginary space . . . is created through music and dance. Traditional Haitian dances are choreographed in such a way that they become balletic. These dances [like music and song] have a dramatic function. . . . they can be regarded as an additional language that the main character has at his disposal. (in Gyssels 2003, 246)

Song, dance, and body movements in *Ton beau capitaine* are not redundant or ornamental modes of expression, but are used by Schwarz-Bart to supplement speech when it proves inadequate in conveying the characters' emotions. After Wilnor has listened to Marie-Ange's confession (1987, 30), he executes the *léroz* dance, which allows him to externalize his devastation through his body movements—"He raises his arms as if to hover in the air" (30)—symbolizing a desperate attempt to escape from his turmoil. The same movements and their meaning are amplified later when he dances the quadrille, but on this occasion he does more than hover. He assumes the position of a bird preparing for flight—"The man has stopped in a position resembling that of a winged creature" (47)—and as the dance movements indicate, he is a caged bird desperately trying to break free from the prison of his condition. A reminder of the futility of this symbolic attempt to take to the air and flee from painful reality is visually suggested by a stage direction and two reflections:

> Wilnor: What a beautiful quadrille! A bit more and I would
> have flown away. [He slowly lowers his raised foot to

the ground, which he scrapes lazily once or twice] The earth. (47)

The use of song in *Ton beau capitaine* has received considerable critical attention (McKinney 1992, 455–56; Montantin 2003, 186; Gyssels 2003, 238–41), but I will make only brief mention here. Marie-Ange's singing in tableau IV (Schwarz-Bart 1987, 52–53), which Wilnor hears in his mind, points to her obsessive presence in his life, but more significant is the song's three rhythms—slow and dragging as if distorted by a synthesizer, semi-normal, and then bright and lively—which are an indication of Wilnor's changing emotions for his wife. From being deeply hurt, his changing mood hovers precariously between "infinite sadness" and "extreme gaiety" (52), culminating in outright joy. As additional visual proof that he has forgiven her, the stage directions indicate that Wilnor "tenderly caresses the cassette" (53).

Marie-Ange's pauses, silences, and shifting rhythms of delivery and, for that matter, Wilnor's gestures, changing attitudes toward the cassette, and movements to and from his bottle of rum, with their appropriate emotional tenor, constitute crucial elements which, if confused or not given the proper weight, can destroy the emotional impact of the play. Additionally, the actors must have some command, at a minimum, of Haitian song melodies and dance rhythms and be able to externalize states of mind through them. Another acting challenge is being able to present onstage the characters in their true complexity. Because both Marie-Ange and Wilnor hide something from each other and even from themselves, it is important to portray their motivations in a manner that brings out their elusiveness and prevents the audience from making reductive moral judgments of condemnation—that Marie-Ange is an unworthy wife, for instance, or that Wilnor is little more than a shallow materialist and domineering husband.

A final challenge, directorial this time, is deciding whether to include Marie-Ange onstage, an option that Schwarz-Bart is said to prefer (Montantin 2003, 186), or to let her be represented by a recorder. Including her onstage, but separating her from Wilnor with a transparent screen, for example, would seem to be the more effective of the two options. While a mere recorder might be a better visual symbol of her absence and therefore be consistent with the mode of communication among illiterate Haitian migrant laborers, having Marie-Ange onstage, invisible to Wilnor, though sufficiently close for him (and therefore the audience) to sense and feel her warmth and body, could accentuate his sense of longing and give it greater poignancy: she will be frustratingly both within grasp and yet distant. The risk that the symbolic value of the recorder as the materialization of Marie-Ange could take second place in the audience's gaze to its status as a mere piece of electronic machinery would be averted by the presence of the actress onstage. After all, the play is, among other things, about bodies in pain, and surely there could be no better way of conveying these emotions than by presenting those bodies onstage.

Francophone Theatres
in the Age of Globalization

The culturalist and political trends in francophone post-nationalist theatre that have been examined in *New Francophone African and Caribbean Theatres* belong to the same temporal framework but constitute different expressions of theatrical transgression against the poetics and thematics of anticolonial nationalism. No sooner had this "new" theatre of the 1970s and 1980s begun to assume a normative status than it was challenged and superseded by yet another new type of francophone drama. The 1990s witnessed the emergence of assertive practitioners who were critical and sometimes polemical exponents of new dramatic forms: Koffi Kwahulé (Ivory Coast), José Pliya (Benin), Kossi Efoui (Togo), Koulsy Lamko (Chad), and Caya Makhélé and Léandre-Alain Baker (both of Congo). Variously described as a theatre "de la traversée" (Chalaye 2004, 22) [of crossings], or "de l'entre-deux" (Makhélé in Chalaye 2001, 9) [of the in-between], these theatrical practices announced a break with the immediate antecedent traditions as radical as the latter's had been with the theatre of the 1960s. The aim, as Makhélé has argued, has been to found a theatre "that conceives of itself as the site of every possible transgression, through a throwing into crisis of those dramatic forms that today pass for 'African theatre'" (2001, 13).

These remarks underscore how 1990s and early twenty-first-century francophone dramatists remained unimpressed by the many efforts at renewal in theatre practice that had preceded their own. Judging from their pronouncements, one might well assume that theirs were the *only* innovative theatre practices to have emerged since independence. (Such claims are partially undermined by the very semantics they adopt: there can be no post- without a pre- just as breaking *away from* a theatrical tradition inevitably inscribes the innovators in an implicit linearity with their precursors.) For dramatists such as Kossi Efoui, Caya Makhélé, and Koulsy Lamko, little difference exists between the 1960s plays of Jean Pliya, Guillaume Oyono-Mbia, and Seydou Badian and the 1980s plays of Werewere Liking and Bernard Zadi Zaourou. In spite of the temporal distance and real artistic differences separating them, Makhélé's periodization of francophone theatre is unambiguous on this point. It distinguishes between a pre-1990s phase that is seen as homogeneous and stuck in what he describes rather vaguely as "the habits and established ways of a conventional theatre" (in Chalaye 2001, 13) and a dynamic and innovative 1990s phase characterized by the "rejection of frozen and institutionalized forms" (in Chalaye 2001, 13).

Koulsy Lamko is even more precise in his periodization. Using an alimentary metaphor to describe issues of innovation, he calls for a new theatrical recipe that does not consist of the "stale" pre-1990s dish of "un bon kilo de palabres, une même mesure de danse, une poignée de chants, un soupçon de récriminations contre les dictateurs, le tout saupoudré de kaolin local" (in Fiangor 2002, 192) [a kilo of palaver, an equal amount of dance, a handful of songs, and a dash of recrimination against dictatorial leaders, the whole sprinkled with kaolin]. Even when genuine innovation is conceded to phases of pre-1990s theatre, that concession is not without reservations. Koffi Kwahulé, for example, readily acknowledges the experimental nature of much 1970s and 1980s theatre only to add that what this theatre sees as its point of originality—its *gesamtkunstwerk* model for the fusion of the arts—is often very unsatisfactorily realized onstage. Furthermore, far from being distinctively African, this so-called originality was extensively theorized elsewhere and was already a feature of many world theatre forms, such as the Indian kathakali and the Japanese kabuki (Kwahulé 1995, 30–31). Whatever their differences of appreciation concerning the degree of innovation of the drama produced between the 1960s and the late 1980s, the practitioners of the 1990s displayed a common hostility to specific shared features and the regulating assumptions of this drama and asserted their originality by systematically subverting them.

Playwrights of the generation of Werewere Liking or Souleymane Koly were primarily concerned with the problematic of cultural authenticity and disavowed the work of their 1960s predecessors for privileging textual values that were associated with the scriptcentric tradition of French theatre and not therefore sufficiently "African." Liking's conception of theatrical culture pertained to a preexistent but repressed stable set of values and beliefs, a cultural and even racial identity waiting to be excavated. Naturally, the culture of orality, with its varied performative idioms, framed that identity's privileged and uncontaminated site of being. In these circumstances, the task of the playwright was to rescue those forms from social marginalization and make them the defining quality of "authentic" African drama (foregrounding a return to origins, historical plays about ancient figures, and cultural plays based on epics or ceremonial performances). This notion of a (theatrical) identity deemed at its most authentic when, and only when, it is expressed in performance idioms native to Africa, or when it figures African characters, situations, and concerns, was firmly repudiated by the more "international" or cosmopolitan playwrights of the 1990s. "A writer's work," Kossi Efoui writes, "must not be reduced to the folklorized image that one has of that writer's origins" (1992b, 44). This is a complicated question, of course. If Efoui is suggesting that to be "African" is not just to exhibit certain predetermined traits but also to be "modern," then these new playwrights are not so much being universal as they are expanding the field of possibilities in terms of what constitutes *being* African; the error, of course, would be to think that using folkloric elements (drums, dances, etc.) would not be universal.

Analogous debates took place in francophone African philosophy during the 1970s. In a sense, the critique articulated by contemporary playwrights of what they see as an "ethnographic" imperative (Chalaye 2001a, 19) in the work of their predecessors is in many ways a belated elaboration of Paulin Hountondji's critique of the then-dominant conception of African philosophy. According to this view, "African philosophy" was to provide an elucidation of a "specific world-view commonly attributed to all Africans, abstracted from history and change" and embedded in their "customs and traditions" (1976, 34) in order to fulfill a task reduced to the retrieval and disembedding of this world view and its translation into an object of modern philosophical/ theatrical activity. The belief, common to both the "ethnophilosopher" (as Hountondji labels such people) and the "ethnodramatist" (as the

1990s dramatists describe their predecessors), about the essence of African philosophical or theatrical identity residing in the cultures of orality explains the hostility of these thinkers and dramatists to the technology of writing. Finally, this belief accounts for the prevalence of binaries—orality/literacy, self/Other, indigenous/foreign, tradition/modernity, and performance/text—that are endlessly reproduced in their work. In the nationalist effort to protect the African self from the Western assimilationist Other—a protection that takes the form of an assertion of that self's radical alterity and total isomorphism—ethnophilosophers and ethnodramatists ironically end up encasing it in a straitjacket and, by sealing it off from cultural exchange and mutuality, folklorize it and potentially render it meaningless. The revolt against such self-encasement is at the heart of both the critical philosophy that emerged in the 1970s and the new theatre of the 1990s. Justifying his critique of his predecessors, Hountondji writes:

> One had to free the horizon, reject any definition of an African that would, by implication, restrict or confine him or her in a conceptual, ideological, religious, or political stranglehold.... To acknowledge Africans' freedom of thought, one had to get rid of all sorts of essentialist and particularist doctrines. (1996, x)

Echoing the arguments made in African philosophy two decades earlier, Lamko evokes the universal appeal of his work, "mon art je le veux universel" (in Chalaye 2004, 58) [I want my art to be universal], insisting that "I feel I belong to the whole world, and no longer to my ethnic group or country" (in Chalaye 2004, 59), statements reminiscent of Hountondji's position that African philosophy need not limit itself to purely African preoccupations but instead aspire to "universality" (2002, xviii). Kwahulé defines the function of the dramatist as being to "expand the field of his own authenticity to render it less limiting and castrating" (1995, 31), joining Hountondji's acknowledgment of a "vocation to enunciate propositions that are valid across frontiers, that are true to all, at all times and in all places" (2002, xvii).

Stark contrasts can be seen between pre- and post-1990s theatre. Whereas the former hankers after origins, the latter is a "future-oriented theatre" (Chalaye 2004, 24), concerned with exceeding binary thinking and with building "pathways" (Makhélé 2001, 11) that connect to the

Other not as irreducibly different and locked in perpetual combat with the self but rather as a determinate expression of the human sameness. Ultimately, the former could be said to privilege locality/roots (anti-colonial and postcolonial statist nationalism) while the latter favors mobility/routes and global translocality/connectivities (Amselle 2001) and internationalizes, in Kwahulé's words, "images of *Dallas, Rambo,* [Diego] Maradona, and Michael Jackson . . . the fall of the [Berlin] Wall and the liberation of Mandela" (in Chalaye 2001a, 21).

In the francophone theatre of the 1990s and beyond, the colonial encounter and its political and cultural aftermath have been expanded to encompass more global and resolutely contemporary subjects (Chalaye 1999). These include youth delinquency, drugs, and urban violence in African cities and in immigrant communities in France and in the French *banlieues* housing projects (Kwahulé, *Bintou,* 1997a; Efoui, *Récupérations,* 1992, and *Le petit frère du rameur,* 1995); family dysfunction, mental imprisonment, bad faith, sadism, and other psychological problems (José Pliya, *Le complexe de Thénardier,* 2001, and *Nègrerrances,* 1997; Kwahulé, *Big Shoot,* 2000a, and *La dame du café d'en face,* 1998a); rape, incest, and other forms of sexual violence against women (Kwahulé, *Bintou,* 1997a, *Jaz,* 1998c, and *P'tite Souillure,* 2000b); war and genocide (Kwahulé, *Fama,* 1998b; José Pliya, *Le complexe de Thénardier,* 2001); commercialized sports (Kwahulé, *Cette vieille magie noire,* 1993); errantry and rootlessness (José Pliya, *Nègrerrances,* 1997; Marcel Zang, *L'Exilé,* 2002; Makhélé, *Picpus ou la danse aux amulettes,* 1995; Efoui, *Le carrefour,* 1990); racism (Kwahulé, *La dame du café d'en face,* 1998a, and *Cette vieille magie noire,* 1993); and artistic creation (José Pliya, *Konda le roquet,* 1997, an obvious intertextual reference to Jean Pliya's 1966 play *Kondo le requin,* and *Concours de circonstances,* 1997; Kwahulé, *Cette vieille magie noire,* 1993). Not the least of the preoccupations of the theatre of the 1990s was the search for identity, not for the recovery of a substantive but repressed or misrecognized African self but rather for a self linked to a field of possibilities, open, to be invented, in a state of perpetual becoming. The fluid notion of identity is expressed in Makhélé's notion of "une africanité vagabonde" (2001, 11) [a nomadic Africanness], accounting for the widespread use of metaphors of liminality that include "crossroads" and "bridges." Sylvie Chalaye, for example, has argued: "These dramaturgies stage traversals because they tend towards an elsewhere. Perhaps, because they are intrinsically the works of authors that are not 'rooted,' of authors who 'traverse the world'" (2004, 25).

Naturally, these concepts are deployed in new representational spaces. No longer located in an African rural imaginary, the 1990s works are predominantly sited in cityscapes in Africa and in global metropolises, such as Paris and New York. Sometimes, the action unfolds in no specific country: Kwahulé's *Blue-S-Cat* (2005a) takes place in an elevator, *Big Shoot* in a glass cage, while José Pliya's *Le complexe de Thénardier* is locationless.

Pre-1990s theatre was not, of course, monocultural, and we observed the confluence of various theatrical traditions displayed in the use of the proscenium arch (a decidedly non-precolonial African stage design) and in the recourse to the scripted text even if it was only to denounce it as a means of valorizing orality. But where the pre- and post-1990s traditions differ most is in their respective attitudes toward their sources of inspiration. Far from being burdened by the anxiety of foreign influence, or preoccupied with purging or nativizing theatre in the name of cultural authenticity like their predecessors had, 1990s dramatists joyously embraced and appropriated that influence. Ancient Greek and European myths, such as stories of Ulysses and Faust, have been central to Kwahulé's *Fama* and *Cette vieille magie noire;* jazz is intrinsic to Kwahulé's *Il nous faut l'Amérique, Cette vieille magie noire,* and *Jaz;* European classical music is found in José Pliya's *Concours de circonstances;* and African storytelling rhythms are used in Kwahulé's *Bintou.* Participating in and shaped aesthetically and experientially by various world cultures (African, European, American) but fully belonging to none, "third"-generation francophone theatre inhabits and explores the interstitial spaces between cultures and nations.

The question of individualism is of paramount importance to the dramaturgy of 1990s practitioners, who struggle with redefining their relationship to the African continent: "When will I be myself and no longer the continent's receptacle?" (Makhélé 2001, 11). Theatre is an invention, an act of individual creation that uses, or gives a personal interpretation of, elements of a culture and not the mere translation, in the sense of transposition onstage, of an already constituted cultural totality. For Efoui, this consists in producing "[a] theatre for those who will come tomorrow" (2000, 8), an affirmation of individual freedom vis-à-vis what he qualifies as a logic of the collective culture. Characters in the first- and second-generation theatre often function as spokespersons for a cause, embodying a collective ideological position or beleaguered ethnic community, nation, or culture. When they are not allegorical figures set up as models or counter-models of good conduct, they are sacred personages charged with the responsibility of initiating their community into cultural self-awareness. Dramatists such as José Pliya deracialize human experience: "The question of writing for black, white, or yellow actors never arises; the material standing on its own should be accessible to any actor" (in Chalaye 2001c, 71). Furthermore, twenty-first-century dramatists do not conceive of themselves as "machines programmed to fulfill specific tasks that define them outright" (Makhélé 2001, 12), but instead as singular and autonomous individuals with "frustrations, hopes, and doubts" (Makhélé 2001, 12). Shorty, in Kwahulé's *Cette vieille magie noire*, is a perfect illustration of the radical singularity of the individual: his life is a constant struggle between the attempts by his sister (Angie) and his manager (Shadow) to force him to assume a burdensome mantle as a representative of the "race"—as *the* black American boxing champion (a symbol of a 1960s ethnic/nationalist consciousness)—and his own intense but tragically unsuccessful desire for anonymity, to simply be himself (1993, 40–41).

Clearly, a broad range of factors serves to circumscribe the specificities of new francophone theatre. But what factors contributed to its emergence? Certainly, the reforms made to the French drama competition supported by Radio France Internationale (RFI) were important. Established in 1966 in collaboration with African broadcasting services, this competition (then named the Concours Théâtral Interafricain) spurred the development of an African theatre in a number of ways. Dramatists were guaranteed large and faithful audiences, and winning entries were sent on tours of various francophone African capitals and provided with publishing opportunities. Such was the importance of this radio drama competition that, by the late 1970s, it accounted for 80 percent of all francophone published plays by African authors (Ligier 1983), and by 1991 a total of ninety-seven plays had support from won the competition (Fiangor 2002). However, the format and rules of the competition were changed in 1992. A competition which had hitherto been restricted to African participants was now thrown open to dramatists from the global francophone world. Economic asymmetries accompanied the introduction into a global space, given that both audiences and competitors would now also include Belgians, French, and French Canadians, who enjoyed certain comparative advantages, notably in terms of publishing outlets (Lansman in Belgium, L'Harmattan and Éditions Théâtrales in Paris), access to established theatre festivals (Avignon, Limoges, Nancy), production teams, and financial support structures for new drama.

Not surprisingly, African drama soon reflected the idioms and concerns of its new global audiences. Innovations made by third-generation francophone dramatists, while partially inflected by a desire to conform to externally imposed criteria, were more significantly influenced by the dramatists' lived experience: "To me, new dramatic writings," Lamko explains, "seem to be more rooted in the individual experience of authors than in a systematic wish to be a witness to Africa's collective adventure" (in Chalaye 2001b, 57). It is worth mentioning in this respect that, with the exception of Kwahulé, who was born in 1956, most of the playwrights of the 1990s are what Franco-Djiboutian writer Abdourahman Waberi (1998) has described as "the children of the postcolony," that is, people born during or after the symbolic decade of African independence. For the offspring of the nationalist generation, their connection to and knowledge of "traditional" African culture is at best tenuous. Furthermore, their lives were influenced by world cinema and other global media, which provided exposure to Chinese and Indian films, American popular culture, and Caribbean musical forms, rather than by the ritual ceremonies that punctuated the lives of their predecessors.

The multilocality of these new writers is extremely important; they belong to that group (like Salman Rushdie, Ben Okri, Kazuo Ishiguro) whom the Sri Lankan–born Canadian author Michael Ondaatje has described as "international bastards, born in one place and deciding to live in another" (in Casanova 2004, 120). Playwrights Kwahulé, Léandre-Alain Baker, Efoui, and Makhélé have moved between countries, including Benin, Burkina Faso, Cameroon, Chad, France, and Rwanda. The result of this mobility is a detachment from place accompanied by sentiments of homelessness and unbelonging. But a corollary to such feelings is the development of a sense of playfulness with notions of Africanness. "What interests me," Efoui comments, "is playing with all the possible figures of identity" (in Chalaye 2001d, 82). The multicultural and migratory subjectivity of these dramatists is movingly captured in a dialogue between Imago and the Inspector in Marcel Zang's *L'Exilé*. To the Inspector, who encourages Imago to return to Africa where, he explains, "you will no longer have to fear bullets and insults" (2002, 30), Imago responds:

> I have no home, no country. . . . I am prepared to acknowledge certain links with Africa. But even if I cannot deny such a link, my identity with Africa is only one among many, many hundreds that have nothing to do with Africa. And even assuming that I do have an identity, then it would have to be the sum total of multiple identities. (30–31)

Like their novelist counterparts (Adesanmi, Cazenave, Chevrier, Jules-Rosette, Thomas 2007, Waberi 1998), Zang and his fellow dramatists can be described as playwrights of "migritude," a "neologism that designates both the issue of immigration that is at the heart of contemporary African works, but also the expatriate status of most of the writers. . . . their inspiration comes from their hybridity and decentered lives, elements that now characterize a kind of French-style 'world literature'" (Chevrier 2004, 96).

The study of what we are describing as second- and third-generation francophone theatre and the existing criticism on these works raise a number of questions linked to a more general cultural politics. The theatre's vexed relationship to the universal/global and the particular can be somewhat confusing or contradictory. Sylvie Chalaye suggests that particular or culturally rooted African theatre (that uses indigenous cultural resources such as ceremonies, masks, and music) betrays its vocation to be universal, for to be truly universal (that is, to be accessible and appreciated by European audiences), this drama would have to divest itself of these elements:

> Most of the Western public does not feel concerned by African theatre, which for it evokes distant images of calabashes . . .

and especially drums, dances, and masks. . . . African creation is believed to be inexorably turned . . . to a mythical search for origins, such that the idea of its reflecting on its modernity seems also incongruous. (2001a, 33)

Rogo Fiangor is in agreement with the 1990s dramatists that the "redoubtable specificities [of pre-1990s theatre] resulted in confining African theatre exclusively to 'the excipients' of folklore, ballet, songs, and dances of the hearth" (2002, 188).

Now, these statements invite several remarks. The first concerns a lack of clarity and precision in the use of the word "universal" that is made by playwrights and critics of 1990s theatre. In the first instance, it refers to visibility beyond national or regional borders in a strictly geographic sense, namely, to designate an international or global presence. But in the other sense it is accorded, "universal" corresponds to a work whose quality of meaning transcends its immediate originating cultural and historical conditions and speaks, at some fundamental level, to the human condition. The two meanings cannot be conflated. A work can be considered universal in the first sense of the word because of deft commercial promotion or a perceived marketable "exoticism"; similarly, a work can be universal but remain unknown beyond its ethnic, national, or regional borders because it is expressed in a minority language or aesthetic form. What interests me here, however, is the 1990s francophone playwrights' constant reference and claim to universality with regard to the human condition in response to critics who perceive of African texts as limited because of their concerns with "African" issues, that is, issues that are not universal. Lamko comments frustratingly about this situation in an interview:

> Our literatures are discussed as local, circumstance-bound epiphenomena whose sole value is to move a narrow circle of initiates and to quench the thirst of some for exoticism. . . . Let people, however, take the trouble to meet the writers that we are, and not the representatives of ethnic groups, tribes, or countries. . . . Let them take the time and show the decency to read in the Africa that we depict the destiny of man. (in Chalaye 2001b, 59)

The problem with Lamko's counter-assertion is not so much its claim to the universality of African drama in terms of its engagement with humanity, it is rather *the means* by which he believes such universality can be attained. His assumption is that it is a quality of human experience that can be artistically explored and attained unmediated by a historically rooted cultural particular.

This assumption is played out in the work of these playwrights through the opposition they set up between the culturally particular, which is African, and the universal, which is global or non-African. This opposition explains their tendency to distance themselves from, indeed ridicule, cultural elements and techniques associated with some of "indigenous" Africa's oral performative forms (ritual/ceremonial, holy figures, music, dance, body decorations, and so on) and to embrace instead global or universal cultural elements and theatre idioms. The former, to them, reduce theatre to exotic folklore, automatically confining it to an African particular, while the latter invest it with universal components. The Freudian parallel that Efoui establishes is telling: a retrieval of the former constitutes a neurotic regression to an infantile (psychocultural) oral stage, while a use of the latter, no doubt, indicates balanced and harmonious progress to (psychocultural) adulthood. He asks: "how many feathers on the backside are necessary for the thing [a play by an African] to be authentic? Unless what is required is an assumed degree of regression to the oral stage" (1992a, 40). Like the claim to universality above, Efoui's angry reaction is natural when read against the background of critics legislating as un-African any play that does not include drums, plumed attire, kaolin powder, and shamans and that does not have a baobab tree for its setting. But it seems to me that it is a reaction based on a confused understanding of the mere *presence* of these elements in the drama and the theatrical *uses* to which they could be put.

If there are examples of such uses being made of "folklore" in first-generation drama or for that matter in the preceding William Ponty School plays of the 1930s and 1940s, these are certainly not features of the drama of the 1980s. Dramatists of this period adopted a creative attitude toward these performance elements, adapted them for the modern stage (with varying degrees of success, it is true), and did not simply transpose them. They sought to use them as the syntax of a modern African dramatic language. Wole Soyinka's work provides a relevant example. The Yoruba deity Ogun is responsible for effecting, like his ancient Greek counterpart, Dionysus, "the union between the human and divine zones" and "mediat[ing] the polar urges of destruction and creation" (Okpewho 2004, 61), among other functions. This African deity's individual creative actions are key to *The Bacchae of Euripides: A Communion Rite* (1973), and one may ask why its function should *necessarily* reduce Soyinka's play to non-universal status or signal cultural regression? The universal is abstract, and it cannot be attained unmediated by a concrete cultural particular, which may be porous to influence and historically dynamic for sure, but nevertheless is a recognizable particular. To claim otherwise would be to misrecognize, and thus to abdicate to, one particular—in this case, the Euro-American—which for complex reasons has universalized or globalized itself to the point of becoming ahistorical. Commenting on the procedures of universalization undertaken by powerful but dehistoricized particulars (for their purposes, the case of American economic, sociological, and cultural doctrines), Pierre Bourdieu and Loïc Wacquant have argued:

> Numerous topics . . . relating to the social particularity of American society . . . have been imposed in apparently de-historicized form upon the whole planet. . . . The neutralization of the historical context resulting from the . . . correlative forgetting of their originating historical conditions produces an apparent universalization further abetted by the work of "theorization" that produces the illusion of pure genesis. . . . Thus planetarized, or globalized . . . these [topics are] now constituted as a model for every other and as a yardstick for all things. (1999, 41–42)

But the symbolic violence that undergirds the universalization of concrete particular models of culture or society is, Bourdieu and Wacquant observe, "never wielded but with a form of (extorted) complicity on the part of those who submit to it" (1999, 46).

Such complicity is precisely what one witnesses in the creative work of the third-generation dramatists and the globalist teleological narrative embedded in the critical discourse on it. This work is presented in this discourse as representing the coming-into-maturity/universality/modernity, finally, of a francophone African theatre hitherto stuck in premodern/particularistic theatrical practices, which it has now had the courage to shun in favor of global/universal ones. This discourse is all the more remarkable precisely because of the manner in which the global is contextualized as a neutral entity, and as such obfuscates the unequal nature of cultural power relations between Africa and the West. The global in this context is indissociable from the process of unidirectional borrowing of the dominant (read: Western) theatre products by francophone African playwrights. If the elements borrowed are not fused within a recognizably African matrix but effectively *replace* preexisting structures, to what degree, one may ask, is the "new" theatre not contributing to the perpetuation of these unequal power alignments?

Of course, to raise these questions is emphatically not to advocate for a parochial cocooning of francophone African theatre from outside influence, let alone to be prescriptive about its nature. This would be both undesirable and impractical. Nor is it to deny the universality of great art. However, I raise these issues to bring out the often unexamined political implications informing the discourse of universality. As Judith Butler has argued, bringing into relief "the contingent and cultural character of the existing conventions governing the scope of the universal does not deny the usefulness or importance of the term *universal*" (1996, 46). I am merely claiming that the existing conventions, by virtue of being historically grounded, do not exhaust all possible forms of the universal:

> If standards of universality are historically articulated, then it would seem that exposing the parochial and exclusionary character of a given historical articulation of universality is part of the project of extending and rendering substantive the notion of universality itself. (Butler 1996, 47)

This point seems lost in some critical readings of contemporary francophone theatre for which the universal is only representable in the idioms of global theatrical practices, even if reshaped and transformed, as they must be, to meet contemporary needs. Given the absence of strong national (theatrical) cultures in African countries, an unreflexive embrace of global forms solely in the name of going universal can only condemn francophone dramatists to latter-day cultural mimicry and dependence. The ideal would not be to abandon local theatre idioms on the grounds that they are particularistic, but rather to modernize and revitalize them with multiple influences, in other words, to foster a practice that is at once rooted and cosmopolitan.

My criticisms regarding the claim to universality by 1990s dramatists should not be associated with an underappreciation of the latter's project. Pascale Casanova's book *The World Republic of Letters* establishes a distinction within a "global literary space" between "national" or "nationalized" and "international" or "denationalized" literatures (2004, 33–44, 108–25). For Casanova, national literature refers to a literature that entertains relations of structural interdependence with the state, because it is the struggle *for,* and eventual establishment *of,* the state that makes possible in the first place the emergence and development of a national literature (Thomas 2002). But to the extent that such a literature, through its mythologizing, constitution of a national language, and recovery of repressed traditions, contributes to the construction of the cultural identity of the state, the latter in turn depends on it. National literature, Casanova argues, functions as a marker of difference with respect to other nations, an instrument of national self-imagining (2004, 35). On the other hand, international literature is one that has achieved a high degree of autonomy from the political and, especially, cultural interests of the nation-state with which it is often at variance. "Emancipated from [the] considerations of political utility" (Casanova 2004, 46) characteristic of nation-building literatures, international literature is more daring and experimental. It extols the writer's creative freedom and his or her singular (as opposed to collective/national) experience. Its novel aesthetic resources confer a self-generating dynamism, an autonomous history that is not necessarily congruent with that of the state.

However, national and international literatures are not static practices rigidly distributed *between* countries or geocultural spaces. They can be found *within* the same country or region (in Europe or Africa, in Ireland or Ivory Coast), although the degree of presence of one or the other within a country or region varies and depends on a number of factors, including, crucially, the question of whether the country belongs to a dominated political and literary space (whether it is an emergent nation-state, in other words), or an ancient one. Thus, pre-

1990s francophone African theatre, indeed literature, can be said to be predominantly national in the sense in which that of France was, for example, in the sixteenth century (when, with its Pléiade poets, it sought to defend and illustrate the virtues of its young vernacular vis-à-vis Latin and its emergent national culture against Italy's cultural hegemony), but in which it has not been since Baudelaire's poetic revolution in the mid-nineteenth century (Casanova 2004, 45–126). If, based upon Casanova's distinction, francophone theatre has been essentially national, then it has sought since the 1990s to claim membership in an autonomous sphere of theatrical activity that is international because it transcends the politics, including the cultural politics, of the nation. In this sphere, dramatists are no longer exclusively Congolese or Ivorian, francophone or French, European or African, black or white, since such qualifiers would nationalize, regionalize, racialize, and particularize them and the practice of the theatre; they are now simply "writers." Referring to the dissent of his theatre practice and that of his fellow dramatists against the prevailing norms, Lamko makes this statement on cultural autonomy: "Indeed these writings lay claim, from the point of view of style and structure, to more freedom of expression; they mount more attacks against the norm, and demonstrate greater heresy with regard to *politically and socially correct* practices" (in Chalaye 2004, 58).

Now, if reading the work of 1990s francophone dramatists in terms of a transition from a national to an international sphere, or from enfeoffment to autonomy, may present their work in a new light, such a reading still does not eliminate my earlier criticism relative to the presentation of this transition in neutral terms and of literary autonomy as a sign of theatrical modernity.

> The great consecrating nations reduce foreign works of literature to their own categories of perception, which they mistake for universal norms, while neglecting all the elements of historical, cultural, political, and literary context that make it possible to properly and fully appreciate such works. In so doing they exact a sort of *octroi* tax on the right to universal circulation. . . . *In this sense the notion of universality is one of the most diabolical inventions of the center,* for in denying the antagonistic and hierarchical structure of the world . . . the monopolists of universality

command others to submit to their law. (Casanova 2004, 154; emphasis added)

In the case of francophone theatre, the center did not need to impose a "tax on the right to universal circulation." The dramatists imposed it on themselves by excising those elements of local culture which, to them, would have nationalized or particularized their work. Such self-taxing might be a necessity given the audiences for which they write, the consecrating authorities from whom they seek recognition, and the globalization of dominant cultural forms. To this end, Koffi Kwahulé's play *Une vieille magie noire* (1993) can help to illuminate a few of these arguments.

If, as we saw in the chapter on Werewere Liking's work, she has been the unchallenged exponent of the culturalist stream in francophone African theatre, then the Ivorian Koffi Kwahulé's work is the embodiment of its transnationalist dimension. The abundance of both writers' creative output, in drama and in prose fiction, their multiple roles as directors, actors, and playwrights, and above all their will to break free from the established canons of their respective ages and to create original forms of theatre, these are the features that distinguish them. But this is, perhaps, where the similarities end since these two theatre practitioners could not be more different.

Born in Ivory Coast in 1956, Koffi Kwahulé received his early formal training in the theatre at the Institut National des Arts in Abidjan. In 1979, he went to France for further professional training at the prestigious École de Théâtre in Paris, commonly known by its street location, l'École de la rue Blanche. He completed his schooling at the University of Paris III with a doctorate in theatre studies. Although some of his unpublished work was initially produced at the cultural center in the popular district of Treichville in Abidjan, in 1993 he came to critical attention with his play *Cette vieille magie noire,* winner of the *grand prix* in Tchicaya U Tam'si's RFI competition. Since then, Kwahulé has published to wide acclaim several more works for the stage, including *Bintou* (1997a), *La dame du café d'en face* (1998a), *Big Shoot* (2000a), *Jaz* (1998c), *Misterioso-119* (2005b), and *Blue-S-Cat* (2005a), many of which have been widely translated and performed in various African and international venues. In 2006, he channeled his creative energies into fiction with his first novel, *Babyface*. Side by side with his creative work, Kwahulé has also pursued theatre scholarship with a book on Ivorian theatre, *Pour une critique du théâtre ivoirien contemporain* (1996), and another on Alfred Jarry co-authored with Sylvie Chalaye.

Kwahulé's scholarship on Alfred Jarry may not be pure coincidence, although his interest in the French author is not the same as that of Tchicaya U Tam'si, who fastened on the grotesque in Jarry's work. Kwahulé is indifferent to this dimension, being instead acutely attuned to the centrality of violence in Jarry's play, something which has come to characterize his own prolific output. Physical and psychological torture, serial killings (*Big Shoot*), rape and sexual assault (*Jaz* and *Misterioso-119*), incest (*P'tite Souillure*), and war (*Fama*) are among the many facets of evil that seem to fascinate him, a fascination that might seem gratuitous, but that he once explained in these terms:

> I'd like to write a play that is not about rape, one in which . . . nature is beautiful. . . . But each time, as if pushed by fate, I catch myself responding to this question that God asked Cain: "What have you done with your brother?" To me . . . this question is what makes theatre art. If asked by God, I want to be able to answer this question. . . . That's what I try to express in my theatre. (in Freda 2004, 103)

In other words, the violence of his theatre relates back to what, from a biblical perspective, he understands as the founding violence of society, namely, Cain's murder of his brother Abel. Rather than shy away from it by evoking a melodious world of twittering birds, Kwahulé feels the obligation to bear witness to it in the most graphic of ways. Although attentive to the religious, Kwahulé's theatrical sensibility is more immediately shaped by a contemporary world of social and domestic violence, a genocidal world of moral ambiguity where victims often are, or quickly become, torturers like Monsieur and Stan in *Big Shoot*, a play born of Kwahulé's visit to Rwanda shortly after that country's fratricidal conflict. As Fanny Le Guen observes of that play: "Although it does not deal with the subject, his play is nonetheless closely linked to a visit he paid to Rwanda after the genocide. And if Kwahulé deals with the fratricidal violence of a people, he'd rather pose the problem as a human rather than a specifically Rwandan one" (2007).

A second feature of Kwahulé's theatre is the centrality of jazz. This is reflected in several titles—*Jaz*, written in homage to Toni Morrison's novel *Jazz* (1992); *Blue-S-Cat*; and *Misterioso-119*—the last two influenced by Louis Armstrong's "What a Wonderful World" and Thelonious Monk's "Misterioso," respectively. There are also multiple references in various plays to jazz composers and to their works: Fats Waller and his "Handful of Keys," Wynton Marsalis and "The Death of Jazz" in *Il nous faut l'Amérique*, unspecified John Coltrane choruses and, more specifically, "A Love Supreme" in *Cette vieille magie noire*. Additionally, compositional techniques such as scatting, improvising, solo performances, and riffing feature in some of the plays. In fact, Kwahulé displays a near obsession with jazz. "Je me considère sincèrement comme un jazzman. C'est mon rêve absolu" [I honestly see myself as a jazzman. It is my most ardent dream], he once confided to the French musicologist Gilles Mouëllic (2000). Referring in particular to the improvisatory nature of some of his works after *Jaz*, he explained:

> In the past, I looked for a story, a theme, and then wrote it down. Today, for *Big Shoot, Petite* [*sic*] *Souillure*, and *Jaz*, I start from a kernel of a story. I can't even tell what the themes of those plays are, even after having completed them. . . . I quite simply felt that I had to pick up a topic and pursue it to wherever it may take me. (Mouëllic 2000)

Similarly, he explained, he draws on certain (rather commonplace) properties of "jazz" (I would say music) to endow his French style with uniqueness and originality. These features include a focus on the materiality rather than the semantics of sound/words and a sensitivity to rhythm along with the superimposition and intersection of dramatic voices: "I think in musical terms: the meaning of a word is not what interests me—meaning will emerge with the right sound, when the rhythm is good" (in Mouëllic 2000). About his style, Kwahulé observes: "I was not born French. One day someone said to me: you speak French. . . . So as not to submit to that language, I have to give it a different ring. Hence the need to have a different relationship to it, a musical one. This is my way of appropriating it" (in Chalaye 2005).

But perhaps the aspect of jazz that makes it most attractive to Kwahulé is its status as the supreme expression of black diasporic consciousness (Congolese novelist Emmanuel Dongala reached similar conclusions in his book *Jazz et vin de palme*, 1982). Resident in France for much longer now than he has been in his native Ivory Coast and shaped by a multiplicity of cultural influences and social experiences, not least that of being an ethnic and social minority in France, Kwahulé has over the years seen his once secure sense of self as "African" eroded. Now unable to adhere to notions of Africanness he once held, and yet marginal to French society, where notions of Frenchness retain an important ethnic dimension in spite of French republican discourses to the contrary, he finds himself inhabiting an interstitial third space where attempts at self-definition are carried out in terms of neither-African-nor-French, where, in other words, the experience of a fullness of being has been cleft apart (Tshimanga, Gondola, and Bloom 2009). He makes this important point in an interview in *Cassandre:*

> In my first plays, the question of identity was posed from a Black African perspective. The change took place when I discovered Jazz. I tried to introduce this into my writing. In terms of how I saw the world and wrote plays, my perspective shifted from an African consciousness towards a diasporic consciousness. . . . we are no longer from where we came and not yet what [we are] becoming. This "in-betweenness" becomes a kind of absolute. (2007)

Kwahulé establishes a parallel between his status in France and that of African Americans; in this connection, jazz emerges as the embodiment of a sense of that cultural in-betweenness that has become his lot. This explains Kwahulé's fascination with jazz and also the prevalence of African American characters, topics, and situations in his plays. When one considers the broad range of themes associated with late twentieth- and early twenty-first-century francophone theatre—the concern with building pathways, the expanded parameters of aesthetic production, and the engagement with the circumstances of global displacement and mobility—nowhere, arguably, are these brought together more convincingly than in Kwahulé's theatrical corpus.

Although theatrical activity in francophone Africa and the Caribbean has been marked since the 1970s by attempts to create new idioms of dramatic expression, this objective has not been uniformly pursued, sometimes not even by the same playwright. Three types of theatrical practice have been distinguished and explored, which have various degrees of overlap: the cultural/aesthetic, political, and transnational traditions. Preoccupied with notions of cultural authenticity, poetics, and politics, the first practice sought to disinter repressed and marginalized performance idioms and make them the defining feature of an authentic theatre with its origins and developments in Africa and the African diaspora, especially in the francophone Caribbean.

As the tradition of the aesthetic avant-garde was flourishing both in Africa and in the Caribbean during the 1970s and 1980s, a different type of oppositional theatre was also developing, namely, that of the post-nationalist critique. Wielding the weapons of the grotesque, fantasy, and ribaldry, the plays in this tradition exposed the crisis of legitimacy of the postcolonial political order. Finally, new theatrical forms emerged, influenced by multiple forms of cosmopolitan hybridity. The very notion of being "African" was now interrogated and, unlike the cultural nationalist tradition of the antecedent period, the "new" theatre of the 1990s repudiated all essentialist notions of origins and roots. In the Caribbean, post-plantation narratives emerged, interrogating the coordinates of a contemporary multiracial society and gauging the impact of new migratory flows and further incorporation into reformulated global networks. Thus, where the former had privileged locality and embedded identities, the latter celebrated translocality and nomadism. Dramatists who initially enjoyed critical acclaim as the cultural avant-garde at such gatherings as the Festival of Francophone Theatre in Limoges and on international theatre festival circuits have now been partially superseded by practitioners of cosmopolitan hybridity. Important French theatre critics such as Sylvie Chalaye now swear by such playwrights as Koffi Kwahulé, Kossi Efoui, and José Pliya, whose works are seen as the embodiment of a nonparticularistic and "universal" francophone theatre.

Ultimately though, whether or not one appreciates these new dramatic forms, or even shares in their critical reassessment of cultural nationalist playwrights like Werewere Liking and Bernard Zadi Zaourou, it is evident that these works and pronouncements have thrown wide open the question of the identity and definition of "francophone" drama. Some dramatists reside in Africa or the Caribbean; others, such as Efoui and Kwahulé, have settled in France; and yet others occupy transversal relationships to geographic locality. This has effectively disrupted the rigid French-francophone binary to the extent that it is now difficult to speak in terms of a theatre that is either "francophone" or "French." In the twenty-first century, these plays inhabit the liminal spaces between bounded national cultures, drawing on their respective cultures but irreducible to none in particular, and contributing therefore to a reconfiguration of the very meaning of Africanness and Frenchness. Certainly, the time has come to abandon references to a monolithic francophone theatre and to talk instead of francophone *theatres*, whose productions will have much to contribute to contemporary debates, including the contested parameters of the 2007 *Manifeste pour une littérature-monde en français* [Manifesto for a World Literature in French] (see Le Bris and Rouaud 2007). The plurality and vitality of francophone theatres—as the title of this book, *New Francophone African and Caribbean Theatres*, emphasizes—should include traditional nation-building/nationalist forms of expression as well as new African diasporic/transnational ones, fruits of the new coordinates of contemporary globalization.

References

Adesanmi, Pius. "Redefining Paris: Transmodernity and Francophone African Migritude Fiction." *Modern Fiction Studies* 51.4 (Winter 2005): 958–75.

Adiaffi, Jean-Marie. *La carte d'identité*. Paris: Hatier, 1980.

Agamben, Giorgio. *State of Exception*. Chicago: University of Chicago Press, 2005.

Ahmad, Aijaz. *In Theory: Classes, Nations, Literatures*. London: Verso, 1992.

Alcoff, Linda M., ed. *Epistemology: The Big Questions*. Malden, Mass.: Wiley-Blackwell, 1991.

Alexander, Jeffrey C., Ron Eyerman, Bernard Giesen, Neil J. Smelser, and Piotr Sztompka, eds. *Cultural Trauma and Collective Identity*. Berkeley: University of California Press, 2004.

Amin, Samir. *Le développement du capitalisme en Côte d'Ivoire*. Paris: Minuit, 1967.

Amon d'Aby, François. *Le théâtre en Côte d'Ivoire*. Abidjan: CEDA, 1988.

Amondji, Marcel. *Félix Houphouët et la Côte-d'Ivoire: L'Envers d'une légende*. Paris: Karthala, 1984.

Amselle, Jean-Loup. *Branchements: Anthropologie de l'universalité des cultures*. Paris: Flammarion, 2001.

Anselin, Alain. "West Indians in France." In Richard D. Burton and Fred Reno, eds., *French and West Indian: Martinique, Guadeloupe, and French Guiana Today*. Charlottesville: University of Virginia Press, 1995.

Anyinefa, Koffi. *Littérature et politique en Afrique noire: Socialisme et dictature comme thèmes du roman congolais d'expression française*. Bayreuth: Eckhard Breitinger, 1990.

Appadurai, Arjun. *Modernity at Large: Cultural Dimensions of Globalization*. Minneapolis: University of Minnesota Press, 1996.

Appiah, K. Anthony. "Is the Post- in Postmodernism the Post- in Postcolonialism?" In his *In My Father's House*. New York: Oxford University Press, 1992, 137–57.

Aristotle. *Poetics*. New York: Dover, 1997.

Arnaut, Karel. "Performing Displacements and Rephrasing Attachments: Ethnographic Explorations of Mobility in Art, Ritual, Media, and Politics." Ph.D. diss., Ghent University, Belgium, 2004.

Artaud, Antonin. *The Theatre and Its Double*. New York: Grove, 1958 [1938].

Awashi, Suresh. "Encounter with Tradition." *Tulane Drama Review* 33.4 (1989): 48–69.

Badian, Seydou. *La mort de Chaka*. Paris: Présence Africaine, 1962.

Balme, Christopher. *Decolonizing the Stage: Theatrical Syncretism and Postcolonial Drama*. Oxford: Clarendon, 1999.

Barkan, Elazar, and Ronald Bush. "Introduction." In Elazar Barkan and Ronald Bush, eds., *Prehistories of the Future: The Primitivist Project and the Culture of Modernism.* Stanford, Calif.: Stanford University Press, 1995, 1–19.

Bayart, Jean-François. *L'État en Afrique.* Paris: Fayard, 1989.

Bayart, Jean-François, Stephen Ellis, and Beatrice Hibou, eds. *The Criminalization of the State in Africa.* Bloomington: Indiana University Press, 1999.

Béart, Charles. *Recherche des éléments d'une sociologie des peuples africains à partir de leurs jeux.* Paris: Présence Africaine, 1960.

Beaumont, Keith. *Jarry, Ubu roi.* London: Grant and Cutler, 1987.

Beckett, Samuel. *En attendant Godot [Waiting for Godot].* Paris: Minuit, 1952.

Belcher, Stephen. *Epic Traditions of Africa.* Bloomington: Indiana University Press, 1999.

Bérard, Stéphanie. "Patrick Chamoiseau, héritier du conteur: Respect ou trahison de la tradition orale dans *Manman Dlo contre la fée Carabosse.*" In Marie-Christine Hazaël-Massieux, ed., *Langue et identité narrative dans les littératures de l'ailleurs: Antilles, Réunion, Québec.* Aix-en-Provence: Publications de l'Université de Provence, 2005, 91–105.

———. "From the Greek Stage to the Martinican Shores: A Caribbean Antigone." *Theatre Research International* 33 (2008): 40–51.

Bernabé, Jean, Patrick Chamoiseau, and Raphaël Confiant. *Éloge de la créolité.* Paris: Gallimard, 1989.

Bernabé, Joby, and Rosy Varesse. *Kimafoutiésa.* n.p.: 1976.

Bharucha, Rustom. *Theatre and the World: Performance and the Politics of Culture.* New York: Routledge, 1993.

Björkman, Ingrid. *Mother, Sing for Me: People's Theatre in Kenya.* London: Zed, 1989.

Bodwin, Paul. "Marginality and Subjectivity in the Haitian Diaspora." *Anthropological Quarterly* 76.3 (2003): 383–410.

Bohui, Djédjé Hilaire. "L'esthétique Romanesque sonienne comme exemple de l'expression de la langue par la parole dans *La vie et demie.*" In Gérard Lézou and Pierre N'Da, eds., *Sony Labou Tansi témoin de son temps.* Limoges: Presses Universitaires de Limoges, 2003, 15–27.

Boiron, Chantal. "Limoges: L'Atelier théâtral." *Notre Librairie,* special volume (September 1993a): 16–19.

———. "Une nouvelle exigence: Werewere Liking." *Notre Librairie,* special volume (September 1993b): 52.

———. "L'auteur et l'interprète: Souleymane Koly." *Notre Librairie,* special volume (September 1993c): 53–54.

Boon, Richard, and Jane Plastow. *Theatre Matters: Performance and Culture on the World Stage.* Cambridge: Cambridge University Press, 1998.

Bordo, Susan. *The Flight to Objectivity: Essays on Cartesianism and Culture.* Albany: State University of New York Press, 1987.

Bouah, Niangoran. "La drummologie, c'est quoi même." *Notre Librairie,* no. 86 (January–March 1987a): 79–83.

———. "Les mots des poids, les poids akan à peser l'or." *Notre Librairie,* no. 86 (January–March 1987b): 70–78.

Boukman, Daniel. *Les négriers.* Paris: L'Harmattan, 1978 [1972].

———. *Ventres pleins, ventres creux.* Paris: L'Harmattan, 1998 [1973].

Boulaga, Fabien Eboussi. "La bantoue problématique." *Présence Africaine* (1969): 1–40.

Bourdieu, Pierre, and Loïc Wacquant. "On the Cunning of Imperialist Reason." *Theory, Culture & Society* 16.1 (1999): 44–58.

Britton, Celia. "'Common Being' and Organic Community in Jacques Roumain's *Gouverneurs de la rosée.*" *Research in African Literatures* 37.2 (2006): 164–75.

Brodwin, Paul. "Marginality and Subjectivity in the Haitian Diaspora." *Anthropological Quarterly* 76.3 (Summer 2003): 383–410.

Bürger, Peter. *Theory of the Avant-Garde.* Minneapolis: University of Minnesota Press, 1984.

Burton, Richard, and Fred Reno, eds. *French and West Indian: Martinique, Guadeloupe, and French Guiana Today.* Charlottesville: University of Virginia Press, 1995.

Butler, Judith. "Universality in Culture." In Martha Nussbaum and Joshua Cohen, eds., *For Love of Country: Debating the Limits of Patriotism.* Boston: Beacon, 1996, 45–53.

Carroll, Noel. "Performance." *Formations* 3.1 (1986): 63–81.

Casanova, Pascale. *The World Republic of Letters.* Trans. M. B. DeBevoise. Cambridge, Mass.: Harvard University Press, 2004.

Cazenave, Odile. *Afrique sur Seine: Une nouvelle génération de romanciers africains à Paris.* Paris: L'Harmattan, 2003.

Césaire, Aimé. *La tragédie du roi Christophe.* Paris: Présence Africaine, 1970 [1963].

———. *Une saison au Congo.* Paris: Seuil, 2001 [1967].

———. *A Tempest.* New York: Ubu Repertory Theatre, 1992 [1969].

Césaire, Ina. *Mémoires d'îles.* Paris: Caribéennes, 1985.

———. *L'Enfant des passages; ou, La Geste de Ti-Jean.* Paris: Caribéennes, 1987.

Césaire, Ina, and Joëlle Laurent, eds. *Contes de mort et de vie aux Antilles.* Paris: Nubia, 1976.

Césaire, Michèle. *La Nef.* Paris: Théâtrales, 1992.

Chabal, Patrick. *Political Domination in Africa: Reflections on the Limits of Power.* Cambridge: Cambridge University Press, 1986.

———. *Power in Africa: An Essay in Political Interpretation.* New York: St. Martin's, 1992.

Chalaye, Sylvie, ed. *L'Afrique noire et son théâtre au tournant du XXe siècle.* Rennes: Presses Universitaires de Rennes, 2001a.

Chalaye, Sylvie. "Africanité et création contemporaine." Round table discussion with Caya Makhélé, Kossi Efoui, and Koffi Kwahulé, January 13, 1999. www.revues-plurielles.org/php/index.php?nav=revue&no=1&sr=2&no_article=8692.

———. "Koulsy Lamko: Semeur de graines de fiction." In Chalaye, ed., *L'Afrique noire et son théâtre au tournant du XXe siècle*. Rennes: Presses Universitaires de Rennes, 2001b, 57–64.

———. "José Pliya, cambrioleur d'émotions." In Chalaye, ed., *L'Afrique noire et son théâtre au tournant du XXe siècle*. Rennes: Presses Universitaires de Rennes, 2001c, 69–72.

———. "Kossi Efoui: Ecrire, c'est avancer masque." In Chalaye, ed., *L'Afrique noire et son théâtre au tournant du XXe siècle*. Rennes: Presses Universitaires de Rennes, 2001d, 81–87.

———. *Nouvelles dramaturgies d'Afrique noire francophone*. Rennes: Presses Universitaires de Rennes, 2004.

———. "Théâtres de l'impossible étreinte." www.africultures.com/php/index.php?nav=article&no=3814. 2005.

———. "A propos de *La Parenthèse de sang* de Labou Tansi, mise en scène de Jean-Paul Delore." www.africultures.com/php/index.php?nav=article&no=4652. 2006.

Chamoiseau, Patrick. *Manman Dlo contre la fée Carabosse*. Paris: Caribéennes, 1982 [1977].

———. *Chronique des sept misères*. Paris: Gallimard, 1986.

———. *Écrire la parole de nuit*. Paris: Gallimard, 1994.

———. *Texaco*. Paris: Gallimard, 1997.

———. *Biblique des derniers gestes*. Paris: Gallimard, 2002.

Chamoiseau, Patrick, and Raphaël Confiant. *Lettres créoles*. Paris: Gallimard, 1999.

Chaudenson, Robert. *Creolization of Language and Culture*. London: Routledge, 2001.

Chevrier, Jacques. "Afrique(s)-sur-Seine: Autour de la notion de 'migritude.'" *Notre Librairie*, nos. 155–56 (July–December 2004): 96–100.

Clark, John Pepper. *Ozidi*. Oxford: Oxford Univesity Press, 1966.

Clifford, James. *The Predicament of Culture: Twentieth Century Ethnography, Literature, and Art*. Cambridge, Mass.: Harvard University Press, 1988.

Condé, Maryse. *Hérémakhonon*. Paris: Seghers, 1988 [1976].

———. *Ségou: Les Murailles de terre*. Paris: Laffont, 1984.

———. *Ségou: La Terre en miette*. Paris: Laffont, 1985.

———. *An tan revolisyon: Elle court, elle court la liberté*. Pointe-à-Pitre: Conseil Régional de la Guadeloupe, 1989.

Conrad, David, ed. *A State of Intrigue: The Epic of Bamana Segu according to Tayiru Banbera*. Trans. Soumaila Diakité. Oxford: Oxford University Press, 1990.

Conteh-Morgan, John. *Theatre and Drama in Francophone Africa: A Critical Introduction*. Cambridge: Cambridge University Press, 1994.

———. "French Critics and African Theatre 1900–1999." *Œuvres et Critiques* 26.1 (Spring 2001): 15–28.

———. "The Color of the Enlightenment." Introduction to Louis Sala Molins, *Dark Side of the Light: Slavery and the French Enlightenment*. Minneapolis: University of Minnesota Press, 2006, vii–xxxvi.

Conteh-Morgan, John, and Irene Assiba d'Almeida, eds. "*The Original Explosion That Created Worlds*": *Essays on the Art and Writings of Werewere Liking*. Amsterdam: Rodopi, 2007.

Crow, Brian, with Chris Banfield. *An Introduction to Post-Colonial Theatre*. Cambridge: Cambridge University Press, 1996.

Dadié, Bernard. *Béatrice du Congo*. Paris: Présence Africaine, 1970.

Dailly, Christophe, and Bernard Zadi Zaourou. "Langue et critique littéraire en Afrique Noire." In *Le critique africain et son peuple comme producteur de civilisation* (Yaoundé Colloquium, 1973). Paris: Présence Africaine, 1977, 441–80.

Damas, Léon-Gontran. "Hoquet." In his *Pigments—Névralgies*. Paris: Présence Africaine, 2003 [1939].

Dambury, Gerty. *Lettres indiennes*. Carnières, Belgium: Lansman, 1993.

Dash, Michael. *The Other America: Caribbean Literature in a New World Context*. Charlottesville: University of Virginia Press, 1998.

Davidson, Basil. *The Black Man's Burden: Africa and the Curse of the Nation-State*. New York: Times Books, 1992.

Davis, R. G. "The Radical Right in American Theatre." *Theatre Quarterly* 5.19 (1975): 67–72.

de Certeau, Michel. *The Practice of Everyday Life*. Trans. Stephen Rendall. Berkeley: University of California Press, 2002 [1974].

Dervain, Eugène. *Saran; ou, La reine scélérate et La langue et le scorpion: Pièces en trois et quatre actes*. Yaoundé, Cameroon: Clé, 1968.

Devésa, Jean-Michel. *Sony Labou Tansi: Écrivain de la honte et des rives magiques du Kongo*. Paris: L'Harmattan, 1996a.

———. "Sony Labou Tansi et les mangeurs d'homme." *Notre Librairie*, no. 125 (January–March 1996b): 123–29.

Dia, Amadou Cissé. *Les derniers jours de Lat Dior*. Paris: Présence Africaine, 1947.

Diabaté, Massa Makan. *Une si belle leçon de patience*. Paris: ORTF/DAEC, 1973.

Diderot, Denis. *Le paradoxe sur le comédien*. 1773. In P. Vernière, ed., *Œuvres esthétiques*. Paris: Garnier Frères, 1988, 290–385.

Dingome, Jeanne. "Ritual and Modern Dramatic Expression in Cameroon: The Plays of Werewere Liking." In Janos Riesz and Alain Ricard, eds., *Semper Aliquid novi: Littérature Comparée et Littérature d'Afrique*. Tubingen: Gunter Narr, 1990.

Diop, Birago. *L'Os de Mor Lam*. Dakar: Nouvelles Éditions Africaines, 1966.

Dongala, Emmanuel. *Jazz et vin de palme*. Paris: Hatier, 1982.

Dozon, Jean-Pierre. "La Côte d'Ivoire entre démocratie, nationalisme et Ethnonationalisme." *Politique Africaine* 78 (2000): 45–69.

Drewal, Henry John, ed. *Sacred Waters: Arts for Mami Wata and Other Divinities in Africa and the Diaspora*. Bloomington: Indiana University Press, 2008.

Dumestre, Gérard. *La geste de Ségou*. Paris: Armand Colin, 1979.

Edwards, Brent Hayes. *The Practice of Diaspora: Literature, Translation, and the Rise of Black Internationalism*. Cambridge, Mass.: Harvard University Press, 2003.

Efoui, Kossi. *Le carrefour*. Paris: L'Harmattan, 1990.

———. *Récupérations*. Carnières, Belgium: Lansman, 1992a.

———. "Post-scriptum." In his *Récupérations*. Carnières, Belgium: Lansman, 1992b, 42–46.

———. *Le petit frère du rameur*. Carnières, Belgium: Lansman, 1995.

———. "Le théâtre de ceux qui vont venir demain." In his *L'entre-deux rêves de Pitagaba*. Paris: Acoria, 2000, 7–10.

Ekeh, Peter. "Contesting the History of Benin Kingdom." *Research in African Literatures* 31.3 (2000): 147–270.

Eliade, Mircea. *Myth and Reality*. New York: Harper and Row, 1963.

Elias, Norbert. *The Civilizing Process*. Oxford: Blackwell, 2000.

Etherton, Michael. *The Development of African Theatre*. London: Hutchinson, 1982.

Eyerman, Ron. "Cultural Trauma: Slavery and the Formation of African American Identity." In Jeffrey C. Alexander, Ron Eyerman, Bernard Giesen, Neil J. Smelser, and Piotr Sztompka, eds., *Cultural Trauma and Collective Identity*. Berkeley: University of California Press, 2004, 60–111.

Eyoh, Dixon. "From Economic Crisis to Political Liberalization: Pitfalls of the New Political Sociology for Africa." *African Studies Review* 39.3 (1996): 43–80.

Fauquenoy, Marguerite. Introduction to Elie Stephenson, *O Mayouri*. Paris: L'Harmattan, 1988, xxviii–xxxiii.

Favre, Isabelle. "Elie Stephenson: Paroles de feu pour un 'pays' nommé Guyane." *French Forum* 29.2 (Spring 2004): 107–26.

Fiangor, Rogo Koffi. *Le Théâtre africain francophone: Analyse de l'écriture, de l'évolution, et des apports interculturels*. Paris: L'Harmattan, 2002.

Fischer-Lichte, Erika. "The Avant-Garde and the Semiotics of the Antitextual Gesture." In James Harding, ed., *Contours of the Theatrical Avant-Garde: Performance and Textuality*. Ann Arbor: University of Michigan Press, 2000, 79–95.

Foucault, Michel. *Ethics: Subjectivity and Truth*. Trans. Paul Hurley et al. New York: New Press, 1997.

Fouchard, Jean. *Le théâtre à Saint-Domingue*. Port-au-Prince: Henri Deschamps, 1988.

Freda, Rita. "Un kaléidoscope de la violence: *Big Shoot* de Koffi Kwahulé." In Sylvie Chalaye, ed., *Nouvelles dramaturgies d'Afrique noire francophone*. Rennes: Presses Universitaires de Rennes, 2004, 104–17.

Freud, Sigmund. *Three Case Histories.* Ed. Philip Rieff. New York: Macmillan, 1963.

Gainor, J. Ellen, ed. *Imperialism and Theatre: Essays on World Theatre, Drama and Performance.* London: Routledge, 1995.

Gandhi, Leela. *Postcolonial Theory: A Critical Introduction.* New York: Columbia University Press, 1998.

Gates, Henry Louis, Jr. *The Signifying Monkey: A Theory of African American Literary Criticism.* Oxford: Oxford University Press, 1988.

Gbagbo, Laurent. *Soundjata: Lion du Mandingue.* Abidjan: CEDA, 1979.

———. *Côte d'Ivoire: Pour une alternative démocratique.* Paris: L'Harmattan, 1983.

Geist, Anthony, and Jose Monleon, eds. *Modernity and Its Margins: Reinscribing Cultural Modernity from Spain and Its Margins.* New York: Garland, 1993.

Geschiere, Peter, and Francis Nyamnjoh. "Capitalism and Autochthony: The Seesaw of Mobility and Belonging." *Public Culture* 12.2 (2000): 423–52.

Gilbert, Helen, and Joanne Tompkins. *Post-Colonial Drama: Theory, Practice, Politics.* London: Routledge, 1996.

Giraudoux, Jean. *La guerre de Troie n'aura pas lieu.* Paris: Bibliothèque de la Pléïade, 1982 [1935].

Glissant, Edouard. *Monsieur Toussaint.* Paris: Gallimard, 1998 [1961].

———. *Le discours antillais.* Paris: Seuil, 1981.

———. *Caribbean Discourse: Selected Essays.* Trans. Michael J. Dash. Charlottesville: University of Virginia Press, 1992.

———. *Introduction à une poétique du divers.* Paris: Gallimard, 1996.

Graver, David. "The Actor's Bodies." *Text and Performance Quarterly* 17.3 (1997): 221–35.

Gyssels, Kathleen. "'I Talked to a Zombie': Displacement and Distance in Simone Schwarz-Bart's *Ton beau capitaine.*" In Mary Gallagher, ed., *Ici-Là: Place and Displacement in Caribbean Writing in French.* Amsterdam: Rodopi, 2003, 227–51.

Haigh, Samantha. "The Return of Africa's Daughters: Negritude and the Gendering of Exile." *Association for the Study of Caribbean and African Literature in French Bulletin* 7 (1993): 3–22.

Hall, Stuart. "Cultural Identity and Diaspora." In *Identity: Community, Culture, Difference,* ed. Jonathan Rutherford. London: Lawrence and Wishart, 1990, 222–37.

Hallett, Cynthia W. *Minimalism and the Short Story: Raymond Carver, Amy Hempel, and Mary Robison.* Lewiston, Maine: Mellen, 1999.

Harding, Frances, ed. *The Performance Arts in Africa: A Reader.* London: Routledge, 2002.

Harding, James M. "Introduction." In James M. Harding, ed., *Contours of the Theatrical Avant-Garde: Performance and Textuality.* Ann Arbor: University of Michigan Press, 2000a, 1–12.

————. "An Interview with Richard Schechner." In James M. Harding, ed., *Contours of the Theatrical Avant-Garde: Performance and Textuality*. Ann Arbor: University of Michigan Press, 2000b, 202–14.

Harris, Susan. *American Drama: The Bastard Art*. Cambridge: Cambridge University Press, 2006.

Hatch, James V. *A History of African American Theater*. New York: Applause, 1987.

Hawkins, Peter. "Un 'néo-primitivisme' africain? L'exemple de Werewere Liking." *Revue des Sciences Humaines* 101.3 (July–September 1992): 233–41.

Hazaël-Massieux, Marie-Christine. "Le théâtre créolophone dans les départements d'outre-mer: Traduction, adaptation, contacts de langue." *L'Annuaire Théâtral* 28 (2000): 21–34.

Herzfeld, Michael. *Cultural Intimacy: Social Intimacy in the Nation-State*. New York: Routledge, 1997.

Heuvel, Michael Vanden. *Performance Drama/Dramatizing Performance*. Ann Arbor: University of Michigan Press, 1991.

Hill, Errol. *The Theatre of Black Americans: A Collection of Critical Essays*. New York: Applause Theatre, 1990.

Hountondji, Paulin. *African Philosophy: Myth & Reality*. Bloomington: Indiana University, 1996 [1976].

————. *The Struggle for Meaning: Reflections on Philosophy, Culture, and Democracy in Africa*. Trans. John Conteh-Morgan. Athens: Ohio University Press, 2002.

Hourantier, Marie-José. *Du rituel au théâtre-rituel: Contribution à une esthétique théâtrale négro-africaine*. Paris: L'Harmattan, 1984.

Hourantier, Marie-José, and Werewere Liking. "*Les mains veulent dire*: Lecture du spectacle." In Werewere Liking and Marie-José Hourantier, eds., *Spectacles rituels*. Abidjan: Nouvelles Éditions Africaines, 1987.

Huggan, Graham. *The Postcolonial Exotic: Marketing the Margins*. London: Routledge, 2001.

Hunt, Lynn. *The French Revolution and Human Rights: A Brief Documentary History*. Bedford, Mass.: St. Martin's, 1996.

Innes, Christopher. *Avant-Garde Theatre 1892–1992*. London: Routledge, 1993.

————. "Text/Pre-Text/Pretext: The Language of Avant-Garde Experiment." In James M. Harding, ed., *Contours of the Theatrical Avant-Garde: Performance and Textuality*. Ann Arbor: University of Michigan Press, 2000, 58–75.

Irele, Abiola. "The Crisis of Legitimacy in Africa." *Dissent* 37.3 (1992): 296–302.

Jack, Belinda. *Francophone Literatures: An Introductory Survey*. Oxford: Oxford University Press, 1996.

Jameson, Fredric. "Postmodernism, Or, The Cultural Logic of Late Capitalism." *New Left Review* 186 (July–August 1984): 53–92.

————. "Third World Literature in the Era of Multinational Capitalism." *Social Text* 15 (1986): 65–88.

———. "Modernism and Imperialism." In Terry Eagleton, Fredric Jameson, and Edward Said, eds., *Nationalism, Colonialism, and Literature*. Minneapolis: University of Minnesota Press, 1990.

Jarry, Alfred. *Ubu roi*. Paris: Fasquelle, 1921 [1896].

Jones, Bridget. "French Guiana." In A. James Arnold, ed., *A History of Literature in the Caribbean:* vol. 1, *Hispanic and Francophone Regions*. Philadelphia: Benjamins, 1994, 389–98.

———. "Quelques choix de langue dans le théâtre antillais 1970–1995." In J. P. Little and Roger Little, eds., *Black Accents: Writing in French from Africa, Mauritius and the Caribbean*. London: Grant and Cutler, 1997.

———. "Theatre and Resistance? An Introduction to Some French Caribbean Plays." In Samantha Haig, ed., *An Introduction to French Caribbean Writing: Guadeloupe and Martinique*. Oxford: Berg, 1999, 83–100.

———. "Comment identifier une pièce de la Caraïbe?" In Alvina Ruprecht, ed., *Les théâtres francophones et créolophones de la Caraïbe*. Paris: L'Harmattan, 2003.

Jouanny, Robert. *Espaces littéraires d'Afrique et d'Amérique*. Paris: L'Harmattan, 1996.

Jules-Rosette, Benneta. *Black Paris: The African Writers' Landscape*. Urbana: University of Illinois Press, 1998.

Julien, Eileen. *African Novels and the Question of Orality*. Bloomington: Indiana University Press, 1992.

Jusdanis, Gregory. "World Literature: The Unbearable Lightness of Thinking Globally." *Diaspora* 12.1 (2003): 103–30.

Kadima-Nzuji, M. "*Le destin glorieux du Maréchal Nnikon Nniku, prince qu'on sort.*" *Présence Africaine*, no. 115 (1980): 249–53.

Kalaidjan, Walter. *American Culture between the Wars*. New York: Columbia University Press, 1993.

Kamara, Cheikh Moussa, and Moustapha Ndiaye. "Histoire de Ségou." *Bulletin de l'IFAN* 40.3 (1978): 458–88.

Kandeh, Jimmy. *Coups from Below: Armed Subalterns and State Power in West Africa*. London: Palgrave, 2004.

Kapalanga, Gazungil Sang'Amin. *Les spectacles d'animation politique en république du Zaire*. Louvain la Neuve, Belgium: Cahier Théâtre Louvain, 1989.

Kayser, Wolfgang. *The Grotesque in Art and Literature*. Trans. Ulrich Weisstein. Gloucester, Mass.: Peter Smith, 1968.

Kerr, David. *African Popular Theatre*. London: James Currey, 1995.

Kesteloot, Lilyan, ed. *Da Monzon de Ségou: Épopée Bambara*. Paris: Nathan, 1972.

Kesteloot, Lilyan, Amadou Hampaté Ba, and Jean-Baptiste Traoré, eds. *L'épopée Bambara de Ségou*. Paris: L'Harmattan, 1993 [1972].

Koly, Souleymane. *Adama Champion*. 1979. Unpublished.

———. "L'auteur et l'interprète." *Notre Librairie*, special issue (1993): 53–54.

Konaké, Sory. *Le grand destin de Soundjata*. Paris: ORTF/DAEC, 1973.

Kotchy, Barthélémy. "Théâtre et public." In *Actes du colloque sur le théâtre négro-africain* (Abidjan, April 15–29, 1970). Paris: Présence Africaine, 1970, 175–78.

———. "New Trends in the Theatre of the Ivory Coast (1972–83)." *Theatre Research International* 9.3 (1984): 232–53.

Kourouma, Ahmadou. *Les soleils des indépendances.* Paris: Seuil, 1968.

Kwahulé, Koffi. *Cette vieille magie noire.* Carnières, Belgium: Lansman, 1993.

———. "Quand l'africanisme dérive vers l'intégrisme culturel." *Alternatives Théâtrales,* no. 48 (1995): 30–31.

———. *Pour une critique du théâtre ivoirien contemporain.* Paris: L'Harmattan, 1996.

———. *Bintou.* Carnières, Belgium: Lansman, 1997a.

———. *Il nous faut l'Amérique.* Paris: Acoria, 1997b.

———. *La dame du café d'en face suivi de Jaz.* Paris: Théâtrales, 1998a.

———. *Fama.* Carnières, Belgium: Lansman, 1998b.

———. *Jaz.* Paris: Théâtrales, 1998c.

———. *Big Shoot.* Paris: Théâtrales, 2000a.

———. *P'tite Souillure.* Paris: Théâtrales, 2000b.

———. "Un théâtre qui cherche la note bleue." In Chalaye, ed., *L'Afrique noire et son théâtre au tournant du XXe siècle.* Rennes: Presses Universitaires de Rennes, 2001, 89–99.

———. *Blue-S-Cat.* Paris: Théâtrales, 2005a.

———. *Misterioso-119.* Paris: Théâtrales, 2005b.

———. *Babyface.* Paris: Gallimard, 2006.

———. "Le Huis-Clos de la Francophonie." *Cassandre* 69 (April 16, 2007). www.horschamp.org/article.php3?id_article=2118.

Kwahulé, Koffi, and Sylvie Chalaye. *Ubu roi: Alfred Jarry.* Paris: Bertrand Lacoste, 1993.

Lamko, Koulsy. *Tout bas . . . si bas.* Carnières, Belgium: Lansman, 1995.

L'Annuaire Théâtral. "Théâtre antillais et guyanais: Perspectives actuelles." No. 28 (special issue). 2000.

———. "Couleurs de la scène africaine." No. 31(special issue). 2002.

Larrier, Renée. "The Poetics of of [*sic*] Ex-île: Simone Schwarz-Bart's *Ton beau capitaine.*" *World Literature Today* 64 (1990): 57–59.

Laude, Jean. *La peinture française et l'art nègre.* Paris: Klinckseick, 1968.

Laye, Camara. *L'enfant noir.* Paris: Plon, 1953.

Léal, Odile Pedro. *La chanson de Philibert.* Paris: L'Harmattan, 1997.

———. "La geste de Fem'Touloulou dans le carnaval créole de la Guyane française: Un théâtre cache-montré." *L'Annuaire Théâtral* 28 (2000): 19–34.

Le Bris, Michel. "Toward a 'World-Literature' in French." Trans. Daniel Simon. *World Literature Today* (March–April 2009): 54–56.

Le Bris, Michel, and Jean Rouaud, eds. *Pour une littérature-monde.* Paris: Gallimard, 2007.

Le Guen, Fanny. "*Big Shoot* de Koffi Kwahulé: Un étrange univers." www.africultures .com/php/index.php?nav=article&no=5938. 2007.

Ligier, Françoise. "La politique de stimulation: Théâtre et radio, une collaboration positive." *Recherche, Pédagogie et Culture* 61 (1983): 30–44.

———. "Lettre ouverte à Monique Blin." *Notre Librairie,* special volume (September 1993): 10–13.

Liking, Werewere. *La puissance d'Um.* Abidjan: CEDA, 1979a.

———. *Le rituel de guérison de Mbeng.* 1979b. Unpublished.

———. *Le rituel du "Mbak" de Nsondo Sagbegue.* In Werewere Liking, Marie-José Hourantier, and Jacques Schérer, eds., *Du rituel à la scène chez les Bassa du Cameroun.* Paris: Nizet, 1979c, 85–99.

———. *Une nouvelle terre suivi de Du sommeil d'injuste.* Dakar-Abidjan: Nouvelles Éditions Africaines, 1980.

———. *Les mains veulent dire: Rougeole arc-en-ciel.* In Werewere Liking and Marie-José Hourantier, eds., *Spectacles rituels.* Abidjan: Nouvelles Éditions Africaines, 1987 [1981].

———. *Elle sera de jaspe et de corail.* Paris: L'Harmattan, 1983.

———. *Dieu Chose.* 1985. Unpublished.

———. *L'amour-cent-vies.* Paris: PubliSud, 1988a.

———. *Les cloches.* 1988b. Unpublished.

———. *Singué Mura: Considérant que la femme . . .* Abidjan: Eyo Ki Yi, 1990.

———. *Perçus Perçues; ou, Esquisse pour un opéra de percussions.* 1991a. Unpublished.

———. *Waramba, opéra mandingue.* 1991b. Unpublished.

———. "Théâtres de Recherche et professionalisme théâtral en Côte d'Ivoire: L'exemple du Ki-Yi Mbock Théâtre." In Ulla Schild, ed., *On Stage: Proceedings of the Fifth International Janheinz Jahn Symposium on Theatre in Africa.* Gottingen: Edition Re, 1992a.

———. *Un touareg s'est marié à une pygmée.* Carnières, Belgium: Lansman, 1992b.

———. "Une nouvelle exigence." *Notre Librairie,* special volume (September 1993): 52–53.

———. *Héros d'eau.* 1994a. Unpublished.

———. *La veuve diyilèm* [*The Widow Dilemma*]. In Françoise Kourilsky and Catherine Temerson, eds., *Plays by Women: An International Anthology.* Trans. Judith G. Miller. New York: Ubu Repertory Theater, 1994b, 87–111.

———. *L'enfant Mbénè.* 1996a. Unpublished.

———. *Quelque Chose-Afrique.* 1996b. Unpublished.

———. *It Shall Be of Jasper and Coral, and Love-across-a-Hundred-Lives.* Trans. Marjolijn Jager. Charlottesville: University of Virginia Press, 2000.

————. *La mémoire amputée*. Abidjan: Nouvelles Éditions Ivoiriennes, 2004.

Liking, Werewere, Marie-José Hourantier, and Jacques Schérer, eds. *Du rituel à la scène chez les Bassa du Cameroun*. Paris: Nizet, 1979.

Lo, Jacqueline. *Staging Nation: English Language Theatre in Malaysia and Singapore*. Hong Kong: Hong Kong University Press, 2004.

Losch, Bruno. "Côte d'Ivoire en quête d'un nouveau projet national." *Politique Africaine* 78 (2000): 5–25.

Mabana, Kahiudi C. *Des transpositions du mythe de Chaka*. New York: Peter Lang, 2002.

MacCannell, Dean. *Empty Meeting Grounds: The Tourist Papers*. London: Routledge, 1992.

Mack, Robert L. *Arabian Nights' Entertainment*. Oxford: Oxford University Press, 1995.

Makhélé, Caya. *La fable du cloitre des cimetières suivi de Picpus ou la danse aux amulettes*. Paris: L'Harmattan, 1995.

————. "L'art du risque." In Sylvie Chalaye, ed., *L'Afrique noire et son théâtre au tournant du XXe siècle*. Rennes: Presses Universitaires de Rennes, 2001, 9–14.

Malina, Judith, and Julian Beck. *Paradise Now*. New York: Random House, 1971.

Malti-Douglas, Fedwa. *Women's Body, Women's Word: Gender and Discourse in Arabo-Islamic Writing*. Princeton, N.J.: Princeton University Press, 1999.

Mambachaka, Vincent. "Rester soi-même." *Notre Librairie*, special volume (1993): 55–56.

Mamdani, Mahmood. "State and Civil Society in Contemporary Africa: Reconceptualizing the Birth of State Nationalism and the Defeat of Popular Movements." *Afrique et Développement/Africa Development* 15.3–4 (1990): 47–70.

Manning, Patrick. *Francophone Sub-Saharan Africa, 1880–1895*. Cambridge: Cambridge University Press, 1988.

Mauvois, Georges. *Agénor Cacoul et Misyé Molina*. Paris: L'Harmattan, 1988.

Mbembe, Achille. "Provisional Notes on the Postcolony." *Africa* 62.1 (1992): 3–37.

————. *On the Postcolony*. Berkeley: University of California Press, 2001.

————. "Necropolitics." *Public Culture* 15.1 (Winter 2003): 11–40.

McKinney, Kitzie. "Vers une poétique de l'exil: Les sortilèges de l'absence dans *Ton beau capitaine*." *French Review* 65.3 (1992): 449–60.

Melone, Thomas. "La vie africaine et le langage théâtral." In *Actes de colloque sur le théâtre négro-africain* (Abidjan, April 15–29, 1970). Paris: Présence Africaine, 1970, 142–57.

Menga, Guy. *La marmite de Koka Mbala*. Yaoundé, Cameroon: Clé, 1976 [1969].

Mielly, Michelle. "An Interview with Werewere Liking at the Ki-Yi Village, Abidjan, Côte d'Ivoire" (June 2002). http://www.postcolonialweb.org/africa/cameroon/liking/2.html.

———. "The Aesthetics of Necessity: An Interview with Werewere Liking." *World Literature Today* (2003): 52–56.

Miller, Judith G. "Simone Schwarz-Bart: Refiguring Heroics, Disfiguring Conventions." In Karen Louise Laughlin and Catherine Schuler, eds., *Theatre and Feminist Aesthetics*. Teaneck, N.J.: Fairleigh Dickinson University Press, 1995, 148–69.

———. "Werewere Liking: Pan/Artist and Pan-Africanism in the Theatre." *Theatre Research International* 21.3 (1996): 229–38.

Mofolo, Thomas. *Chaka: A Historical Romance*. Oxford: Oxford University Press, 1931.

Montantin, Michèle. *Vie et mort de Vaval*. Point-à-Pitre, Guadeloupe: Association Chico-Rey, 1991.

———. "Ton beau capitaine/An tan revolisyon: À bâtons rompus." In Alvina Ruprecht, ed., *Les théâtres francophones et créolophones de la Caraïbe*. Paris: L'Harmattan, 2003, 183–92.

Monteil, Charles. *Les empires du Mali: Étude d'histoire et de sociologie*. Paris: Larose et Maisonneuve, 1968.

Morrison, Toni. *Jazz*. New York: Random House, 1992.

Moudileno, Lydie. *Parades postcoloniales: La fabrication des identités dans le roman congolais*. Paris: Karthala, 2006.

Mouëllic, Gilles. Interview with Koffi Kwahulé. *Jazz Magazine* 510 (December 2000). http://jfprevan.club.fr/perso.club-internet.fr/jfprevan/BLAYE/Auteurs_Blaye/photos_auteurs/auteurs_dossiers_parents/Kwahule.htm.

Mwantuali, Joseph. "La 'Parenthèse' de Sony; ou, L'Espace palingénésique." In Drocella Mwisha Rwanika and Nyunda ya Rubango, eds., *Francophonie littéraire en procès: Le destin unique de Sony Labou Tansi*. Ivry-sur-Seine: Silex/Nouvelles du Sud, 1999, 129–42.

N'Da, Pierre. "*Le destin glorieux du Maréchal Nnikon Nniku, prince qu'on sort*." *Recherche, Pédagogie et Culture* 47–48 (1980): 59.

Ndagano, Biringanine. *La Guyane entre mots et maux: Une lecture de l'œuvre d'Elie Stephenson*. Paris: L'Harmattan, 1994.

———. *Nègre tricolore: Littérature et domination en pays créole*. Paris: Maisonneuve and Larose, 2000.

Ndao, Cheikh. *L'exil d'Albouri suivi de La décision*. Paris: Oswald, 1973.

Neale, Caroline. *Writing "Independent" History: African Historiography 1960–1980*. Westport, Conn.: Greenwood, 1985.

Ngal, George. "Les 'Tropicalités' de Sony Labou Tansi." *Silex*, no. 23 (1982): 134–43.

Nietzsche, Friedrich. *The Birth of Tragedy and the Case of Wagner*. New York: Knopf, 1967 [1872].

Nkanga, Dieudonné-Christophe Mbala. "Multivocality and the Hidden Text in Central African Theatre and Popular Performances: A Study of the Rhetoric of Social and Political Criticism." Ph.D. diss., Northwestern University, 1995.

Nketia, Kwabena. *Funeral Dirges of the Akan People.* New York: Negro Universities Press, 1969.

N'Zembele, Luftatchy. "L'envers du miracle." *Peuples Noirs/Peuples d'Afrique,* special issue (1984): 69–87.

Okagbue, Osita. "The Strange and the Familiar: Intercultural Exchange between African and Caribbean Theatre." *Theatre Research International* 22.2 (1997): 120–29.

Okpewho, Isidore. *The Epic in Africa.* New York: Columbia University Press, 1979.

———. *Once upon a Kingdom.* Bloomington: Indiana University Press, 1998a.

———. "African Mythology and Africa's Political Impasse." *Research in African Literatures* 29.1 (1998b): 1–15.

———. "Soyinka, Euripides, and the Anxiety of Empire." In John Conteh-Morgan and Tejumola Olaniyan, eds., *African Drama and Performance.* Bloomington: Indiana University Press, 2004, 55–77.

Olaniyan, Tejumola. *Scars of Conquest/Masks of Resistance.* New York: Oxford University Press, 1995.

Ossouma, B. Ekome. "Laideur et rire carnavalesque dans le nouveau roman africain." *Politique Africaine* 60 (1995): 117–28.

Oyono-Mbia, Guillaume. *Trois prétendants, un mari.* Yaoundé, Cameroon: Clé, 1964.

Pavis, Patrice. *The Intercultural Performance Reader.* London: Routledge, 1996.

Pillot, Christine. "Le 'Vivre vrai' de Werewere Liking." *Notre Librairie,* no. 102 (1990): 54–58.

Pirandello, Luigi. *Tonight We Improvise.* Trans. Marta Abba. New York: Samuel French, 1932.

Placoly, Vincent. *Dessalines; ou, La passion de l'indépendance.* Ciudad de la Havana, Cuba: Casa de la Américas, 1983.

Pliya, Jean. *Kondo le requin.* Yaoundé, Cameroon: Clé, 1981 [1966].

Pliya, José. *Nègrerrances suivi de Konda le roquet et de Concours de circonstances.* Paris: L'Harmattan, 1997.

———. *Le complexe de Thénardier.* Paris: L'Avant-Scène Théâtre, 2001.

———. *Une famille ordinaire.* Paris: L'Avant-Scène Théâtre, 2002.

Pont-Hubert, Catherine. "Gabriel Garran et le théâtre international de langue française." *Notre Librairie,* no. 102 (1990): 101–109.

Porquet, Dieudonné Niangoran. *Soba ou grande Afrique.* Abidjan: Nouvelles Éditions Africaines, 1978.

———. *Masquairides-Balanfonides (Griotorique).* Abidjan: Le Qualitorium, 1994.

Pradel, Lucie. "Du ka au langage scénique: Fondement esthétique." In Alvina Ruprecht, ed., *Les théâtres francophones et créolophones de la Caraïbe.* Paris: L'Harmattan, 2003.

Price, Richard, and Sally Price. "Shadow Boxing in the Mangrove." *Cultural Anthropology* 12.1 (February 1997): 3–36.

Quayson, Ato. *Strategic Transformations in Nigerian Writing.* Oxford: James Currey, 1994.

Rakotoson, Michèle. *La maison morte.* Paris: L'Harmattan, 1991.

Rotimi, Ola. "Much Ado about Brecht." In Erika Fischer-Lichte, Josephine Riley, and Michael Gissenwehrer, eds., *The Dramatic Touch of Difference.* Tubingen: Gunter Narr, 1990, 253–61.

Roumain, Jacques. *Gouverneurs de la rosée.* Port-au-Prince, Haiti: Imprimerie de L'État, 1944.

Ruprecht, Alvina. "Théâtres antillais et guyanais: Perspectives actuelles." *L'Annuaire Théâtral* 28 (2000): 11–19.

Ruprecht, Alvina, ed. *Les théâtres francophones et créolophones de la Caraïbe.* Paris: L'Harmattan, 2003.

Rushdie, Salman. *Imaginary Homelands.* London: Granta, 1991.

Rwanika, Drocella Mwisha, and Nyunda ya Rubango, eds. *Francophonie littéraire en procès: Le destin unique de Sony Labou Tansi.* Ivry-sur-Seine: Silex/Nouvelles du Sud, 1999.

Said, Edward. *The World, the Text, and the Critic.* Cambridge, Mass.: Harvard University Press, 1983.

———. "Yeats and Decolonization." In Terry Eagleton, Fredric Jameson, and Edward Said, eds., *Nationalism, Colonialism, and Literature.* Minneapolis: University of Minnesota Press, 1990, 69–95.

———. *Culture and Imperialism.* New York: Vintage, 1994.

———. *Representations of the Intellectual: The 1993 Reith Lectures.* New York: Vintage, 1996.

Sala-Molins, Louis. *Dark Side of the Light: Slavery and the French Enlightenment.* Trans. John Conteh-Morgan. Minneapolis: University of Minnesota Press, 2006.

Salifou, André. *Tainimoune.* Paris: Présence Africaine, 1973.

Salzman, Michael, and Michael Halloran. "Cultural Trauma and Recovery: Cultural Meaning, Self-Esteem, and the Reconstruction of the Cultural Anxiety Buffer." In Jeff Greenberg, Sander Koole, and Tom Pyszczynski, eds., *Handbook of Experimental Existential Psychology.* New York: Garland, 1994, 231–46.

Savory, Elaine. "Strategies for Survival: Anti-Imperialist Theatrical Forms in the Anglophone Caribbean." In J. Ellen Gainor, ed., *Imperialism and Theatre: Essays on World Theatre, Drama and Performance.* London: Routledge, 1995, 243–56.

Schechner, Richard. *Public Domain: Essays on the Theatre.* Indianapolis, Ind.: Bobbs-Merrill, 1969.

———. *Between Theatre and Anthropology.* Philadelphia: University of Pennsylvania Press, 1985.

———. *The Future of Ritual: Writings on Culture and Performance.* London: Routledge, 1993.

Schérer, Jacques. *Le théâtre en Afrique noire francophone.* Paris: Presses Universitaires de France, 1992.

Schwarz-Bart, Simone. *Ton beau capitaine*. Paris: Seuil, 1987.

Scott, Virginia. *The Commedia Dell'Arte in Paris: 1644–1697*. Charlottesville: University of Virginia Press, 1990.

Sen, Amartya. "Indian Traditions and the Western Imagination." *Dedalus* 126.2 (1997): 1–26.

Senghor, Léopold Sédar. *Chaka*. In his *Poèmes*. Paris: Seuil, 1964 [1956].

Serres, Michel. "Le Christ noir." *Critique* 29 (1973): 3–25.

Shelton, Marie-Denise. "Primitive Self: Colonial Impulses in Michel Leiris' *L'Afrique fantôme*." In Elazar Barkan and Ronald Bush, eds., *Prehistories of the Future: The Primitivist Project and the Culture of Modernism*. Stanford, Calif.: Stanford University Press, 1995.

Sièyes, Abbé. *What Is the Third Estate?* 1789. In Lynn Hunt, ed., *The French Revolution and Human Rights*. New York: St. Martin's, 2001, 63–70.

Silenieks, Juris. "Marronage and Canon: Theatre in the Negritude Era." In A. James Arnold, ed., *A History of Literature in the Caribbean:* vol. 1, *Hispanic and Francophone Regions*. Philadelphia: Benjamins, 1994a, 507–16.

———. "Towards Créolité: Postnegritude Developments." In A. James Arnold, ed., *A History of Literature in the Caribbean:* vol. 1, *Hispanic and Francophone Regions*. Philadelphia: Benjamins, 1994b, 517–25.

Smelser, Neil J. "Psychological Trauma and Cultural Trauma." In Jeffrey C. Alexander, Ron Eyerman, Bernard Giesen, Neil J. Smelser, and Piotr Sztompka, eds., *Cultural Trauma and Collective Identity*. Berkeley: University of California Press, 2004, 31–59.

Smith, Bernard. *Modernism and Post-Modernism: A Neo-Colonial Viewpoint*. London: London University Institute for Commonwealth Studies, 1992.

Soyinka, Wole. *A Dance of the Forests*. Oxford: Oxford University Press, 1963.

———. *The Road: Collected Plays*. Oxford: Oxford University Press, 1973 [1965].

———. *The Bacchae of Euripides: A Communion Rite*. New York: Norton, 2004 [1973].

———. *Myth, Literature, and the African World*. Cambridge: Cambridge University Press, 1990.

———. *King Baabu*. London: Methuen, 2002.

Steadman, Ian. "Race Matters in South Africa." In Richard Boon and Jane Plastow, eds., *Theatre Matters: Performance and Culture on the World Stage*. Cambridge: Cambridge University Press, 1998, 55–73.

Steins, M. H. W. "L'influence de l'ethnologie sur l'avant-garde française et allemande du XXe siècle." In Béla Köpeczi and György Vajda, eds., *Proceedings of the VIIIth Congress of the ICLA* (August 12–17, 1976). Stuttgart: Erich Beiber, 1980, 725–33.

Stephenson, Elie. *Les Voyageurs*. 1974a. Unpublished.

———. *O Mayouri*. Trans. Marguerite Fauquenoy. Paris: L'Harmattan, 1988 [1974b].

————. *Une flèche pour un pays à l'encan.* Paris: Oswald, 1975.

————. *Un rien de pays.* 1976. Unpublished.

————. *Les Délinters.* 1978. Unpublished.

————. *Catacombe de Soleil.* Paris: Caribéennes, 1979.

————. "Y-a-t-il un théâtre en Guyane?" *Notre Librairie*, no. 107 (1990): 77–79.

Szabolcsi, Miklós. "Avant-Garde, Neo-Avant-Garde, Modernism: Questions and Suggestions." *New Literary History* 3 (1971): 49–70.

Tansi, Sony Labou. *La vie et demie.* Paris: Seuil, 1979.

————. *L'État honteux.* Paris: Seuil, 1981a.

————. *La parenthèse de sang.* Paris: Hatier, 1981b.

————. *Qui a mangé Madame d'Avoine Bergotha?* Morlanwelz, Belgium: Promotion Théâtre, 1989.

————. *La résurrection rouge et blanche de Roméo et Juliette.* Arles: Actes Sud, 1992.

————. *La rue des mouches.* Paris: Théâtrales, 2005 [1985].

Taoua, Phyllis. *Forms of Protest: Anti-Colonialism and Avant-Gardes in Africa, the Caribbean, and France.* Portsmouth, N.H.: Heinemann, 2002.

Thomas, Dominic. *Nation-Building, Propaganda, and Literature in Francophone Africa.* Bloomington: Indiana University Press, 2002.

————. *Black France: Colonialism, Immigration, and Transnationalism.* Bloomington: Indiana University Press, 2007.

Thompson, Philip. *The Grotesque.* London: Methuen, 1972.

Toulabor, Comi. "Jeu de mots, jeu de vilains: Lexique de la dérision politique au Togo." *Politique Africaine* 3 (1981): 55–71.

Touré, Abdou. *La civilisation quotidienne en Côte d'Ivoire.* Paris: Karthala, 1981.

Touré, Aboubacar C. "Controverses sur l'existence de l'art du théâtre en Afrique." *Revue de Littérature et d'Esthétique Négro-Africaine* 8 (1987): 46–54.

Towa, Marcien. *Essai sur la problématique philosophique dans l'Afrique actuelle.* Yaoundé, Cameroon: Clé, 1971.

Traoré, Bakary. *Le théâtre négro-africain et ses fonctions sociales.* Paris: Présence Africaine, 1958.

Tshimanga, Charles, Didier Gondola, and Peter J. Bloom, eds. *Frenchness and the African Diaspora: Identity and Uprising in Contemporary France.* Bloomington: Indiana University Press, 2009.

Turner, Victor. *The Drums of Affliction.* Oxford: Clarendon, 1968.

Upton, Carole-Anne. "Words in Space: Filling the Empty Space in Francophone Theatre." In J. P. Little and Roger Little, eds., *Black Accents: Writing in French from Africa, Mauritius, and the Caribbean.* London: Grant and Cutler, 1997, 235–51.

U Tam'si, Tchicaya. *Le Zulu suivi de Vivène le fondateur.* Paris: Nubia, 1977.

————. *Le destin glorieux du Maréchal Nnikon Nniku, prince qu'on sort.* Paris: Présence Africaine, 1979.

————. *Le bal de Ndinga*. Lausanne: L'Age d'Or, 1989 [1987].

Waberi, Abdourahman A. "Les enfants de la postcolonie: Esquisse d'une nouvelle génération d'écrivains francophones d'Afrique." *Notre Librairie*, no. 135 (1998): 8–15.

————. "Écrivains en position d'entraver." In Michel Le Bris and Jean Rouaud, eds., *Pour une littérature-monde*. Paris: Gallimard, 2007, 67–75.

Walcott, Derek. *Dream on Monkey Mountain and Other Plays*. New York: Farrar, Straus and Giroux, 1971 [1967].

————. *What the Twilight Says: Essays*. London: Faber and Faber, 1998.

Warner, Gary. "L'histoire dans le théâtre africain francophone." *Présence Francophone* 11 (1975): 37–48.

Watts, Richard. "'Toutes ces eaux!' Ecology and Empire in Patrick Chamoiseau's *Biblique des derniers gestes*." *Modern Language Notes* 118.4 (September 2003): 895–910.

White, Bob. "Modernity's Trickster: 'Dipping' and 'Throwing' in Congolese Popular Dance Music." In John Conteh-Morgan and Tejumola Olaniyan, eds., *African Drama and Performance*. Bloomington: Indiana University Press, 2004, 198–218.

Wilson, August. *Joe Turner's Come and Gone*. New York: Samuel French, 1988 [1986].

Wrigley, Peter. "Historicism in Africa: Slavery and State Formation." *African Affairs: Journal of the Royal African Society* 279 (1971): 113–24.

Yansane, A. Y. "The Impact of France on Education in Africa." In G. Wesley Johnson, ed., *Double Impact: France and Africa in the Age of Imperialism*. Westport, Conn.: Greenwood, 1985.

Yudice, George. "Rethinking the Theory of the Avant-Garde from the Periphery." In Anthony Geist and Jose Monleon, eds., *Modernity and Its Margins: Reinscribing Cultural Modernity from Spain and Its Margins*. New York: Garland, 1993.

Zang, Marcel. *L'Exilé*. Arles: Actes Sud-Papiers, 2002.

Zaourou, Bernard Zadi. *Sory Lambré*. 1968. Unpublished.

————. *Les Sofas suivi de L'œil*. Paris: Oswald, 1975 [1974].

————. *Le secret des dieux*. 1984. Unpublished.

————. *La guerre des femmes suivie de la Termitière*. Abidjan: Nouvelles Éditions Ivoiriennes, 2001 [1985].

Zinsou, Senouvo Agbota. *On joue la comédie*. Lomé: Haho and Haarlem: In de Knipscheer, 1984 [1975].

————. *La tortue qui chante*. Paris: Hatier, 1987.

INDEX

ab origine period, 64, 66. *See also* originary source of African theatre
Abidjan, 4–5, 32, 62, 170
absurd, the, 67, 128
"acephalous" African societies, 53
Adama Champion (Koly), 9, 12
Adamov, Arthur, 128
Adiaffi, Jean-Marie, 31, 40
afflictive rituals, 63–64
African Americans, 24–25, 173
African Studies Institute, 31
Africanness, xvii, 10–11, 18, 33–35, 163, 173–175
Ahmad, Aijaz, 142
Akan society, 40, 128
Algeria, 20, 29
allegory, 22, 39, 68, 95, 104, 125–126, 144, 147–148, 161
allochthonous, 40, 45
Amerindians, 36, 110
Amin, Samir, 26–27
amnesia, 60, 65, 68
Amondji, Marcel, 26
L'amour-cent-vies (Liking), 68
"amputated memory," African, 68
An tan revolisyon (Condé), 144
anamnesis, 60, 64, 68
Anansi the Spider, 23
anarchistic freedom, 44–45
Angela Davis Troupe, 19
anglophone theatre, 43; in Caribbean, 16–18, 43
animal characters, 23–25, 102, 104–106
Anthony of Padua, 147
anticolonialism, xi, xiv, 11, 20–21, 49–50, 53, 57, 155, 159; and Schwarz-Bart, 144–146; and U Tam'si, 127
Antigone (Sophocles), xii, 94
antillanité (Caribbeanness), 30–31, 101, 105, 146

Appiah, K. Anthony, xi
Arab Islam, 87–88
Archinard, Louis, 77
Ariane space station (Kourou), 110
Aristotle, 9
Armstrong, Louis, 172
Arnaut, Karel, 31, 39
Arnold, James, 150
Artaud, Antonin, 6–7, 41–44, 57–58, 73
assimilation, 29–30, 70, 97, 101, 109, 158
atalaku, 135–136
audience participation: in African theatre, 5, 10–15, 35, 46; in Caribbean theatre, 22–23, 35–36, 39, 103–107; Chamoiseau's use of, 103–107; Dervain's use of, 81–82; experimentation in, 43–44, 46–48; internal, 90; Liking's use of, 63; of multi-ethnic audiences, 12, 22, 35–36; Stephenson's use of, 112; Tansi's use of, 135; Western, xv, 36–38, 46, 112; Zaourou's use of, 87–88, 90–91
audiovisual technology/instruments, 62
authenticity, cultural, xv, 36–40, 45, 51–53, 160, 174; in African theatre, 2, 6, 9, 12, 32–34, 122–123; in Caribbean theatre, 18, 21, 32–34; postmodern fantasy of, 37–38; rejection of, xvii–xviii, 156–157; U Tam'si's use of, 122–123
authoritarianism, 52, 56, 98, 109, 115, 136, 142
autochthony, 30–32, 39–40
autonomy, 23, 39, 49, 51, 161, 168–169; Chamoiseau's use of, 101; Liking's use of, 60, 70; Stephenson's use of, 109–110; U Tam'si's use of, 127
avant-garde theatre, xv–xvi, 5, 9, 15, 27, 29, 32–34, 174; characteristics of,

42–49; and Liking, 63, 73; problems of, 35–41

avant-texte, 77

Ba, Amadou Hampaté, 77
Babemba epic, 76
Babyface (Kwahulé), 171
The Bacchae of Euripides: A Communion Rite (Soyinka), 166
Badian, Seydou, 1, 47, 51, 54–55, 73, 156
Bakaba, Sidiki, 6
Baker, Léandre-Alain, 155, 162
Le bal de Ndinga (U Tam'si), 125–130
Balinese theatre, 7, 41
Bambara epic of Ségou, 77–80
Baraka, Amiri, 16
Bassa people (Cameroon), 33, 61, 63–64; women of, 33
Basutho people, 54
Baudelaire, 169
Baye-nerfs-le-crikette (cricket), 102
Béatrice du Congo (Dadié), 51
Beck, Julian, 42
Beckett, Samuel, 5, 150
Bédié, Konan, 39
Béhanzin, 17
békés (white settler class), 29
Benin, xvii, 19, 51, 116, 155, 162
Bérard, Stéphanie, 102, 105
Bernabé, Jean, 45
Bernabé, Joby, 141, 143
Bété people (Ivory Coast), 84–85, 88
Bhabha, Homi, 146
Biafra, 79
Biblique des derniers gestes (Chamoiseau), 99
Big Shoot (Kwahulé), 159–160, 170–172
Bin Kadi-So, 31
Bintou (Kwahulé), 159–160, 170
Blacher, Louis Placide, 17
Black Arts movement (U.S.), 16–17
Black Consciousness movement (S. Africa), 16
blackness, 34–35. *See also* Africanness
Blin, Roger, 5
Blue-S-Cat (Kwahulé), 160, 170, 172

body, focus on, 12–14, 20, 35–38, 48–49, 58, 165; in Schwarz-Bart, 152–154
Boiron, Chantal, 36, 42
Bokassa, 116, 141
Boni Maroons, 36, 110
bossonisme, 40
Bouah, Niangoran, 31, 39
Boukman, Daniel, 20, 39, 141–143
Boulaga, Fabien Eboussi, 52
Bourdieu, Pierre, 166
Brazil, 28
Brecht, Bertolt, 42, 128
Brer Rabbit, 23
Breton, André, 53
Britton, Celia, 115
Brook, Peter, 42
Bullins, Ed, 16
Bureau pour le développement des Migrations dans les Départements d'Outre-Mer (BUMIDOM), 142–143
Bürger, Peter, 46–47
Burkina Faso, xvii, 6, 27, 116, 162
burlesque, 52; burlesque satire, 133–134; Tansi's use of, 132–134
Burton, Richard, 23
bushinenge (bush Negroes), 36, 110
Butler, Judith, 14, 167

call and response, 20, 103, 129
Cameroon, 60–61, 63–64, 162
capitalism, 30–31, 45–46
Carabosse, 23, 95–102, 104–107
Carib Indian languages, 23
Caribbean Asians, 36
Caribbean Discourse (Glissant), xiii–xiv
Caribbean theatre, xiii–xiv, 16–25, 28–37, 39, 43, 141, 174; *Manman Dlo contre la fée Carabosse* (Chamoiseau), xiii, xvi, 18–19, 21–22, 25, 94–107; *O Mayouri* (Stephenson), xiii, xvi, 18–20, 25, 28, 108–115; *Ton beau capitaine,* xiii, 20, 28, 141–154
Caribbeanness (*antillanité*), 30–31, 101, 105, 146

caricature, 51, 97; fantastic caricature, 119–120, 122

carnival, xvi, 20, 124–125

Le carrefour (Efoui), 159

La carte d'identité (Adiaffi), 31

Cartesian thought, 48. *See also* dualism

Casanova, Pascale, 168–170

Cassandre, 173

cassé-co (dance form), 111

cassette letters, 143, 145, 147–150, 153–154

Catacombe de Soleil (Stephenson), 108

catharsis, 48, 64, 71

Catholicism, 92

Central African Republic, 116

Césaire, Aimé, 34, 47, 95–96, 108, 126, 137–139, 142, 144–145, 151

Césaire, Ina, 17, 19, 23, 39

Césaire, Michèle, 19–20

Cette vieille magie noire (Kwahulé), 159–161, 170, 172

Chad, 155, 162

Chaka, 13, 51–52, 54–55

Chaka (Senghor), 1, 54–55

Chaka: A Historical Romance (Mofolo), 54

Chalaye, Sylvie, 139–140, 163–164, 171, 174

Chamoiseau, Patrick, xiii, xvi, 18–25, 32, 34, 39, 41, 45, 50, 146; *Manman Dlo contre la fée Carabosse,* xiii, xvi, 18–19, 21–22, 25, 94–107, 108–112, 114

La chanson de Philibert (Léal), 20

charismatic leaders, xvi, 51–52. *See also* leaders, African

Chekhov, Anton, 150

Chevrier, Jacques, 123

Chronique des sept misères (Chamoiseau), 95

Cinderella, 23

cityscapes, xvii, 160

civil society, 55–57; in U Tam'si, 119, 128

La civilisation quotidienne en Côte d'Ivoire (Touré), 27–28

Clark, John Pepper, 16

class, 35–36; Chamoiseau's use of, 114–115; U Tam'si's use of, 116–118, 122, 129

Les Cloches (Liking), 37

coded musical language, 20, 85, 135

Cold War, 52

collective consciousness, 65, 67

collective creation, 14–15, 20, 43–44, 47–48, 161–162; Liking's use of, 62

colonialism, Belgian, 125–127

colonialism, French, xiv, 1, 6–10, 17–18, 20–23, 50–52; Chamoiseau's use of, 95–101; as cultural trauma, 66–68, 72; Liking's use of, 66–68, 72

Coltrane, John, 172

commedia dell'arte, 7

communism, 131

Le complexe de Thénardier (Pliya), 159–160

concert-party spectacle, xv, 9, 33

Concours de circonstances (Pliya), 160

Concours Théâtral Interafricain, 161

Condé, Maryse, 29, 144, 147

Confiant, Raphaël, 19–20, 23–25, 39, 45

Congo-Brazzaville, 50–51, 125, 131

conte théâtralisé (theatricalized folktale), 102

conteur (storyteller), 102–107. *See also* storytelling

Corneille, 7, 76

coumbite (peasant association), 112

countercultural space, 24, 44, 47, 62

coups d'états, 52; U Tam'si's use of, 117–119

Coups from Below: Armed Subalterns and State Power in West Africa (Kandeh), 116

"creative mystery," 101–102

Creole, xii–xiv, 19, 21–23, 30, 33–38, 45; Chamoiseau's use of, 94, 101, 105, 107, 108; Creole studies, 32; *créolité* (Creoleness), 30, 32; creolization, 146; creolized French, xiii, 22, 94, 105, 108; creolized spaces, xviii; Stephenson's use of, 108–112, 114

Duvalier, François "Papa Doc," 137, 141
dyali (praise singer), 128
dystopian theatre, 57, 117–119

Eboué, Felix, 17
École de Théâtre (Paris), 170
École Nationale de Théâtre (Canada), 84
École William Ponty, xv, 1, 10, 165
economic problems, 45–46, 52; of Caribbean territories, 28–30, 110–114, 142; of Ivory Coast, 25–28; Liking's use of, 68, 70; Stephenson's use of, 110–114. *See also* globalization
Éditions Théâtrales (Paris), 162
Efoui, Kossi, xvii, 155–157, 159, 161–163, 165, 174–175
Ekeh, Peter, 54
Eliade, Mircea, 64–65
elites, xii–xiii, xv, 10, 26–30, 32, 46, 49, 52, 56; as "fake locals," 39–40; and militariat, 116–118; in Stephenson, 112; in Tansi, 138; in U Tam'si, 116–118
Elle sera de jaspe et de corail (Liking), 3, 33, 64, 66, 68
Éloge de la créolité (Bernabé, Chamoiseau, and Confiant), 45
emigration, Caribbean, 28, 110–111, 113, 142–154, 174
L'Enfant des passages; ou, La Geste de Ti-Jean (Césaire), 19
L'enfant Mbénè (Liking), 61
L'enfant noir (Laye), 112
L'Ensemble Kotéba, 12, 31
environmentalism, 99–100
epic performance, xv–xvi, 9, 21, 32, 61; Chamoiseau's use of, 106–107; Dervain's use of, 75–83; Zaourou's use of, 84, 86
Erzulie Freda Dahomey, 147
L'État honteux (Tansi), 123
ethnophilosophers/ethnodramatists, 53, 55, 157–158
etiological tales, 18, 66, 104

Europe, 28, 37–38, 53–54, 160; European Common Market, 27. *See also* Western cultural/economic influences; *names of European countries*
European theatre, xv, 6–7, 10, 16, 23, 41–43, 46, 53
Ewe language, 56
L'exil d'Albouri (Ndao), 9, 11, 73, 76
exile, 142–154
L'Exilé (Zang), 159, 163
exoticism, xiv–xv, 10, 22, 36–37, 44, 46–47, 164–165
expatriates, 163
Experimental Theatre, 6
Eyadema, 116

fairground tradition, 7
Fama (Kwahulé), 159–160, 171
Fanon, Frantz, 17, 20
fantastic grotesque, 119–120, 125
fantasy, 3, 11, 15, 57, 59, 63, 73, 174; Chamoiseau's use of, 94, 106; Dervain's use of, 75; Tansi's use of, 131–132; U Tam'si's use of, 119; Zaourou's use of, 84, 86, 89
Fauquenoy, Marguerite, 108–109
feminism, 146–150
festival circuit, 36–37, 62, 162, 174
Festival International des Francophonies (Limoges, France), 62, 84, 174
Fiangor, Rogo, 164
flashbacks, 125
Une flèche pour un pays à l'encan (Stephenson), 108
folktale performance, xv–xvi, 57, 157–158, 164–165; in African theatre, 9–10, 21, 33; in Caribbean theatre, 18–21, 32, 94–106, 111; Chamoiseau's use of, 94–106, 111; *théâtre conté* vs. *conte théâtralisé*, 102; U Tam'si's use of, 122; Zaourou's use of, 86
folly, human, 80–81
France, 162, 172–173; and Caribbean territories, 28–32, 37; and Haiti, xii,

xiv; and Ivory Coast, 25–29, 31, 39; modern "high" culture of in overseas territories, 6–10, 29; and modernist theatre, 42, 45–46. *See also entries beginning with* French

French Antilles, xii–xiv

French Guyana, xii, 6, 18–20, 28, 36, 108–113, 125

French language, xiii–xv, 4–6, 10, 22, 27, 35, 46; Chamoiseau's use of, 105, 108; denationalization of, xviii; Dervain's use of, 76–77; Stephenson's use of, 108–109; Tansi's use of, 139–140; translations of, xiii, 108; U Tam'si's use of, 125

French theatre, xiv, 29, 42, 169; Chamoiseau's rejection of, 104; Dervain's use of, 76–77, 79–81, 86; epic narratives in, 76–77, 79–81; Liking's rejection of, 63, 73; as literary drama, 6–7, 46–47, 81; rejection of, 6–12, 20, 32–34, 45–46, 48–49, 63, 73, 104, 156–157

Freud, Sigmund, 64–65, 165

funerary rituals, 33

Gabon, 61

Galliéni, Joseph Simon, 77

Gandhi, Leela, 67–68

Garran, Gabriel, 125

Gates, Henry Louis, 25

Gbagbo, Laurent, 39

gender inequality, 88–89, 92–93

genocide, 159, 171–172

Geschiere, Peter, 30–31

gestures, symbolic, 11–14, 20, 35–37, 44; Liking's use of, 63, 73

Ghana, 26

Gilbert, Helen, 17–18

Giraudoux, Jean, 77, 79–81

Glissant, Edouard, xiii–xiv, 28–30, 37, 39, 95, 97, 144, 146–147

globalization, xvi, xvii–xviii, 2, 28, 30–31, 45–46, 141, 159–160, 162–168, 170, 173–175

Gouverneurs de la rosée (Roumain), 112, 115, 144

grajé (dance form), 111

Le grand destin de Soundjata (Konaké), 76

Greco-Latin culture, xii, 43, 76–77, 79–80, 97–98, 160, 166, 169

griot, West African, 4, 9, 23, 39–40; Dervain's use of, 77–82

griotique movement, 4, 8, 12, 39–40

the grotesque, 3, 119–121, 125, 136, 171, 174

Groupe de Recherche sur la Tradition Orale (GRTO), 31

Groupe d'Études et de Recherches de la Créolophonie (GEREC), 32

Groupement de l'organisation nationaliste guadeloupéenne (GONG), 20

Guadeloupe, xii, 18–21, 35, 143–144

Les Guérivoires, 31

La guerre de Troie n'aura pas lieu (Giraudoux), 77, 79–81

La guerre des femmes (Zaourou), xvi, 18, 84–93

Guingané, Jean-Pierre, 6, 12

Guireaud, Rose Marie, 31

Guyanese Movement for Decolonization (MOGUDE), 20

gwoka, 20

Haigh, Samantha, 150

Haiti, xii–xiv, 22, 28, 34, 112, 125, 137–138, 143–154

Hall, Stuart, 21

Hallett, Cynthia, 151

Halloran, Michael, 65

"Handful of Keys" (song), 172

Harrison, Paul Carter, 16

Hatch, James, 17

Hawkins, Peter, 44

healing ceremonies, 63–64, 69–74, 93, 135

Hérémakhonon (Condé), 29, 147

Héros d'eau (Liking), 61

hieratic gestures, 44, 73

historical memory, 75–77

holy theatre. *See* religious ceremonial theatre

Union for the Liberation of
Guadeloupe (UPLG), 20–21
United States, 16, 18, 34, 36, 42, 160–
162, 166; African Americans, 24–25,
173. See also Western cultural/
economic influences
universalism, 34, 94, 98–99, 157–158,
163–170, 174
University of Abidjan, 4–5, 32
University of Paris III, 170
University of the Antilles and Guyane,
32
utopian theatre, 57, 115

vanguardism, political, 115
Varesse, Rosy, 141, 143
Ventres pleins, ventres creux
(Boukman), 141
La veuve diyilèm (Liking), 61
videos, 62, 90
La vie et demie (Tansi), 132–133
Vie et mort de Vaval (Montantin), 20
Villa Ki-Yi, 62
violence: Chamoiseau's use of, 97,
99, 101; of colonialism, 67, 97, 99;
Kwahulé's use of, 171–172; Liking's
use of, 67, 74; male, 88, 91; of
militariat, 116–117; modern, 159;
U Tam'si's use of, 118–119, 124;
Zaourou's use of, 88, 91
virility, Congolese, 127
vodou, 112
Les Voyageurs (Stephenson), 108

Waberi, Abdourahman, xviii, 162
Wacquant, Loïc, 166
Waiting for Godot (Beckett), 5
Walcott, Derek, 17, 18, 22
Waller, Fats, 172
war, 159; Chamoiseau's use of, 106–
107; Dervain's use of, 75, 77–80, 82;
in epic narratives, 75, 77–80, 82,
106–107; U Tam'si's use of, 117–
118; Zaourou's use of, 87–88, 91
Waramba, opéra mandingue (Liking),
61

warrior ethic, 51, 54, 57, 79, 150
water fairies, 102. See also Mamy Wata;
Manman Dlo
Watts, Richard, 99
Western cultural/economic influences,
27, 30–32, 34, 36–38, 43, 166–167;
Liking's use of, 70; in medicine, 63;
and modernist theatre, 41–46, 163–
164. See also globalization; names of
Western countries
"What a Wonderful World" (song), 172
What Is the Third Estate? (Sièyes), 32
White, Bob, 135
Wieland, Christoph Wieland, 119
Wilson, August, 18
women: Bambara women, 78; in Bassa
society, 33; in Enlightenment ratio-
nality, 48; in La guerre des femmes
(Zaourou), 86–93; as "media-
trix," 150; in Ton beau capitaine
(Schwarz-Bart), 146–150
World Bank, 27
The World Republic of Letters
(Casanova), 168–170
writerly texts, 5
writers, African, persecution of, 93
writing (literacy), 94–95, 98, 102,
104, 158. See also textualization in
theatre

yoga, 14
Yoruba (Nigeria), 34, 165–166

Zaire, 116
Zambia, 63
Zang, Marcel, 159, 163
Zaourou, Bernard Zadi, 1–3, 7, 9, 11,
32–33, 39–41, 45, 49–50, 156, 174;
as director, 12, 14, 31, 85; La guerre
des femmes, xvi, 18, 84–93
Zinsou, Senouvo Agbota, 3, 5–6, 9,
13–14, 33, 46, 48, 134
Zouzou, 88, 91
Zulu, 54

JOHN CONTEH-MORGAN (1948–2008) was Professor of French and Italian at the Ohio State University. He is author of *Theatre and Drama in Francophone Africa* and editor (with Tejumola Olaniyan) of *African Drama and Performance* (Indiana University Press, 2004). He was editor of *Research in African Literatures*.

DOMINIC THOMAS is Chair of the Department of French and Francophone Studies and Professor of Comparative Literature at the University of California, Los Angeles. He is author of *Nation-Building, Propaganda, and Literature in Francophone Africa* (Indiana University Press, 2002) and *Black France: Colonialism, Immigration, and Transnationalism* (Indiana University Press, 2007).